# Memorable

*Lessons to Leave a* **legacy**

## Kalyna Miletic

*KBM*

Heather,
Thanks for supporting this book from
the very beginning!

**SUNBURY PRESS**®
Mechanicsburg, PA USA

12.22

Published by Sunbury Press, Inc.
Mechanicsburg, Pennsylvania

**SUNBURY**
**PRESS**
**www.sunburypress.com**

For information about special discounts for bulk purchases, please contact Sunbury Press Orders Dept. at (855) 338-8359 or orders@sunburypress.com.

To request one of our authors for speaking engagements or book signings, please contact Sunbury Press Publicity Dept. at publicity@sunburypress.com.

FIRST SUNBURY PRESS EDITION: November 2022

Set in Adobe Garamond | Interior design by Crystal Devine | Illustrations by Ricardo Moreira | Cover by Victoria Mitchell | Edited by Sarah Peachey.

Publisher's Cataloging-in-Publication Data
Names: Miletic, Kalyna, author.
Title: Memorable : lessons to leave a legacy / Kalyna Miletic.
Description: First trade paperback edition. | Mechanicsburg, PA : Sunbury Press, 2022.
Summary: *Memorable* changes the way we define the nature of work. International career coach Kalyna Miletic provides 22 vital skills to take your life from one filled with obligation to one of contribution and meaning. She discusses how to build careers based on choice, fulfillment, and impact and seeks a happier, more alive workforce one reader at a time.
Identifiers: ISBN 978-1-62006-953-0 (hard cover).
Subjects: SELF-HELP / Personal Growth / Success | BUSINESS & ECONOMICS / Careers / General | BODY, MIND & SPIRIT / Inspiration & Personal Growth.

Product of the United States of America
0 1 1 2 3 5 8 13 21 34 55

*Continue the Enlightenment!*

*This book is for you.*
*For every time you thought there must be more to life.*
*For the voice inside you that whispers your big dreams.*
*For the part of you that doesn't want to give up on them.*
*May your bravery shine through as you walk toward your vision.*
*May your time be well spent.*

# Contents

# Impact

# Introduction

WHEN I FIRST set out to write this book, I thought I was writing about how to build a "successful" career. The writing process has been an evolutionary one as I realized that what I was exploring wasn't really about success in the workplace but about something bigger.

Throughout, I will introduce you to people, both public figures and friends and family, who have acted as mentors to me. I'll share client stories, anonymously, of course, as they've taught me just as much as I've taught them. I've realized that the skills in this book aren't solely about moving up the corporate ladder or making the most money. They're skills that are vital for fulfillment beyond that. They're for creating a meaningful legacy through your contribution to the world. This book is about building your character to become someone who pursues their calling in order to light up the world.

I've contemplated the role of time my entire life. When I turned ten, I told my mom I didn't want to rush to be older and felt I was at the perfect age. I've kept this philosophy of appreciating the present far past my tenth birthday and it's served me well. What I know for certain is that time is limited. We have roughly 100,000 hours to dedicate to work—a sizable chunk of our lives. I'm determined to spend that time being exceptionally deliberate about where I put my efforts. And so, the mission of this book is to help you fill your metaphorical career time bucket with many meaningful hours so you can leave a legacy you feel proud of.

Whether you're developing software in Silicon Valley or creating art in Vienna, we're all looking for that feeling of flow that we experience when we *enjoy* our work. What if that's possible . . . while also making money?

I've dedicated my life to making this dream come true for myself and helping others do the same. My goal is to help you feel confident enough to declare what you love and spend more of your precious time on it.

This is a three-part journey. First, we'll look at defining what your meaningful legacy is. We all have our own version that evolves throughout our lives, and understanding what legacy means for you right now is the first step. Next, you'll identify what fulfills you and feels like your true vocation. You'll be asked to think about what you want to do with your 100,000 hours at work and cultivate faith in the path you're on. Finally, we'll talk about amplifying the impact you make on others to produce a lasting legacy in the areas you're dedicating time to.

You'll discover that the three pillars will support you to build a meaningful legacy, ensure you have clarity of vision, cultivate faith, and feel valued for your unique impact on the world. By the end, you'll have twenty-two different hats you can put on to effectively handle any situation that comes your way.

## What is building a meaningful legacy about?

Success is such a deeply personal thing: It means one thing to me, another to you, and probably something entirely different to our great-grandparents. Over nearly a decade of coaching others, I've identified that our ideas of success are tied to our sense of fulfillment, which is driven by our daily actions. Coming home at the end of the day and feeling like you've done your part to improve the world around you delivers a deep sense of satisfaction. There are three key aspects to finding meaning: choice, fulfillment, and impact. Within these three factors, there are various life skills we can employ to get us closer to our personal idea of living a meaningful life.

Choice means being deliberate about the life you're creating. If we choose our work environment and responsibilities carefully, we're less likely to end up blaming others when we dislike what we're doing day in and day out. In the first part of this book, we'll examine where you're at, where you want to be, and, most importantly, what's holding you back from your vision. Then, you'll choose whether you want to stick with what you've been doing or forge a new path.

One thing that seems constant in our society is that success is linked to money. I believe that success is having autonomy over how you spend your time. This includes the health and wherewithal to be able to spend it as you wish.

# Introduction

Money often means safety, a sense of security, and, once our needs are met, freedom. It factors in as an enabler for us to do what we want. You'll make varying amounts of money over the course of your life no matter what you choose to do for work. It's also critical to note that it's about the wealth you create along the way. Spending all you make is a zero-sum game and doesn't get any of us far. So, instead of allowing money earned to be the main conscious driver, we'll focus on building character—being proud of your work and the person you are. We'll start with figuring out what you enjoy doing, then find ways those activities can bring you a level of income you would consider "successful." No job comes with any guarantees, so it's crucial that you garner a level of fulfillment out of what you do.

Enjoying something doesn't just mean it's fun. Sometimes, I find enjoyment in developing a solution to a seemingly impossible situation. Sometimes I enjoy working from my bed. At other times, I want to be around lots of people. Enjoyment is fluid, it's contextual. Fulfillment, on the other hand, is deeper and more enduring. It gives you a sense of satisfaction. This book isn't here to tell you to impulsively jump from the lifeboats and leave your stable job to travel to Vietnam because it would be fun. But it will make you question how you're navigating the boat you've chosen to drive.

In the second section, you'll discover what fulfillment means to you and use that to build out the terms of your career so you're satisfied with it. That might mean staying exactly where you are and tweaking a few smaller things, or it might mean you *do* need to pack your bags and fly to Hanoi. Either way, this section will help you get real with yourself about what you truly care about and build faith in pursuing your unique path.

The last section of the book is about impact, and this is where you'll focus on your contribution to the world. It is your legacy via your reputation and the value you provide others. Once you've established your non-negotiables and are clear on your path, then you're ready to impact others. Having a refined idea about what you want to create and achieve in your career is crucial and is often the difference between people that are constantly complaining about work and those that are actively finding solutions and innovating. This final section is where we'll talk about how to identify the ideal receivers of your work; how to deliver your work to make the most meaningful impact and, yes, how to get paid well for delivering value to others.

You may be thinking, why not skip to the last part? Well, you can. I often skip to the parts of books I want to read the most, too. But when I do that, I've found that the information I'm resisting (skipping over, criticizing, or deeming irrelevant) is often the stuff I need to be reading the most. You'll get more from this experience if you come along for the entire ride. The choice is yours, but I invite you to come on this journey with me and bring a journal to record your thoughts. Take your time with each chapter. The most important realizations you'll have from this book are the answers you'll generate from the questions asked throughout it.

# What to Expect

I N THE COMING chapters, we'll explore twenty-two skills that can help you become a person you deeply respect and admire.

In each chapter, we'll follow a similar structure:

1. **Core Question:** This is the question I invite you to consider regarding the skill we're discussing. Core questions will clarify what we're exploring and how you want to harness the skill via your actions going forward.

2. **Real Life Experiences and Client Anecdotes:** In the opening section, I will offer my thoughts, personal anecdotes, and client stories to explore the key skill and main concepts under discussion. This isn't a one-size-fits-all book by any means, and neither are the real-life examples included throughout. Take from them what you will. They're exemplary in nature by definition, not prescriptive.

3. **Mentor's Table:** This is a coaching tool I regularly use with clients, especially when they feel uncertain or are approaching something new. There are a few ways to think about the Mentor's Table. One is a literal "table" that you gather your mentors around. These are people you work with personally and know. They help you toward your goals and often directly impact your life, giving you advice, anecdotal support, or perhaps coaching. The other version is where you pick people you admire and then draw upon their work for inspiration and guidance.

If you create this "roster" of individuals, you'll always have a group of people that you know personally or that you follow from afar that act as a support network throughout your career. One great way to harness their wisdom without their physical presence is to ask yourself "what would my mentor do in this situation?" It's a powerful version of a perspective shift.

4. **Ask Yourself:** In this section, you'll answer questions to clarify your thinking and record your responses in your preferred note-taking tool. You will also be asked to rank how satisfied you are with your skill development on a scale of one to ten. This number will fluctuate based on the day, the specific situation you have on your mind while reading a chapter, or the season of work you're currently in. That's okay. This serves as a barometer to give you a means of scaling how you feel you're doing. As it's completely subjective, there's no right or wrong answer. The scale's purpose is to draw your attention to the qualities in this book you might like to focus more attention on, or the areas you feel you might like to improve the most.

5. **One-Degree Shift:** You'll establish some next steps and actions to take based on your new realizations. If you'd prefer to continue reading, then commit to the action in your calendar and do it as soon as possible to create a new habit loop (more on this later). I advise reading this book with time in between chapters so you can implement your new insights. If you're looking for information only, breeze through as you please.

6. **Takeaways:** A summary of the skills and strategies you've learned from the chapter. It's easy to refer to and a reminder of the insights you're collecting along the way.

# PART ONE
# CHOICE

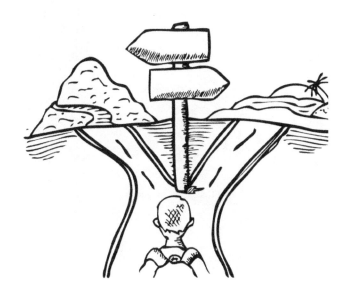

*"Life is not a having and a getting,*
*but a being and a becoming . . ."*
—MATTHEW ARNOLD

# *One*
# Responsibility

## CORE QUESTION

**"What part of this situation can I take responsibility for?"**

In 2019, I was in a car accident and sustained a traumatic brain injury. My life, along with the writing of this book, got put on hold. I lay in my bed for months on end. I wore sunglasses everywhere due to light sensitivity. Sleeping roughly eighteen hours a day, I felt like I was in an isolation chamber. This gave me some time to question how I'd been living my life. When my accident happened, I had all sorts of people to blame, like the driver who ran a stop sign. It was a pivotal moment in my life when everything seemed to collide. I felt down and out. Was I going to fold and give up? Or was I going to use this as a springboard to better things?

The choice presented to me after my car accident has everything to do with your career. Think of this moment, right now—reading this book—as if it is a reset button, an opportunity to choose change at all costs because there's no turning back.

What if you could create a different life without needing the injury or the totaled vehicle?

The thing that's holding you back, to put it lightly, is you.

Today's the day to make a change—if you want it to be.

## MENTOR'S TABLE

### My Dad

My dad started fixing cars at sixteen years old in his parents' garage, and he now owns several autobody shops. He worked hard for every penny, putting in long hours, and he often talked about how he sacrificed for our family. Simultaneously, he also *loved* fixing cars and helping others. He gave up time with his family to work, but he got something else: He got enjoyment out of his contribution and made an impact while also earning the money his family needed. He always reminded me to work hard and that I would be okay if I gleaned lessons out of the challenges I faced. My parents didn't shelter me from difficult situations—they invited me to learn and grow through them.

We all choose where we put our focus, but society (and sometimes even our parents, partners, or friends) can make us feel like it's only noble if the story we tell is one of sacrifice and pain. There's no question that true suffering exists in the world. The question is, are you truly suffering or just complaining? When it becomes a competition to see who can suffer the most it's a good sign we're dealing with the latter. Is it healthy for life to be about comparison? I'd say we can approach it differently. You can tell your story like it's been an awful time, dwelling on it being difficult, or you can talk about all the challenges you've had from a place of learning and gratitude. My dad taught me to be grateful for everything I have, especially the struggles. They are what sharpen us into the person we need to be in order to fulfill our contribution to the world.

Look, I know what you're thinking. Every mindfulness and self-help book talks about gratitude, and it can seem played out. I say "thank you" every time someone opens a door. Isn't that enough? Well, yes and no. If you're connected to your heart, you start realizing that being human is an amazing gift. You get to be in a body, feel things, go on adventures, and change lives. Little things can be more joyful than we often recognize.

In my life, I've noticed that the challenging times really do pile on all at once, and so do the good times. When things are good, they somehow keep getting better. But when I'm in a downward spiral, a parking ticket, car accident, and sprained ankle all happen in the span of a month.

So, how do we cultivate gratitude and use it to our benefit? Consider this: What is the best thing that's happened to you over the past year?

Now, think about the worst thing that's happened.

Which one did you learn more from?

Exactly.

We can learn a lot from the difficult, the challenging, and the not-so-polished. So, rather than making it a bad thing, let's call a spade a spade. Personal transformation often comes from the dark and challenging moments we experience.

---

THE GOOD IS EASY TO MINE FOR JOY.
LET'S START FINDING GOLD IN THE BAD AND THE UGLY.

---

And if all else fails, try showing others gratitude for their efforts. I've heard that honestly thanking someone or showing appreciation rubs off on the giver, too.

## Jordan B. Peterson and Tammy M. Peterson

Jordan B. Peterson is a best-selling author, clinical psychologist, and an acclaimed public thinker. He's authored many books, including *12 Rules for Life* and *Beyond Order*. He's the host of the number one education podcast, "The Jordan B. Peterson Podcast," and applies eternal truths to modern problems. Jordan's lectures and books have transformed the lives of millions. One simple but forgotten premise he's brought to the forefront of people's minds is: take responsibility for your life. How does the idea of taking responsibility translate when we talk about things that seem unavoidable or out of our control? What does this mean when it comes to earning that promotion, requesting more vacation days, or landing your next client? I'd say it starts by identifying what's in your control. I'm perpetually asking, what can I take responsibility for? And what can I let go of? Those two questions help me consciously filter out what should stay on my radar and what needs to go.

Tammy M. Peterson is Jordan's wife, and she expertly investigates biblical symbolism, prayer, and living in relationship with God. She has the goal of understanding how ancient scripture has affected our modern world.

I had the great privilege of interviewing Tammy on my podcast, Lead Today. Her profound relationship with God and prayer inspired me to return to my own connection with Him. Tammy embodies how to gracefully take responsibility for ourselves and our circumstances. We do this by listening to the wisdom God is whispering into our conscience through the Holy Spirit. When it comes to taking responsibility in our careers, I believe it is of the utmost importance to consider what elements of your work you're ready to take ownership of. In truth, everything you contribute to is what you must take responsibility for. We find the most meaning from taking on challenges bigger than ourselves. The grace is in knowing that your fufillment isn't derived from external recognition, rather from acting with integrity. As we continue this journey, your willingness to take personal responsibility for the way you experience your life is what I believe will dictate your long-lasting fulfillment.

It's clear that when we abdicate our responsibilities, we feel lousy. It can feel good in the moment to push off a deadline or commitment. In the long run, however, it only mounts feelings of anxiety, doubt, and powerlessness. If you want to be proud of who you're looking at in the mirror, the first step is to choose that *you* alone are the one responsible for the life you're creating.

## ASK YOURSELF

**What does "responsibility" mean to me?**

**Why is it important?**

**How satisfied am I with how I take responsibility in my life?**

**On a scale of 1 (being low) and 10 (being extremely satisfied), how would you rate your current level of satisfaction with taking responsibility for your work and daily life:**

1     2     3     4     5     6     7     8     9     10

**Where in your life might there be room to own more responsibility?**

**What's the biggest learning experience ("failure") you've had so far at work?**

Identify at least one thing that makes you glad it happened. Great! Now you're an expert at finding the silver lining in situations. Let's do it again and make it bigger.

To create a life that's different, better, and more exciting than "normal," we've got to craft a personal story that compels us to act. We'll be working on this concept throughout the book, but let's start with where you are right now. My personal story could go several ways. I could harp on the challenges I've faced, focus on the amazing parts, and pretend everything is perfect, or I could appreciate all parts of the spectrum for what they are. To make any changes in my life, I've realized I need to identify where I'm starting from. So where are you now? What choices have you made so far?

Let's explore your current situation.

- What do you regularly tell yourself, family, friends, or co-workers about your work?

- Use ten adjectives to describe your boss, co-workers, and position.

- What do you notice?

- What would you like to change about your current job?

- How would you change your employer?

- Do you work in a pleasant environment?

- Why did you choose to pursue what you're currently doing?

- List the things about your current work that are important to you.

- Reflect on your answers. Are most of the reasons externally focused (pay, obligation, status) or internally focused (fun, skills, interests, your values)?

- What other areas in your life do you find yourself complaining about (e.g., health, relationships, learning, hobbies, finances etc.)?

- What have you established as your situation so far?

- Considering all you've answered above, what's in your control that you're willing to take responsibility for?

## ONE-DEGREE SHIFT

1. Choose one thing about your work situation that you're ready to take responsibility for and decide what you can change about it right now.

2. Ask someone to partner with you as you work through the exercises in this book. I have *many* accountability partners who support me to reach my goals. They regularly check in to ask about my progress and help me to stay on track. Reach out to someone you trust who may also benefit from embarking on this journey with you. It's much more enjoyable to create change together!

## TAKEAWAYS

✦ Learn to find the gold in work blunders to maximize learning and future success.

✦ Assume responsibility from now on when it comes to what you create over the course of your life. It's in *your* hands.

✦ Take ownership of what's within your control to have the biggest bang for your buck when you act.

# Purpose

*"Every man's work, whether it be literature or music or pictures or architecture or anything else, is always a portrait of himself."*
—SAMUEL BUTLER

## CORE QUESTION

**"Why are you doing the work you're doing?"**

A client comes into a session and says, "I can't take it anymore. My boss isn't listening to a word I say about what we need to do for our sales team. I've been doing a sales role for six months, and I'm his executive assistant! I'm completely fed up." Sure, in that scenario, we can all imagine needing to make a change. But what about a scenario where you have a dull, nagging thought in your head that says, "Maybe I can do better? But I'm not sure. Maybe I can't? So, I'll stay safe. I'll stay the same."

After my accident, I faced seven months of daily rehabilitation. My life changed instantaneously, and it *had* to because I had no other choice. My body was telling me to rest. My head hurt if I did too much, and doctors gave me a whole host of changes to make. Those months have led to permanent changes. I have changed how I work: I take frequent breaks from screen time. I committed to stop drinking alcohol for my healing and gave up drinking coffee, a big one for me. I made these changes because I wanted to recover as quickly and completely as possible. They had a purpose.

Events occur unexpectedly to all of us at random points throughout our lives. Some of these events can spark sudden and drastic changes. Others make themselves felt slowly and over time. The most dangerous is the latter, because it's easy for the small things to build up and go unnoticed.

What about you?

Are you fed up enough?

Have you reached the final straw where you can't bear it anymore?

Or are you hearing the slow, dull murmur of dissatisfaction in some parts of your career or life trajectory?

---

YOU CAN DECIDE, RIGHT NOW,
TO TAKE MATTERS INTO YOUR OWN HANDS AND MAKE A CHANGE.
IT DOESN'T HAVE TO TAKE A NEAR-DEATH EXPERIENCE
FOR YOU TO DECIDE YOU DESERVE BETTER.

---

In doing so, you open yourself up to pursue a purpose larger than yourself and make a meaningful impact you feel proud of. This, of course, means deciding to take a risk.

I'd like to clarify that I don't think there's only one way to live out your purpose. We're here to pursue various roles as we impact the world. Who and what we involve ourselves with during our time here becomes the legacy we leave behind. Your sense of purpose is derived from feelings of being valued and making an impact. In this chapter, we'll seek to define your greater purpose and why you feel compelled to pursue it at this point in your life. Know that it will inevitably twist and turn as you walk your unique path. As a result, it's best not to attach your entire sense of purpose to a single role, whether that be at work or personally. Your calling changes as you grow throughout the seasons of your life. So be present in where you're being called now to make the most of your current season of life.

If the call feels unclear where you currently sit, one way to hone in on it is to explore your unique set of gifts. The way you use them will evolve and change, but they are core parts of who you are. Others may recognize them in you and call them out. You may feel fulfilled when you're using them. Your gifts are another way to categorize the traits that are compiled to make you unique. We are all a mix of many gifts to varying degrees and some can come out of the blue in situations when you need them. There might be a few foundational gifts that resonate with you deeply.

# Purpose

Consider these as you contemplate walking toward your purpose in life:

1. **Leadership:** You have a vision to tackle.

   You're drawn to motivating others to work together toward common goals.

2. **Administration:** You bring order to chaos.

   You're detail oriented and help bring visions to life.

3. **Teaching:** You enjoy instructing others to learn and grow.

   You thrive when sharing information whether that be one on one or in groups.

4. **Knowledge:** You're an avid learner.

   You derive joy from studying and exploring information.

5. **Wisdom:** Your intuition gives you the way to go and make choices.

   Ask for wisdom and you shall receive it.

6. **Prophecy:** You are willing to share uncomfortable truths.

   You help people by being direct and speaking up boldly.

7. **Discernment:** You recognize the true intentions of others.

   You assess if someone is genuine by closely observing their words and actions.

8. **Encouragement:** You inspire others to be enthusiastic.

   You are a good counselor and motivate others to act and serve.

9. **Shepherding:** You find that people regularly confide in you.

   You walk with and look out for others along their path.

10. **Faith:** You act with the belief that everything will work out.

    You remind others to be bold and unwavering in difficult times.

11. **Enthusiasm:** You can strike up a conversation with anyone.

    You lead others joyfully toward a goal.

12. **Starter:** You love to start things and delegate the details.

    You see the gaps in a situation and how to fill them.

13. **Service:** You are willing to step in and tangibly meet needs.

    You enjoy hands on work and practically helping others, even if it's behind the scenes.

14. **Mercy:** You empathize strongly with people who are hurting and meet them where they are.

    You cheerfully give compassion and don't judge others for past mistakes or struggles.

15. **Giving:** You give freely, liberally, and joyfully.

    You love to share with others and fulfill their needs, even if you get nothing in return.

16. **Hospitality:** You make visitors, guests and strangers feel at ease.

    You enjoy using your home to entertain guests.

- Which ones resonate with who you are?
- Which ones come more easily than others?
- Have you noticed yourself using some regularly in your life?
- Which gifts have you used in times of struggle?
- Which ones would you like to strengthen?

And finally, the most important element of purpose is finding meaning in daily occurrences. Everything that happens in your life is defining your calling. Even challenging events are molding you into who you need to be to grow, one step at a time. It can be derived via the inner work of healing or the outer work of leaving the world a bit better than it was yesterday. The key is to find a sense of meaning in every little thing we do by being present. Your gifts shine through in the fleeting moments throughout your day. There is magic in the seemingly mundane.

## MENTOR'S TABLE

### Simon Sinek

Simon Sinek, British-American author of *Start with Why: How Great Leaders Inspire Everyone to Take Action* (2009), says that people do things based on *their beliefs*—the "why"—rather than based on the logistics—the "what." Inspiration and purpose, he argues, are what motivate us.

Purpose is why something is done or exists. So, let's start with "why." Why do you do what you do every day?

The word "purpose" is so played out and even clichéd in career books. "Find your purpose," they say. Well, rather than *finding* it, Sinek says that you can define it yourself. Take the lead here and define your legacy and your own "brand." Your brand is how you define yourself as a leader, not only in your work but in your daily life.

**Why are you spending your time the way you are?**

**Why are you doing the job you're doing right now?**

**Why are you still doing things the way you did five or even ten years ago?**

**Do those ways still work?**

The more you ask yourself *why* (six times at least), the closer you are to your real purpose, the reason you embarked on your career path in the first place. And if you think you've had a series of jobs rather than a defined career, I'd offer up the idea that perhaps there are similarities and benefits from those jobs that are crafting themselves into a meaningful career across multiple roles and industries. Money is not a deep enough answer. There's always something more to why you're doing things the way you are right now.

### James Clear

James Clear is the author of *Atomic Habits: An Easy & Proven Way to Build Good Habits & Break Bad Ones*. The main premise behind Clear's argument is that you change your habits by deciding to change who you believe yourself to be. Your perceived identity directs your actions. If you *believe* you're an author, you start doing author-y things, including writing and publishing work. If you decide you're a runner, you will run each day. Decide you're a singer and you'll sing and perform whenever you can. If you *believe* you possess the capabilities to be a certain type of person, then you'll practice them and continue improving. Start believing you're successful at what you do, and you'll start thinking of and doing things that you believe a successful person in your position would do. It's a simple and genius model:

1. Answer: What type of person do you want to be (e.g. adventurous, successful, a CEO, a writer, a kind parent, a good friend, etc.)?
2. Prove it to yourself (and others) with small wins.

I'd take this a step further and add that everything in your career and beyond has to do with your perception. Your perception of your purpose is based on your self-imposed limitations, fears, strengths, and experiences. Only you can define it based on what you perceive to be the best fit. This often stems from your senses. Add your conscience, or inner voice, to that list. Check in with yourself about what you've perceived as your purpose so far in your head, then cross reference that with your actions to bring Clear's point to light. If you think you're meant to work with animals but your actions don't line up with anything related to them, that's your moment of reckoning. Be honest with yourself and decide if it's truly your purpose or if it's what you think you "should" be doing.

Have you been running up a corporate ladder only to discover in your thirties or forties that you think being a stay-at-home parent is truly what you want? We often think the grass is greener on the other side. So, test out your assumptions before jumping ship. Base your decision on what you're willing to undertake day in and day out. Developing your purpose is not linear and is, in fact, a series of different projects, roles, tasks, and skills. Perhaps you don't need an outward-focused purpose at all but a guiding star to identify what type of person you want to be at the identity level, as Clear suggests. If you're being the type of person you want to be—kind, resilient, and adaptable, for example—then the actions you take as a result will define what you create.

The truth about your greater purpose is that it is slowly being revealed to you over the course of your life. We often have dreams that don't come to fruition and feel discouraged or wonder why. It's only at the end of your story that everything will be clear. You must have faith that what is meant for you will find you. Your work is to be willing to receive aligned opportunities as they come your way so you can use your experiences to become the best version of yourself.

## ASK YOURSELF

**What does "purpose" mean to me?**

**Why is it important?**

**How satisfied am I with how I bring purpose to my work?**

**What kind of person do I want to be?**

**How do I want to leave the world a better place than it was yesterday?**

**On a scale of 1 (being low) and 10 (being extremely satisfied), rate your current level of satisfaction with how much purpose you have in your daily life:**

1    2    3    4    5    6    7    8    9    10

- Where in your career might there be room to bring more purposeful action?

- What do I want to leave behind as a result of my efforts in life?

- What small actions will I take to prove to myself that I'm the person I want to be daily?

- How do I currently derive meaning at work?

- What does work mean to me?

- What do I want my work and career to mean to me?

- What is so meaningful to you that the suffering of life becomes worth it?

- How can I turn my dissatisfaction into an opportunity for growth?

## Formula for Change

We know that life is a continuous series of changes strung together. What about the changes we want to proactively make that somehow evade us? David Gleicher's famous formula for change, developed in the sixties, is relevant here. It shows that change happens when dissatisfaction outweighs the resistance to change. He adds that you also need a desire for improvement and a visualization of the first steps needed to reach that state of improvement.

$$C = D * V * F > R$$

Where **C** is the Change

Where **D** is the Dissatisfaction with the present state

Where **V** is the Vision of the future state

Where **F** is the First Steps or plan to get there

Where **R** is the Resistance to change

**Consider:**

- What's your level of dissatisfaction with your work?
- How clear is your vision of where you'd like to head next?
- How clearly can you visualize the steps that will get you there?
- How willing are you to take these steps? What stands in your way?

## ONE-DEGREE SHIFT

1. Take the time to journal on the above questions regarding the meaning you want to derive from your life and the Formula for Change.

2. Decide where you're deriving your sense of purpose from in this season of your life so you can further develop it as we continue in the book.

3. Fill in your mission statement using the gifts you feel resonate with you:

   **I have the gifts of** (*list your top three gifts*) **for** (*people, places, things you're passionate about*).

   **Therefore, I will look for opportunities to** (*list ways that you can develop and use your gifts*).

   For Example:

   I have the gifts of *hospitality, leadership, and encouragement* for *women, outcasts, the doubtful, and the burdened.*

   Therefore, I will look for opportunities to *make those around me feel at ease, encouraged, and supported to bring their visions to life.*

4. Do one thing you know will get the ball rolling based on your answers above.

   • Send the text.
   • Write the email.
   • Tell the person.
   • Do it now.

## TAKEAWAYS

- ✦ Identify your readiness for change in your career.

- ✦ Clarify your vision about what legacy you want to leave behind through your work.

- ✦ Understand the "why" of your work beyond societal pressure and bills.

- ✦ Define your purpose based on the person you want to be.

- ✦ Build new habits by asking yourself, "What would a [insert role] do?" Your answer to this question will lead you to act with integrity.

  (e.g., "What would a successful CEO do?" "What would a runner do?" "What would a comedian do?" "What would a loving parent do?")

- ✦ Consider your gifts and use your mission statement to relate them to what your calling might be at this point in your life.

# Awareness

*"The question is not what you look at, but what you see."*
—HENRY DAVID THOREAU

## CORE QUESTION

**"What parts of this (situation, problem, topic) need attention?"**

We go through the motions and try to "do the right thing" much of our lives. I applied to business school at eighteen because it was the "right" thing to do. It would give me the most career path options and biggest chance at success, or so I thought. Was it the only path open to me? No, however, I appreciate all the schooling I've been privileged enough to have access to. I also know that there are multiple journeys you can take to a career destination. We often base what we believe to be the "right" and the "wrong" path on what society expects. Sure, as a doctor, medical school is probably the "right" move. However, there are many nuances when it comes to the sort of medical doctor you want to be, where you want to practice, and who you want to serve. Some health professionals don't go to medical school. Same thing goes with any profession; we're in an age of many choices. Being aware means considering all our viable options. We must tune in to what is best for us, not just what sounds like the right decision superficially or doing it for external stakeholders, like our parents, partners, or friends.

One way to become more aware of our true selves is to consider how we feel about others. Carl Jung once wrote, "Everything that irritates us about others can lead us to an understanding of ourselves."[1] This is often a tough pill to swallow. It can be hard to accept that we have anything to learn from others' bad behavior. When I've asked myself, "Why am I so irritated by X?" "What about this is something I'm resisting?" Sometimes, I've received answers I didn't want to hear. They were things like, "I wish I could relax like they do," or "I admire how they don't take things so seriously all the time." I realized that the qualities that were irritating me were true opportunities for growth and learning on my part.

Learning to be more self-aware is one of the most valuable skills I continuously cultivate. I know I'm off track when I lean toward blaming, self-numbing, or distracting behaviors. Connecting to my heart means being real with myself, and it shines through in how others perceive me as well. At times I still complain about the annoying things that transpire—I'm human. But, when it comes to getting yourself out of a rut and feeling like the world is against you, remember that the first step is being aware of your thoughts in order to be able to consequently shift them to better places.

The same idea goes for different responsibilities or tasks you routinely avoid. We often shy away from the things that would help us the most. Make your list. On mine, you can find daily accounting and administrative paperwork. What is it about these tasks that you're trying to avoid? Where's the discomfort or fear? By shining light on the difficult things you create awareness and can proceed to make better choices toward your desired behaviors.

---

1. Jung, Carl. Essay. In *Memories, Dreams, Reflections,* 247. New York: Vintage Books, 1989.

# MENTOR'S TABLE

I believe there are different forms of conscious awareness: awareness of our environment, others, and how they perceive us; awareness of our physical body; awareness of the Holy Spirit within and around us, and awareness of the dialogue in our minds. Yoga and mindfulness started me on the journey of cultivating conscious self-awareness. I've had a few brilliant mentors throughout my learning. The main idea they all share is that the better we can distinguish the truth about what we're feeling, thinking, wanting, and needing, the better we can make decisions. This idea transcends downward dog and meditation.

Our bodies constantly signal what we need, like a tightness in our stomach or a lump in our throats. We need to listen to these signals instead of ignoring them or shutting our bodies down with painkillers, stimulants, and the like. I'll be the first to admit to emotional eating or using alcohol and caffeine as a crutch prior to my accident. Since adopting these practices (albeit imperfectly—I'm still learning), I've gotten pretty in tune with what my heart believes is the best next move. This has served me well in choosing clients to work with, interviewing potential team members, signing with vendors, picking products, and making decisions. I listen to my instincts. And when I don't? I often have buyer's remorse, feel burnt out, or feel uneasy. As we go further from what our bodies and minds tell us is true and necessary, we feel less grounded and further removed from our true selves. Building this skill is critical for us to learn how to tune back in to that inner guidance.

## Rachel Brathen

Yoga instructor, author, and influencer Rachel Brathen inspires millions online via her social media, website YogaGirl.com, and podcast. I'm grateful to have spent six months practicing at her yoga studio in Aruba. She's remarkably successful for someone who takes time out to meditate and spend time with her daughter. Having a global reach means that Rachel is subject to wide scrutiny. Despite her audience size, she has managed the public's perception of her well. She uses awareness to follow her heart and balances her brand reputation with her core values. She is truly someone who allows herself to *feel* and enables those around her to do the same. A large part of this is about allowing herself to be vulnerable enough to change her mind if new learnings come her way.

How others perceive us is largely out of our control, but we need to manage others' perceptions of us in order to succeed in society. Rachel taught me that you can be aware of your public persona and how you're viewed by the outside world while being true to yourself and your feelings. We can balance the times we compromise with the times we acknowledge and are honest about our stance on issues. We can manage and cultivate our personal brand while ensuring we're authentic and true to ourselves. There's no need to be disingenuous about feeling disappointment or anger. Name it, share it respectfully, and find a solution.

---

**IT TAKES BEING AWARE OF YOUR VALUES AND BELIEFS TO SHOW UP WITH AUTHENTICITY IN THE WORLD.**

---

Rachel is a brilliant example of someone moving through life with a commitment to building awareness of herself in order to show up and help others do the same.

## Carolien Gaarthuis

Carolien is another yoga instructor I met in Aruba, and she taught me that my body is my home. The more I listen to what it tells me, the better I can navigate life. This concept alone changed me. Often it's easier to hide from the messages our bodies are sending. It might be saying things like "I'm tired," "I need a break," or "This makes me uncomfortable." The moment you start paying attention to your body's physical cues, your decisions will make you better, not tear you down. Don't ignore the physical signals and instincts of your entire body. They're guiding you toward the right choices. Turning off your mind and listening to your body is a powerful form of awareness.

Your body has the answers. Are you willing to listen? During yoga practice, Carolien invites her classes to put their hands on the parts of their body where they're experiencing physical sensations, like tightness or soreness, and feel what their body is telling them to do—is it asking to be stretched or released? You can translate this in a less literal sense to situations both in work and life. Ask yourself how it feels when you're in a particular situation. Turn off the rational side of your mind and listen to what your body or your gut instinct tells you. Say goodbye to indecision and looking to others for answers about what you truly want. The most difficult part about this is intentionally creating the space where you can listen to your body's whispers. You have to make a conscious decision to regularly dedicate time to be still and listen to your body. Practicing this can be the most powerful ten minutes of your day if you prioritize making decisions that are a full resonant yes. If you find yourself taking action out of guilt, obligation, outward acceptance, or shame, then this type of practice is for you. Taking time to ask my body what it wants, needs, or desires has changed my life, even if it simply prompts me to take a nap or drink more water.

## Sadhguru

A yogi, author, and public speaker, Sadhguru is a renowned spiritual guide and shares meditations, including the effective *Isha Kriya*, which increases clarity and awareness and reduces stress, anxiety, and anger. It's a meditation used worldwide by people who want to find a sense of peace. It's in quiet peacefulness that we can hear the messages of the Holy Spirit. Some call it our intuition or inner knowing. The overall idea is similar—it is the force sharing God's wisdom with us, often in small doses. Inspired by Sadhguru, I've created my own meditation practice and have shared two below that I frequently use. If you've never tried this before, I encourage you to give it a chance, even if it feels like you're doing it wrong at first. Meditation brings moments of calm as well as moments of clarity and understanding. It will enhance all forms of your awareness.

### MEDITATION 1: BODY SCAN
You can use this meditation to focus on your physical self and release tension. It takes around five minutes and can be practiced daily.

- Get yourself into a comfortable position with your eyes open or closed as you prefer.
- Breathe in and out and notice your breath.
- Tune out any noises around you and focus on your body.
- Where in your body does it feel tight or constricted? Do you feel pain anywhere?
- When you inhale, think "inhale," and when you exhale through the mouth, think "exhale."
- Now, when you inhale, focus on the part of your body that feels tight and visualize the breath going straight to that spot.
- As you exhale, envision that tightness leaving your body with your breath.
- Repeat this breathing exercise ten times.
- If you have other areas of tightness or pain in your body, do the same breathing exercise, focusing on them.
- Now thank yourself for spending some time focusing on yourself.

## MEDITATION 2: GETTING ANSWERS TO QUESTIONS AND CHALLENGES YOU'RE FACING

Has something been swirling around in your mind? Perhaps you've noticed an issue that won't leave you alone. Day after day, your mind keeps returning to it. You feel uncertain about it. This meditation is designed to allow you to focus and gain some clarity on an issue that is bothering you or a decision you're having trouble making.

- First, taking the time to be alone with this is huge, so congratulate yourself for sitting on your own with a book and without technology, notifications, or expectations.

- Get yourself into a comfortable position with your eyes open or closed as you prefer.

- Take three deep breaths, in and out.

- Whether your eyes are open or closed, bring your chin up a little bit so your face is pointed toward the sky.

- Open your shoulders and your chest.

- Breathe in through your nose and exhale through your mouth.

- Inhale.

- Exhale.

- Inhale.

- Exhale.

- Now, bring that issue or choice you need to make to the forefront of your mind.

- Ask yourself what you want to know.

- Think about what you want to be or do, and ask yourself, "How can I . . . ?"

- Keep breathing and pay close attention to the little sparks of thought and inspiration as you contemplate. Listen for the answers and trust that you have them within you.

## Natalie Chapron

Natalie Chapron is a global women's empowerment coach. She helps women align their inner and outer beauty. She shows emotion, is present, and takes time to listen to what her heart says. Natalie taught me how to harness my intuition in business and showed me the art of intuitive pricing. Natalie's philosophy is to not only look at what goods or services cost, but to consider what your intuition believes is a fair and aligned value provided.

She believes that women need to bring their hearts and feminine wisdom into their businesses. She urges them to take time to make important decisions. Results are always better when care is taken. Sit in silence and set an intention before starting on your to-do list. Wear clothes and represent yourself physically in a way that makes you feel confident because it'll change how you carry yourself in business and around others. Your physical body shows people how you feel about yourself. A photoshoot in Paris, reluctantly accepting training in how to shop for myself, and a retreat to the caves in the south of France were what it took for me to finally accept and adopt Natalie's philosophy on this.

If you think this part is superficial, it is. They say dress for the job you want. This is true because how you physically show up indicates how you would like others to treat you. You're sending a congruent message about what you stand for and your self-worth. Use James Clear's theory of habits built around purpose (see *Chapter 2: Purpose*) and combine this with Natalie's thinking on self-presentation. Act and look like the person you want to be and embody your purpose in every way possible. When someone is attractive to others, it's because their self-awareness is congruent with how they portray themselves to the world.

MANY SAY, "FAKE IT TILL YOU MAKE IT," BUT
WHEN YOU'RE SHINING FROM THE INSIDE OUT,
YOU DON'T NEED TO FAKE ANYTHING.

The confidence I felt during my photoshoot in front of the Eiffel Tower didn't need bolstering. It emanated from me, and the photographs reflected the radiance within me. That is our work, being aware of the qualities we value so we can radiate them outward to the world.

## ASK YOURSELF

**What does being "aware" mean to me?**

**Why is it important?**

**How satisfied am I with the level of awareness I bring to my life?**

**On a scale of 1 (being low) and 10 (being extremely satisfied), rate your current level of satisfaction with the way you cultivate awareness:**

1    2    3    4    5    6    7    8    9    10

### Career

- Put aside any whispers about what's "unrealistic" or things you haven't "thought through."
  What is your inner wisdom or heart telling you is the right next career move?

- What do you *believe* is the next step?

- If you knew you couldn't mess it up, what would you do today?

- How might you take your new awareness about your desires at work and bring them to life?

### Relationships

- What is your inner knowing telling you about your relationships?

- Which relationships require more of your attention?

- Where might you like to change your approach?

- How is your relationship with yourself?

- What do you need more or less of in your current relationships?

- What would it be like to be more aware of your own needs?

## Health

- What messages might your body be trying to send you?
- Where are you feeling constricted or closed off?
- What movement or activity would feel restorative?
- What areas of your health need more attention?

## Spirit

- How do you characterize the wisdom or intuitive messages you get?
- What's your relationship with the Holy Spirit?
- What messages are trying to come to you when you're in silence?
- What messages are you avoiding by ignoring the signs or using distractions to stay busy?

## ONE-DEGREE SHIFT

1. Embrace your intuitive next step today as something that can happen.

2. Write yourself the prompt, "What do I want to do next in my work?" and spend twenty-five minutes writing your thoughts. More of a talker? Call the person you talk to about your work and let it out. Like drawing? Create a visual to express what you see.

3. Meditate in a class or alone using guided breathing or focused awareness of the present moment. Give it a try. Adding this to my day makes a world of difference in how present I can remain with myself and the events of my day.

4. When you've cultivated new awareness about an area of your life, decide on one thing you can do to move closer to what you want in that area. This could be as simple as cleaning up your living room or as big as realizing you need to make a complete life change. Map out (visually, in written form, or verbally) how you can make changes based on your new awareness.

## TAKEAWAYS

✦ Realize that intuition is as valuable as thoughts when analyzed accurately and acted upon responsibly.

✦ Learn to tune into your body's messages when it comes to your needs and wants.

✦ Use the information you receive from both your mind and heart when you make important decisions about your life.

✦ Take time to cultivate awareness of your current situation and map out opportunities for change.

# *Four*

# **Perspective**

*"The world only exists in your eyes.*
*You can make it as big or as small as you want."*
—F. Scott Fitzgerald

## CORE QUESTION

**"How might you look at the situation differently?"**

If everything is about how you look at it, then how frustrating is it when there are cold, hard facts to consider? How can a roadblock possibly be overcome by the way you look at reality? In this chapter, we're going to explore that.

Sometimes, your interpretation of your skillset changes what you're willing to try or do at work. Specialization has its place. I'm happy that the doctor who assessed me after my accident was a specialist in traumatic brain injuries. But have you ever felt that, because something wasn't within your range of practiced skills, you didn't want to bother attempting it? Have you ever found yourself saying, "Oh, I'd love to but . . . ?" This section is about what happens when we shut ourselves down before we even pursue the success we hope to create.

The roadblocks to your success are often self-created and based on untruths rather than reality or facts. Let's assume that there are *no* roadblocks. Am I suggesting that anyone can do anything and that we should allow people to create havoc with no set plan or specialized skillsets? Not exactly. However, if there's something constantly nagging at you—the thing that has popped into your head right now as you read this—then I say you may as well give it your best go. The alternative to trying is lifelong regret, and that one can sting a little. No one wants to be the eighty-five-year-old saying, "I would've, I could've, and I should've." We admire our elders with epic tales of adventure to share, the stories that keep us grasping for every last word.

This is not a cry for everyone to abandon ship and become yoga teachers in Bali. (Although if that's your next step, I believe in you!) This is a call for you to take another look at the things standing between you and the idea that keeps swirling around in your head and then aim to approach them differently. Getting our big, wild ideas out into the world so we can contribute to it in a meaningful way is the whole point of this book. Considering new ways of looking at your life is the first step to bringing about change in it.

## A Word on Limiting Beliefs

Often the stories we tell ourselves in the present come from something that happened in our past. I've heard many renditions of three similar beliefs: *I don't have the time, money, or experience to go after the things I really want out of my life.* Repeatedly, we work through the underlying fear, envision a brighter future, and take action, one step at a time, toward creating it in reality.

I heard about a great approach to moving through limiting beliefs at a church service I recently went to. I didn't think church was about self-development, but there's one of my limiting beliefs shining through. The pastor said:

"First, find awareness. Become aware of the belief you're having. Then, address the thoughts." She said, "lousy story, lousy state; lousy state, lousy story." Our thoughts are often a cycle of stories we tell ourselves repeatedly, for better or worse.

WHAT STORIES HAVE YOU BEEN REPEATING IN YOUR MIND?
REPROGRAM THEM BY TAKING ACTION.
WHEN YOU TAKE ACTION TO PURSUE WHAT YOU WANT,
YOU'RE PROVING THE LIMITING BELIEFS WRONG.

A great example of this is my mom who retired from her corporate job and completely changed careers. She worked on a doctorate-level degree for seven years while still in her full-time job to become a Jungian Analyst. Now she's fulfilled running her own practice and doing the work she's always wanted to do. It's not too late, you're not too old, it's not silly to want more, and you can do it. You are worthy of good things, and you deserve to spend your time on meaningful work. Become aware, address your thoughts and beliefs, and take action toward the life you desire.

## MENTOR'S TABLE

### Elon Musk

Elon Musk serves as a major inspiration for many. He is a guy who takes "That's impossible!" and turns it into "Watch me." From electric cars to space exploration, he defines what he wants, finds others who believe in the cause, and figures out a way to make it happen. If anyone embodies a growth mindset, it's Elon Musk. Having a third party tell you "no" can be a comforting roadblock, in a way, because it means you don't have to keep trying. And, as we all know, "trying" can be hard. Deciding to give something a chance is much easier once you draw your line in the sand. Then there's no turning back.

Again, choice matters here, both for yourself and others. If the first response someone gives you is "no," it doesn't mean there's no room to negotiate a better solution. Maybe somebody says "no" to your pie, so you figure out how to make a cheesecake instead—something you'd both enjoy more anyway. When it comes to new horizons, consider how someone like Elon, with seemingly unlimited resources, would approach your situation. Would he shy away from an unpractical option? Who would he recruit to help him with a new project? How would he tackle the criticism and judgment floating around in your mind about potential roadblocks and failures?

### Emma Hughes

Emma was a supervising flight attendant, and I'm grateful to have crossed paths with her in life. Emma is, by far, the most positive person I know. She has an almost super-human ability to put everything into perspective. She mostly lets stress roll off her shoulders, but more than that, Emma expertly takes problems and turns them on their head, approaching them with wisdom. Perspective can also be about bringing some humor and levity to a situation. I've seen this first-hand when Emma and I have traveled together. No matter what may happen or go wrong, Emma is calm, cool, and collected with a chipper tone and a smile. I constantly ask myself, "How does she do it?" Always resilient, she's never made me feel guilty for complaining about jet lag or feeling sad even though her situation may have been infinitely worse. The type of quiet strength Emma possesses is important in leadership. She leads and inspires without a direct word. That's powerful influence.

Whenever I have a work issue or something in my daily life that feels like the end of the world, I think of Emma and how she would approach it.

Emma doesn't pretend or deny it when things are challenging, and I'm in no way saying we should put on a fake smile when we face roadblocks. I admit, I'm the last one to do this in any scenario. If I'm upset, it's written all over my face. Emma's skill at reframing challenges is the key.

---

NOW I ASK MYSELF, "HOW CAN I?"
INSTEAD OF SAYING, "HERE'S WHY I CAN'T."

---

Her demeanor has helped me to direct my perspective toward the opportunities that abound in a difficult situation. Reframing a thought can help you realize that, although the present moment may feel insurmountable, if you look just beyond the horizon, there is possibility and room for growth to be found.

So, you can be sad about losing the job or the client. You're free to feel angry about the difficult co-worker or the presentation that didn't go according to plan. But then make like Emma and face the possibilities that lie ahead of this current twist in the road.

## Georgia's Dad

Years ago, I was with my friend Georgia and her dad, Joe, and we were sitting around the dinner table. I was pretty sure my boyfriend had cheated on me while I was away for work, and I was obsessing over it. Suddenly, with a calm, steady resolve and a face that says he's seen many things over the course of his life, Joe looked at me and said, "Is it worth it?"

At first, in my state of anger, sadness, frustration, and panic, my knee-jerk reaction was "Yes!" Joe went on to tell me about a time when he was frustrated at work. As a teacher, he had found himself volunteering too much time and energy to after-school math programs that weren't funded by the school. He was frustrated because he was giving so much of his time and the school wouldn't contribute to his efforts. However, once the school year was finished, he would move on to a new school, and he wouldn't continue the program unpaid. His pain and frustration had an expiration date. In that moment, my anger and upset at my boyfriend dissipated, and I realized that, no, this really wasn't worth it. I couldn't change what he'd done. I would move on, and eventually, the disappointment I felt would lift, and it wouldn't seem as important as it did in the moment. Things are rarely as dire as they seem in the heat of emotion. And they often resolve themselves somehow. What you can do is decide how much of your time and emotional energy you're willing to give to challenges or whether you decide to channel your energy elsewhere.

This is not a nod to push an issue down and act like you're fine or don't care. It's an invitation to fully feel while considering other possible ways to look at the scenario at hand. I've experienced many losses in my life. When it comes to mourning, grief, sadness, and the range of emotions surrounding deep loss, it often feels supportive to create an emotional container for difficult feelings. I get it—they can still come up out of the blue when you're at the mall and see a shirt that reminds you of your ex, but giving yourself dedicated time and space to feel, grieve, recover, rest, and reset is hugely valuable. And after a few days, weeks, or months, when the fog begins to lift and the pain fades, you can start a new day with a hint of the willingness to try again. When we ask ourselves, "is it worth it?" and the answer is, "for right now, yes," we know to continue healing, resting, and examining our situation. If we continue to check in and take little steps forward, that's all anyone can ask of themselves while navigating tough times with the wisdom of a broad perspective.

## Five by Five Rule

There's a rule floating around in the personal development world that distills the wisdom that Joe shared with me that day:

"If something won't matter in five years,
don't waste more than five minutes worrying about it now."

Talk about a reframe. The five by five rule is perfect for gaining some perspective when you're facing a challenging moment in life.

Having the skill to consider different vantage points when addressing a situation is vital. At work, it can be the difference between being so lost in the weeds you forget about the business as a whole and losing sight of your industry's evolution. Or being so pie-in-the-sky that you fail to look at your daily numbers and operational efficiency slips right through your fingers. Perspective is paramount when it comes to being a leader in any field. The five by five rule also lends itself to resilience. The ability to bounce back from challenges is a core trait of someone who others want to follow. Decide if what you're stewing about is worth the five minutes or five days of upset. Give it the time it deserves, then shift into what's next.

## Buddha's Two Arrows

In Buddhism, there is a concept of two arrows. The primary arrow is something you cannot change and will be accompanied by immediate feelings of pain, sadness, or grief. The secondary arrow is the stories you tell yourself about the scenario. You can choose which stories and judgments you repeat and think of in your mind. The work of cultivating perspective is recognizing that you're bringing secondary arrows upon yourself via the stories in your mind. We add to our pain by judging ourselves as lazy, unproductive, unsuccessful, or a failure when something outside of our "plan" happens.

To support yourself, you can sort out which thoughts and feelings are coming from the primary arrow or the secondary one. After my third pregnancy loss, I found myself saying, "Why me?" and "Why *not* me?" all at the same time. The level of judgment and the stories I was telling myself were amplifying my sadness and simultaneously taking me away from my true grief. The work was to focus my perspective on the true primary arrow, the loss we had experienced. My body was in pain, and I was exhausted from laboring for twenty-four hours and walking out of the hospital empty-handed. I was grieving the loss of yet another child. In sorting through the primary arrow, I could feel the true pain I was experiencing.

The secondary arrows were things like, "I'm not good enough," or "This shouldn't be happening to me," or "Will I ever be a mom?" They are stories we create in our minds that aren't pertaining to the event itself. They take us away from the true pain and into painful ideas. The stories are not grounded in facts or emotions from the event. Keeping my perspective on healing the true wound has allowed me to recognize when I was being pulled into feeling like a victim and realign with the perspectives that helped me heal. In this situation, that was changing my story to, "I did all that I could. My body knows what to do to heal from this." We're all human and it's natural to get pulled into secondary arrows when we're hurting. The point is not to avoid the pain, but rather to direct our focus toward healing the true pain of the first arrow, the actual event that transpired, so that we can heal. The secondary arrows emanate from not healing the primary one.

For me, healing has meant taking the time to grieve, then shifting the dialogue in my mind surrounding our babies to one of love and hope. It's noticing that the thoughts I have now are: "I trust my body," "The past doesn't dictate the future," or "I am feeling sad right now, and I can handle feeling that." Grief certainly comes in waves as we heal, and I focused on allowing myself to feel those waves fully, even when it was inconveniently happening in the car or during a meeting. We'll discuss more about emotions in *Chapter 10: Courage*. When something challenging happens that is out of your control, stay present in your thoughts. Focus on feeling and healing the primary arrow surrounding what happened rather than allowing yourself to ruminate and spiral into secondary arrows like judgment and victimization. When you notice yourself moving into storytelling, realign your focus to "What really happened? What is this pain about?" It's in the acknowledgment of the arrow and opening up to feel the hard feelings that we heal our pain.

Using this tool, we learn that sometimes the perspective shift we need is focusing on the present instead of looking to the future. Our emotions might feel as though they will swallow us whole, but I assure you there's no true way around them, only through. Give yourself grace while you're walking through difficult times in life. It's only after we've walked through them that we can come out the other side and look back with a different perspective to see the personal learning and growth we've undergone. Being in a valley can feel isolating, but there's an opportunity to go inward during these moments. This method of shifting my perspective toward the real pain of an event has helped me to face some of the lowest moments of my life. Oddly enough, the more I'm willing to go toward and face the pain, the stronger I feel, and the easier it is to get to the other side of it.

## ASK YOURSELF

**What does "perspective" mean to me?**

**Why is it important?**

**Where is there room to build more of a sense of perspective in your life?**

**How satisfied am I with how I consider different perspectives in my life?**

**On a scale of 1 (being low) and 10 (being extremely satisfied), rate your current level of satisfaction with the perspectives you bring to your work and daily life:**

1    2    3    4    5    6    7    8    9    10

## Limiting Beliefs

Which one of the following statements do you find yourself gravitating toward the most?

1. **I don't have enough time.**
   Things are too busy right now. I barely have enough time to read this book. How on earth do I have time to change the course of my career?

2. **I have bills to pay.**
   I don't have the money to take three months to build a business or switch jobs. The economy isn't good. Are there even jobs in that industry? Will people pay for the product or service I want to provide?

3. **I have the time and I have the money. But not enough experience.**
   When I think about switching to a new industry, a new job, or doing my own thing, I wonder how I can do it since I have zero experience or am not sure what exactly I would like to do. I'm also too old—I can't make a change now.

4. **All the above.**
   These are the most common rationalizations for being stuck in a situation you don't particularly want to be in. Which one do you lean toward most? Could the voice in your head be what is keeping you from building a meaningful legacy? You know better than I ever will.

## Perceived Roadblocks

- What are the roadblocks you've created for yourself?

- What's the nagging excuse you keep making?

- What's the thing you keep putting off because mundane, mindless activities seem more appealing? (Think mindless technology use, cleaning your entire closet out again, etc.)

- What's the thing you'd *love* to do but find every reason under the sun not to as it's unreasonable?

- What primary arrow am I avoiding because I'm scared I can't handle the emotions that come with it?

## Use the Five by Five Rule

- Re-examine the small steps you decided to take at the end of the last chapter.

- What's the most challenging thing before you right now?

- Ask yourself, is it worth it?

- Will it matter in five years?

If the answer to those last two questions is "yes," ask yourself:

- Who do I want to be in order to solve this?

- What perspective is the one that'll help me grow?

- What are the primary and secondary arrows in my thought process?

## Changing Perspectives

- Who is someone you admire for seeing the bright side of life?

- When do you feel most resilient to consider different perspectives?

- How much time and mental space are you willing to dedicate to this challenge you're facing?

- How might you find the opportunities or possibilities created as a result of the roadblocks you've identified?

- Answer "How can I?" as it relates to the core areas you'd like to change in your life.

## ONE-DEGREE SHIFT

1. Compile a list of the limiting beliefs you identified above. Put an arrow beside it and write the opposite belief you're going to use instead. Then define an action to take to reinforce the new story you're telling yourself.

   For example:

| Limiting Belief ➤ | New Story ➤ | Aligned Action ➤ |
|---|---|---|
| I'm too busy to start something new. | I make time for what's important to me. | Schedule thirty minutes per day to read this book, reflect on the questions inside, and take steps toward my goals. |

2. Check in with your accountability partner(s) to report your progress. This works. Do it regularly at whatever time interval makes sense (daily, weekly, monthly). Start a book club accountability group to go through each chapter. If you haven't found a partner already, send a message to someone you trust and ask them to accompany you on this journey. (Thank you to all my accountability partners for helping me with countless tasks that would've otherwise fallen to the wayside.)

3. Make a list of primary and secondary arrows swirling around in your mind lately. Decide to focus on the primary arrows. If you notice that you've started to swirl around in secondary arrow stories, pause and take a moment to shift your perspective.

## TAKEAWAYS

✦ Start to define the stories that have held you back so far.

✦ Give yourself a dose of honesty by naming what you want to do but haven't done yet.

✦ Record your limiting beliefs and the new stories you will tell yourself along with the aligned actions to reinforce them.

✦ Identify primary and secondary arrows in your day-to-day thoughts.

✦ Act—even one small step—toward what you know you want to do but have avoided.

# *Five*
# Vulnerability

*"Why do you stay in prison when the door is so wide open?"*

—RUMI

## CORE QUESTION

**"How do I *truly* feel about this, and what needs to change as a result?"**

I've battled being vulnerable my whole life, and I'm not the only one. Looking at our most fragile parts takes faith to believe that we'll be better off if we remove the band-aid and expose what's underneath. It also means being truthful enough with yourself to admit you have vulnerabilities in the first place.

I had a client named Mary, whom I admire deeply for what she's accomplished in her career. Not only is she a single mom to two lovely boys, but she has enjoyed a twenty-year successful tenure in a large corporation. Well, she *did* enjoy it up until a few years ago. Mary found that her work was causing stress and anxiety, and she felt pressured to work more hours and commit to more projects than she could reasonably handle. She started worrying about the effect her work was having on her mental and physical health and the well-being of her family. But she had a good salary, great benefits, and corporate perks. If she spoke out about her stress, asked for more time on a project, or took a vacation with her boys, perhaps that would show she lacked commitment. Would her boss and co-workers see her as a failure if she said she needed help? Maybe she would miss out on that promotion to vice-president if she took her eye off the ball. Mary carried on as she had been and her work-life balance didn't improve. That's when she found me and dug deep into where she felt vulnerable.

We addressed those vulnerabilities using second-order thinking, and she mapped out her next career step. She would ultimately leave her corporate position but wanted to start with a secondary source of income by freelancing as a human resources consultant and trainer before completely going out on her own. Sometimes going down the rabbit hole and considering a variety of potential good and bad consequences of our decisions allows us to move forward, with vulnerabilities in tow, excited about what's next and mitigating what risks we can along the way.

## Second-Order Thinking

MARY'S DECISION: PURSUE FREELANCING PART-TIME AND ULTIMATELY QUIT MY JOB

| Immediate Effects: (1st Order) | And then what? (2nd Order) | And then what? (3rd Order) | And then what? (4th Order) |
|---|---|---|---|
| More income | More time working | More stress, less fun | Need for boundaries, time off, less overtime with current job |
| Less free time at night and weekends | Need childcare/ help with the house | See kids and boyfriend less | Feel distant/like a "bad" mom/ girlfriend |
| Need to find clients | Marketing budget or spend time on client acquisition | Find marketing agency or learn how to do client acquisition | Budget the first ninety days for client acquisition and asking for referrals from my network |
| Quit job (eventually) | Loss of major income source | Need to replace income stream with freelance income | Use savings until income is replaced or do not quit until primary income is replaced |

Using second-order thinking, Mary was mindful of potential pitfalls, like missing out on family time, while she built her freelance business. By freelancing part time, it made the vulnerability of going after a new income stream more manageable and less scary.

We know that work involves dedication and it won't be easy all the time. Realism—the act of accepting the truth of a situation—is something we need to have a sense of, but what happens when reality causes you continued emotional hardship, stress, or burnout?

What happens when, like Mary, we become trapped in the need to avoid appearing like a failure, where the need to cover up our vulnerabilities means we stay in a situation we know isn't right for us? Saying no to something or someone can be an act of vulnerability.

OFTEN, LIKE A METAPHORICAL ELEPHANT IN THE ROOM, WHEN WE CALL OUT AND ADDRESS OUR VULNERABILITIES, THE FEAR OF THEM TAKING OVER IS SEVERELY DIMINISHED.

Vulnerability is about acknowledging and being honest about your boundaries. After my accident I had no choice but to acknowledge my physical limitations. The word "vulnerability" comes from the Latin "vulnus," which means "wound." We're always open to all sorts of potential emotional and physical wounds. We also have past wounds we care for and patch up with time. I had to learn to prioritize my health and recovery, which meant being open with clients and collaborators about what I could and couldn't do. By acknowledging my limitations, I could perform better and set realistic expectations for others.

Sometimes vulnerability is about saying yes to something and ignoring that nagging dread that you might fail. I will readily admit that realism makes the world go around. It allows us to depend on systems and organizations to continue doing what they do and keeps people in their defined roles. However, innovation, growth, and success can come from being unrealistic until that thing becomes realistic through your actions. "Be more realistic" is something I've heard my entire life.

Would following that advice have put me in a different spot?
Absolutely.
Could I have made more money if I'd chosen a more "realistic" path?
Maybe.
Would I be doing what lights me up?
No.

I've learned that being committed to my decision, even if the outcome isn't guaranteed, is what has allowed me to take big risks in my career. If I only focused on being realistic, I would have dismissed many opportunities that have changed my life for the better.

Using vulnerability to propel ourselves forward can be about doing something you might fail at in order to learn and grow. At twenty, I decided that a traditional nine-to-five job wasn't for me. I became a digital nomad (bear in mind that this was a decade before working away from the office was common) and started my own online business. I knew it might fail, and my father told me he was worried I'd made the wrong decision. I had some understandable worries, but acknowledging those and doing it anyway was an act of embracing vulnerability. They say there is no bravery without fear.

Writing this book has been on my mind for years, but something in me thought I could never do it. The truth was that I was afraid of failing. I was afraid of people not liking it or saying it wasn't valuable. At school, I had an English teacher tell me I had no real talent in writing. So, I've put off making a start. But now here we are. This is a book. And I've written it (admittedly with a lot of help), but these words would not be in front of you today if I didn't get comfortable being vulnerable with myself and in front of others, for their ultimate benefit. For when we expose our true selves to the world, it improves those around us as well.

## MENTOR'S TABLE

### Brené Brown

The first time I watched Brené Brown's now-viral TED Talk on vulnerability, I was in a headspace of "Yeah, I know all this. I'm already open and happy with being vulnerable." Brown's research is largely centered around shame and how that shapes the way we present ourselves. I thought I was already showing everyone my true colors at work and beyond. What I realized after delving further into her content was that I was really showing only a curated version of myself. I was deleting the unfavorable parts and being vulnerable only about what was "acceptable" to show. Her work on perfectionism is particularly brilliant and made me realize that nothing will ever be "perfect." In truth, we are meant to seek continual personal growth and improvement.

I began developing a podcast series in 2020. I've always been a "talker" and preferred learning in an auditory way. Since my accident, my eyes grow tired much faster than before, meaning that listening to an audiobook is more comfortable than reading a page of text. Podcasting seemed like an ideal medium for me to work in. But as I embarked on this project, I realized how vulnerable I felt about it. What if people didn't like it? What if they judged me? What if nobody even listened? What if I failed? My fears about nobody listening were unfounded after the first episode—even if the listeners were mainly family and friends. I felt bolstered by their support and belief in me. The self-expression I'd regained by taking the leap into podcasting invigorated me. It was scary to reclaim my voice, to know I was committing my thoughts to record and I couldn't take anything back once it was out there. But it also felt like I was presenting my real self—nothing hidden or held back—and that is a good feeling.

Acknowledging my vulnerability in my personal life has been revelatory too. My parents divorced when I was young. They were sad and my reaction was to bury my feelings and be strong for them—or at least pretend to be strong for them. Ignoring the fact that I was, quite understandably, devastated, I built the habit of hiding my true feelings from that experience. I married my husband in 2020, but in the early days of our relationship, it was challenging for me to let him see my "soft" parts as it had been with anyone in my close circle of friends and family. I was still in the habit of hiding anything that could be regarded as weakness. I avoided showing that I was scared at all costs.

Marriage has taught me that good relationships are about sharing all aspects of ourselves. We avoid deep misunderstandings when we come to a relationship with our whole selves because we can be honest about what we're feeling and thinking. This kind of vulnerability has improved my relationship with my husband and others in my life. It can also change working relationships. I find that clients respect me more when I'm realistic and honest with them and likewise when they can be the same way with me. One client shared that he was sick and needed the week off from our sessions. I didn't feel let down or annoyed. I told him to rest up, feel better, and let me know when he was ready to resume sessions. The alternative would have been him bringing half his presence to our meeting, making himself feel even worse and possibly resentful of me.

SHARE YOUR VULNERABILITIES WITH OTHERS.
BEING PERFECT ISN'T A PREREQUISITE TO BEING LOVED OR RESPECTED.

Learning how to acknowledge the good, bad, and weird is exactly what landed me in the place I'm at now. It takes a good helping of vulnerability and courage. Thanks to Brené's work and the support of those closest to me, I've slowly brought vulnerability to the forefront of how I show up. It takes knowing that it's better to have few people truly know you than to worry about the many who superficially spectate from the sidelines. That's what social media feels like, and while it is a curated space for people's highlight reels, it's important to remind ourselves of that when we engage. No one's entire life is showcased publicly, and being aware of that allows us to remember that even the most perfectly manicured accounts are just highlights of someone's journey.

# Vulnerability

## Jesse Koren and Sharla Jacobs

When I started coaching, I charged clients what I thought I was "worth." I thought that because I was doing something I'd dreamed of doing, because I enjoyed my work, I couldn't charge much for it. My dreams of building a team and bringing in six, seven, or eight figures weren't even fully crystallized. Then I met Jesse and Sharla, a couple running Thrive Academy, a seven-figure coaching business. They taught me that we can be successful, respected money earners *and* enjoy the work we do. They do this with vulnerability about their limitations and integrity in resolving situations as they arise. Working with them was one of the first times I saw a coaching business that was filled with vulnerability and hugely successful. I realized that being successful didn't mean having to "sell my soul." I could build a great company I believe in and stay true to my most important values.

My work with Thrive and many other entrepreneurs has proved to me that you can generate serious profits while being real about what you stand for. Being vulnerable means being open to attack or wounding. The thing is, in our most vulnerable moments, we showcase such a meaningful part of our humanity. It's what allows us to strengthen ourselves and fortify our blind spots and weaknesses. We need to acknowledge our vulnerabilities. It's in that acknowledgment that we cultivate deeply meaningful relationships with others. Our wounds are soft spots where our friends, clients, and family can support us and help us heal. It's in our vulnerabilities that our greatest opportunities are found.

## ASK YOURSELF

**What does being "vulnerable" mean to me?**

**Why is it important?**

**How satisfied am I with how I live with (and honor) my vulnerabilities?**

**On a scale of 1 (being low) and 10 (being extremely satisfied), rate your current level of satisfaction with the way you show vulnerability:**

1    2    3    4    5    6    7    8    9    10

### Career

- What idea, dream, or achievement would you love to make a reality?

- What have you taken off the table as possible because it seems too unrealistic, too big, too scary, too expensive, too hard, or something you're bound to fail at?

- Where in your career might you benefit from being more honest about your vulnerabilities?

### Relationships

- What's my personal relationship with vulnerability?

- What areas of my life do I feel comfortable being vulnerable in?

- Which ones cause me to shy away from being real with myself?

- Which relationships make me feel safe?

- What relationships make me feel insecure and like I can't share my vulnerabilities?

- How would I like to approach vulnerability within the context of my relationships going forward?

## Health

- Where do you feel vulnerable when it comes to your health, be it mental, physical, emotional, or spiritual?

- What are you avoiding admitting to yourself in regard to your health and wellbeing?

- Where might you put some attention to healing where you feel vulnerable?

## ONE-DEGREE SHIFT

1. Spend some time (twenty minutes, perhaps) reflecting on the idea you'd love to achieve. Write out the first five to ten steps that need to occur.

2. Bring out your "start process" and build some momentum on your work idea. Do the first thing on your list. Don't try, don't think anymore—do it. We need to act. Ready is a fallacy.

3. Reflect on your core relationships. Pick three to five people you're closest with. Who might you choose to be more vulnerable with? Maybe about your new work or business idea?

4. Try out second-order thinking when it comes to a vulnerable decision or area of your life. What are the consequences of things staying the same? What's possible if you choose to make a change?

## TAKEAWAYS

- ✦ Realize we're all human and that means facing vulnerability every day.

- ✦ Learn to reflect on where you could be more vulnerable and real with yourself and others.

- ✦ Use second-order thinking to harness vulnerability as a source of ideas and growth.

- ✦ Identify an idea, dream, or goal you find daunting.

- ✦ Take the first steps to implement your big, exciting idea. It's the whole reason you bought the book, isn't it? To shake up your life?

# Self-Advocacy

*"Those who stand for nothing fall for anything."*
—ALEXANDER HAMILTON

## CORE QUESTION

**"What do I believe in?"**

You learn a lot about self-advocacy when your ability to do so is taken away. I've experienced this personally and have had loved ones stripped of their voice on more than one occasion. My grandfather lost his leg due to a medical error at the hospital and couldn't self-advocate during his treatment and recovery. This led to family members putting their hats in the ring to help and be there for him. At every turn, there were decisions to be made about medications, rehabilitation, and more. It took most of the qualities in this book to show up, ask questions, be persistent, and not settle for mediocre care. Standing up for yourself takes a base level of knowledge or research in the subject matter, creating time and space to have your needs heard, and the willingness to stand up for yourself under pressure from others or the situation. That can be remarkably hard when "experts" are forcing your hand to make decisions in a medical setting or any other environment where you feel unprepared or pressured. One model that has helped me advocate for myself when I need to make an important decision is the BRAIN model. It was given to me by a doula when I was going into the hospital to birth my third baby that ended in pregnancy loss. Talk about an emotionally charged, can't-think-straight kind of situation. This model helped me advocate for myself at a time when I felt most alone.

## The BRAIN Model

1. **Benefits: What are the benefits?**

   Ask what the benefits are given your unique situation. Seek out data, research, testimonials, or case studies from a variety of sources to gather a holistic understanding of the solution(s) being presented to you. Perhaps get a second or third opinion on the solution being proposed to you.

2. **Risks: What are the risks?**

   There are trade-offs and drawbacks to every single choice. Don't let someone ever sell you on risk-free—it doesn't exist. Be sure you know and are okay with what you're giving up in every big decision you make.

3. **Alternatives: What alternatives are available?**

   This might mean getting a second or third opinion elsewhere. Shop around. No one doctor, company, or institution is the end all be all. There is always another way of doing things with a different benefit or risk profile that might be more suited to you and your situation. If someone avoids giving you alternatives, it's most likely the case that they're benefitting from the recommendation they're giving you.

4. **Intuition: What does my intuition say?**

   Cultivate self-awareness from *Chapter 3: Awareness.* Give yourself space and time to consider how you truly feel about the decision. If the environment feels like it's creating a sense of urgency, find a way to take a step back to check in with yourself. Ask yourself "what feels right to me?" Your gut feeling matters. Don't let anyone take that away from you. If something doesn't feel right, stop and say something.

5. **Nothing: What happens if I do nothing?**

   This one is so important. Most things aren't as dire as we make them out to be. Of course, if it's truly a life-or-death moment, you'll know it. Outside forces might ask you to decide because of an artificial deadline. Anyone who uses a false sense of urgency to compel your actions isn't looking out for your best interest. More often than not, you have time to make choices.

Are you the sort of person that advocates for your own needs? What about the needs of those closest to you? I find that many women I coach are much more practiced and confident in speaking up for their children or family members. Isn't that interesting? We're ready to stand up and protect those around us but often languish and brood about our issues in silence and isolation.

When I choose to advocate for myself first, I can do more for others, too. I'm more insightful and show up as the version of myself I'm most proud of. What happens to you when you skip the things you care about? Think of the times you've wanted to do something important for you, but someone or something comes up and you sacrifice that thing to help them instead. We've all been there. If you're not taking care of yourself, the reality is, you're not operating at one hundred percent, and resentment often starts to creep in.

Take the nap, take the day off work, and we will all be better off when you do.

The idea that you should invest time in looking after yourself doesn't mean you get to cop out of the responsibility of helping others. In fact, it means that when you put a new hierarchy in place that ensures your needs are looked after first, the way you help others is enhanced.

I've set up an automatic response on my emails. It reads:

> Hello,
> Thanks for your message!
> Due to my email batching approach, I will answer time-sensitive inquiries once per day. My aim is to reply to all within a week's time. I do this as a part of my compassionate technology policy, where I limit screen time. It is a part of my concussion recovery and prioritization of a balanced lifestyle.
> If it is an urgent matter, please email team@bechiefly.com.
> If you need to speak with me directly, please message or call
> ******
>
> I appreciate your understanding.
>
> Warmly,
> Kalyna

I've received many positive replies, but one in particular stuck with me. One day, a client wrote to me and included the following in the postscript of their email: "I love your auto-reply about giving yourself time to answer emails. It's such a beautiful expression of self-care and models your respect for self and others." The fact that I've received encouraging feedback multiple times says a lot about the world of work we inhabit. We've reached a time in society when being effective has become nearly synonymous with being quick to respond. My email policy of allowing a week to reply is my way of advocating for my time.

On a surprisingly high number of occasions, I notice that people not only resolve issues themselves but, in the future, they think twice before pressing send on an email when they aren't guaranteed a swift response. It means they take more time to craft their message, include all the relevant points, and have a realistic expectation for my response time. I always ensure that clients have a method for contacting me if they truly believe the matter is urgent, in which case I reply as soon as possible. This system instills self-respect and efficiency.

I've had only one executive call me out, saying this is unprofessional. I asked what she thought was a better approach to setting realistic expectations. I also asked if she personally replies to all emails she receives. She sheepishly admitted she doesn't and had no alternatives for me to employ other than to get an assistant to answer on my behalf. I have yet to receive a better approach to this method to ensure no one slips through the cracks of my personal inbox. If I don't reply quickly enough, I find those with urgent inquiries will check in again or wait to see my response within one business week. This has been the only way I can give myself a break when needed, reply with compassion, and compartmentalize email time rather than being beholden to my inbox.

This is not a replacement for customer service. If you run a company, it's imperative someone is always at the helm. However, in addition to a real person, it's remarkably useful to try and answer as many questions as possible via a knowledge repository.

But what if you can't set up something for yourself? Would your boss have your head if they received a reply from you stating that their question wouldn't be answered for up to a week?

When it comes down to it, the example of my email response system is not necessarily direct advice. Rather, it's about asking you to identify and carve out your own boundaries based on your priorities, and then advocate for them with others.

Let's look at two different but realistic options for a typical Monday morning:

**Individual A:** Overworked, overtired, and resentful. You haven't had a second to enjoy your lunch. You end up in a one-upping conversation with a similarly tired colleague about how little sleep you've had this week. After work, you head out to the bar with a friend and end up staying out until 3 a.m. Your friend has tomorrow off, but whatever, you'll get a big coffee, and it'll be fine. Congratulations! You're depleted, and when 7 a.m. shows up, you're also miserable. Your brain is foggy. You forget your keys. And you roll into your 8 a.m. meeting fifteen minutes late. Not a great feeling.

**Individual B:** You went to bed early and told your friend you wouldn't be able to make it to the bar tonight. He was a little annoyed, but he's already planning drinks for next week. You wake up feeling revved. You take the morning to scan your favorite sites, have your coffee in peace, and maybe even do some physical activity. You leave the house on time. When 8 a.m. hits, you're ready to go for the meeting with your team. Solid.

Which one of these is closest to you at least eighty percent of the time? If I'm honest, in my early twenties, I was a lot like the first one—and I thought I'd be fine. When relating the situation of the first individual to clients I have in their forties and fifties, I notice that the bar is often replaced with late nights at sports practice with kids or feeling like they must squeeze in domestic chores at all hours. Either way, they aren't doing anyone a favor by showing up resentful because their martyrdom rose above their own needs. The thing to remember here is that everyone loses when you run yourself to the edge. You're a shell of yourself, unmotivated, and lashing out at whatever poor soul gets in your way. And all those people you're trying to satisfy aren't getting the best of you either.

I've also realized that if I won't take a break or stand up for myself, the forces that be often find a way to do it for me. Won't take a break? A cold or other physical ailment will crop up to force me to rest.

Do I always make the right choices when it comes to my needs and the work I need to do for others? Of course not. But what I try to do is make careful, deliberate choices so I can show up as who I want to be as often as possible.

- When you make sure you're in top-notch shape (physically, emotionally, mentally, spiritually), what is that like?

- How are you operating?

- How are you making decisions?

- Who are you when you're at your best?

Clarify what boundaries you need to put in place to show up as your best self more often than not. Once you're clear on the boundaries you'd like to set, the next step is to advocate for the things you need. I've found there are a few criteria:

- What sort of advocacy is it? Examples may include mental or intellectual, emotional, spiritual, physical, time or space needs, or wants.

- How would you like to advocate for yourself?

Examples may include verbally, in written format, visually, using body language, or creating space between you and the situation.

Once you know what boundaries around work and responsibilities look like, you've got to master upholding them. Hence, I created my email auto-responder. It isn't enough to be clear about your needs. You need to advocate for them and uphold the boundary in practice.

That concept is one of the most challenging things for me. It's so much easier to abandon myself, say yes, and then feel bad about it later. The best way I've found to prioritize myself is to set up systems that help me stay true to the needs I've identified I have. That might take the form of a reminder on my phone, booking in regular massages, or asking for help on a project that I realize is larger than I can complete on my own. It's not about perfection, but rather noticing where you have the tendency to go beyond what you know is best for you. Then, you can create support systems to be like guardrails to guide you in your desired direction. If others are asking something of you and you want to deliver, how can you do that while maintaining your boundaries? What can you automate, delegate, or batch to create meaningful boundaries around work and beyond? You must find ways to make your needs non-negotiable or else you run a risk of the rest of the world finding a way to creep in.

## MENTOR'S TABLE

### Desiree

My first manager in a corporate environment was also my first advocate in the professional world. From the moment I began at the firm, Desiree had my back. She taught me that asking for what I needed to do my best work possible was reasonable. Des was the mentor of mine who taught me I wouldn't reliably get what I wanted at work without:

- Asking for it
- Having clear, justifiable reasons for asking
- Backing it up with numbers and facts

One of the most brilliant women I had the pleasure of working for, Des always had numbers to support what she proposed. This approach works wonders, not only in a conventional sales capacity but whenever you're reinforcing an idea. Having the data and facts prepared will usually help you come out ahead. You can muffle your way through a pitch, but you can't truly advocate for your ideas until you've deliberated both sides. Be sure to have as many relevant facts as possible for the key decision-makers involved. Show proof of what you expect will result from a vendor switch, your raise in comparison to your additional value delivered, or what the cost of an additional employee will bring to the output of the team. This is what I learned from Desiree.

She supported me in moving to remote work by allowing me, at eighteen, to work from home. That's in the 2000s when it wasn't cool to work from home. I remember a director saying she never got to work from home, so who was I to think I could? Des didn't flinch. She supported me because I got my work done at a high quality and on time. I always went above and beyond, regularly working late and overtime, which I did, of my own volition, unpaid. I wanted Desiree to be proud of me—*I* wanted to be proud of me.

She advocated for me to the rest of the team and showed me she was a supporter, so I did everything I could to deliver for her. That's the sign of an exceptional manager. Crucially, Desiree knew how to advocate for *her* ideas and *her* needs, which meant she could equally do so for those she cared about and managed. She convinced the firm to purchase a digital software service for $58,000 per year, not by expounding on the software itself but by showing that the benefits and value that would be delivered by using it would exceed $500,000 in new business for *them*. I remember sitting in that meeting and being in awe of her approach to sales and negotiation. Desiree was skilled at identifying and explaining the specific benefits things would bring her clients. She was always logical with pitching and clearly showed the advantages of making a purchase. Her ability to simultaneously advocate for the company *and* her needs made her indispensable.

At eighteen years old, I gave that job my best effort while learning what self-advocacy meant by watching Des. It made me realize I didn't have to let my needs be trampled. I just needed to ask for what I wanted in a compelling fashion.

## My Mom

It doesn't matter if you're negotiating with a multi-million-dollar client or serving someone that walks through the door of your shop, your ability to understand your needs and advocate for them will directly impact your ability to do the same for your clients. Of course, it's possible to negotiate billion-dollar deals one day and still cave the next day when your toddler wants ice cream. Negotiations are everywhere and situational. That being said, when you don't *ask* for what you want, your metaphorical ice cream won't come anytime soon. Living in the land of resentment starts to suck after a few months, years, or decades.

Think about it. The first section of this book is your opportunity to focus solely and completely on yourself so you can help others more fully in the following sections. Relish this moment of self-advocacy because there is plenty coming on how you'll impact others.

SUPPORTING OTHERS STARTS WITH STANDING UP FOR YOURSELF. WHEN YOU DO THAT, OTHERS WILL FOLLOW YOUR LEAD.

My mom is my first and perhaps most powerful example of this skill. Raised in a traditional Croatian family, her choices growing up were limited due to parental expectations—I believe this is something many of us face with our families. As we mature, our ability to separate ourselves from their view of the world and align more closely with our desires and dreams is what nurtures our ability to advocate for ourselves.

Historically, my mom and I had different approaches to negotiating. Where she would approach a negotiation with patience and calm, eager to avoid confrontation, I would show up and say, "It's my way or the highway." My mom would ask for something she needed diplomatically, whereas I would come in like a bulldozer and make demands. I used to think her approach was weak and that she needed to have a stronger approach to get things done. What I've learned, by her example, is that gentle persuasion can be as powerful as stern demand. She always had a breaking point where she would walk away; she was just calm and collected until she reached that point.

The core idea to remember here is that you need to know when you're willing to walk away and what your non-negotiables are. Without those, you risk becoming a doormat.

At work, this means knowing when to be direct and when to embody the role of the diplomat. Cultivating self-advocacy at work doesn't mean being the bulldozer. It means making your boundaries and needs known because no one else will do it for you. Don't be the one who settles uncomfortably into a mediocre position at a mediocre desk with mediocre pay because that's what landed in your lap and you don't want to ask for more. This isn't a criticism of corporate life, but it *is* a criticism of settling because it's the low-conflict way to coast through your career without ever really thinking about what you truly want.

*Your* time and *your* contribution are far too important to allow that to happen.

## ASK YOURSELF

What does "self-advocacy" mean to me?

Why is it important?

How satisfied am I with the way I advocate for myself in life?

On a scale of 1 (being low) and 10 (being extremely satisfied), rate your current level of satisfaction with your level of self-advocacy:

1    2    3    4    5    6    7    8    9    10

Making the safe assumption that you're the one who knows yourself best, where do you need to start advocating for yourself in your work?

What other parts of your life might need to be advocated for?
(e.g. health, relationships, spirituality, emotions, etc.)

## ONE-DEGREE SHIFT

1. Make a list of things that, if they changed, would make your current work more enjoyable.

2. Pick one thing to speak up about (or more if you're feeling bold).

3. Define what needs to be taken off your plate to make room for your biggest goals.

4. Set up a batching, delegation, or automation system for the busy work you notice gets in the way of your goals.

5. Find a way that feels good to you to communicate your new boundaries to key stakeholders by respectfully advocating for your needs and wants.

6. Identify which areas of self-advocacy you'd like to focus on: emotional, intellectual, task-driven, spiritual, or physical.

7. Name how you'd like to advocate for yourself: verbally, with space or time, in writing, or visually.

## TAKEAWAYS

✦ Use the BRAIN model for self-advocacy.

✦ Self-advocacy helps you be better for others and isn't an act of selfishness.

✦ Define areas to advocate for yourself at work and beyond.

✦ Set up a batching, delegation, or automation system to stay focused and advocate for your time.

✦ Take a bold action that requires you to stand up for yourself.

# *Seven*

# Focus

*"Rule your mind or it will rule you . . ."*
—HORACE

## CORE QUESTION

**"What do I want the end result to be?"**

Another of my pivotal life-changing conversations was with my friend Alexander. "Kalyna, you want to do it all, but you're getting nowhere with anything as a result." Ouch. After taking a step back, I accepted that parts of what he had said to me held truth. I had certainly been moving forward in my work and building my business, but I was being pulled in a million directions. I had "shiny object syndrome," and I had lost focus on the important things. I wanted to say yes to everything and everyone, but the magic of focus is that it clarifies when saying "no" is necessary. Being deliberate about what and who I let into my career, both as a client and as a mentor, was a huge shift. It has helped me be clear about the type of service I want to provide and where my key areas of growth for my business are. Narrowing in on what I deem important and then keeping my attention centered on that is extremely useful.

Let's think about what this means for you. We need *your* definition of success to make the rest of this book relevant. When you picture what your legacy looks and feels like, what parts of this vision are your *own*? Which parts are motivated by other influences or individuals in your life? Separate the different voices. It'll be the biggest favor you ever do for yourself.

What I've noticed with a lot of my clients is that they often have some-one else's version of success clouding their vision. This can be a result of their upbringing (what a parent views as success for their child), societal pressures, and close relationships, like their boss, colleagues, or friends. Because of technological advancements, we have more choices in our careers than ever before. The notion of traditional retirement is no longer the only or best option, and many of us can design a future we really look forward to while enjoying our present. Having a plan for the legacy we want to leave behind matters in the long run. As I have throughout this book, I'm going to ask you to look deep and find your own definition of this—to focus on what creating a meaningful legacy means for you. The value you will derive directly correlates to your willingness to get clear about what you think, want, and are willing to do to get there. This will also change throughout the different seasons of your life, so coming back and re-focusing is even more important than crafting an initial version of "success" in any given endeavor.

Free writing is an effective tool to get clarity of focus. Refined by Peter Elbow in 1973, it was originally intended as a creative writing tool. The aim is to write without stopping, letting your ideas flow onto the paper before your brain has a chance to censor them.

Free write about your vision of a memorable legacy based on the differ-ent aspects of life that are important to you. This need not be solely work-related. Legacies come in many forms. Some ideas to consider before you begin might include: health (physical, emotional, and mental), spirituality (relationship with God/the divine), environment or location (either work or home), daily routine (how would your day look if you were successful?), relationships (family, friends, romantic, colleagues), learning and growth, contribution and impact, finances, fun, adventure, or recreation.

Be honest with yourself.

I like to rank them in terms of importance, then prioritize tasks based on the ranking.

Now, I'll ask again. (You get closer to real clarity of focus in the second or even third time of asking a question, as we've learned in previous chap-ters. The most valuable insight is rarely the first thought that comes to our minds.) What does building a meaningful legacy mean to you? For me, I knew I wanted part of my legacy to be in changing hearts through speaking engagements online and in person. I want to leave behind a sea of people whose lives have been impacted by my words and example.

With that big vision in mind, in 2018 I narrowed my focus to landing a TED Talk. I created a spreadsheet of TED events, hired a speaking coach, and concentrated my efforts on applying until I was accepted. In September 2018 I reached my aim, speaking at TEDxWLU (Wilfred Laurier University in Waterloo, Ontario.) It was by considering my desired legacy, defining a specific goal to achieve within it, and then planning with the end in mind that I was able to realize my goal. When you're clear on your big vision, pick one major focus of what you want to achieve this year. One. It'll give you a North Star to aim toward which will make you unstoppable.

## MENTOR'S TABLE

### Tim Urban

Tim Urban is the co-creator of the blog Wait But Why. The website special-
izes in long-form blog posts about subjects ranging from artificial intelligence
to procrastination. They are uniquely illustrated by Urban's drawings, which
are both charmingly simple and powerfully incisive. In one post titled "How
to pick a career (that actually fits you)," Urban introduces his "Yearning
Octopus." On a simple doodle of a five-tentacled octopus, Urban explores
the many desires and fears that feed into our ideas of success and happiness.
Urban chooses the octopus, a creature traveling through water, as a clever
analogy to the journey we all take through life.

Each tentacle outlines a group of concerns or priorities when it comes
to how we measure our success in life and work. There are personal ones
like passion, self-esteem, personal identity, and fulfilling our potential. On
the societal tentacle are things like the approval of others, status, respect,
fame, and inclusion. There are moral concerns on another tentacle, including care of our loved ones and our impact on society and the future. Practical

concerns are covered in the basic needs tentacle, like having enough money to survive and ensuring we have security. This feeds into the fifth tentacle, habits, which covers lifestyle concerns such as freedom, work-life balance, and ease of living and working.

Urban talks about finding a balance using these tentacles. The importance you give to each one will depend on your personality and your values. Perhaps we're happy to put in long hours if it means we secure wealth and security for ourselves and our loved ones, but we're not willing to undertake work that compromises our morals. Urban's octopus can be used as a prompt for free writing exercises where we can dig deep into our values and priorities. We can use it as a roadmap to consider our wants and needs—the things that are non-negotiable for us. Understanding our values, our priorities, and our goals can help us see what matters most to us and find our focus.

## Stephen Hawking

Professor Stephen Hawking was the brilliant mind behind a theory that fundamentally changed the scientific community and the author of the groundbreaking book *A Brief History of Time*. He was a Fellow of the Royal Society, a recipient of the Presidential Medal of Freedom, and became a regular face in popular culture. Hawking also suffered from debilitating motor neuron disease for more than fifty years, which eventually left him paralyzed and only able to communicate through a series of artificial voice devices.

Hawking is one of the purest examples of using laser-sharp focus to achieve greatness in one's field. Regardless of whether Hawking's motivation came from wanting acclaim (societal), material wealth (basic needs), or a want to further mankind's understanding of the universe (values), his focus was what drove him to make the scientific breakthroughs he did during his lifetime. He gets a seat at my Mentor's Table because of his remarkable focus despite his circumstances. It's easy to see our personal situations as hindrances or get distracted by limitations. Hawking's legacy reminds me to focus on my unique characteristics and to capitalize on them. I'm not going to be brilliant at everything, but if I zero in on utilizing my gifts to make an impact, I'll bring something unique to the table that no one else can. No setback, personal situation, or delay in progress can stop me. Hawing's legacy is a reminder that if we remain focused on our goals, we can do the seemingly impossible.

## Warren Buffett's Fictitious Rule

Buffett is considered one of the greatest businessmen in the world. A brilliant man with a clear track record of success in an objective sense is something worth listening to, right? Well one of the things he is (falsely) credited with is creating a strategy for focus: The 25/5 rule. Apparently, he has denied creating it, but funnily enough, no matter the creator, the value is there just the same. The premise is that you write down twenty-five goals you want to achieve in your lifetime. For the next stage, you identify and select the five most important goals from your list. Once you have your five goals, give your focus and energy entirely to them until they're complete. After you bask in the glow of crossing one out, go back to your master list and add a new one to your top five focus list.

This process forces us to look at our real priorities and concentrate on achieving the most important things. I love it because I'm multi-passionate, and I find that the clients I work with gravitate to this framework when they want to do a lot all at once. I'd say to check in with this semi-regularly as well. Sometimes goals become obsolete or you pivot directions.

---

BEING FOCUSED EMPHASIZES YOUR LARGER AIMS AND ENSURES YOU PUT ENERGY INTO WHAT'S CRITICALLY IMPORTANT.

---

This is great to do as an audit of how we've spent the week and to check in on how our time is spent daily. How much time have you dedicated to your top five goals? Where are you allocating time that is unfocused or creating "busy work?" It's a wonderful way to remind yourself that, while you can accomplish many things on your list, they don't all need to happen at once but rather a few at a time. My husband would probably debate me on this, but there will always be something special to me about writing a list out on paper and being able to see it tangibly in front of me. Regardless of what medium you choose, keeping your point of focus nearby will ensure you remember what you're aiming at.

## ASK YOURSELF

**What does being "focused" mean to me?**

**Why is it important?**

**How satisfied am I with the level of focus in life?**

**On a scale of 1 (being low) and 10 (being extremely satisfied), rate your current level of satisfaction with your level of focus:**

1    2    3    4    5    6    7    8    9    10

Use the strategies we've explored above or a method of your own to identify what's important to you. Identifying non-negotiable items in your life is about setting priorities, so let's start with what is at the top of your list:

- What's the single most important thing for you to create this year?

- If you achieved one thing this year, what would it be?

- Why is that important to you?

You hold the key to all of this. This book is a conduit. Your answers and the subsequent actions you take are what will create true change in your life. Keep coming back to this one anchor whenever you feel swept away in the hundreds of possibilities that bombard you regularly. This point of focus will remind you why you're putting in the effort and time on a daily basis. Once you have the North Star clear, visualize the details about what it will be like and how it will feel when you reach it. Envision every single detail of what it'll be like when you reach it. Including all your senses in this really helps. The clearer you can imagine this North Star, the easier it will be to bring it to life. Your ideas may shift and evolve, so continuously clarify what your greatest priority is. Having one pointed focus on your biggest goal will give you the best shot at making it a reality.

## ONE-DEGREE SHIFT

1. Free write for twenty-five minutes to get all your ideas, priorities, values, and wishes out in front of you.

2. Make your 25/5 list of goals.

3. Set up your primary goal for the year, your North Star.

4. Make sure your personal version of a meaningful legacy is recorded somewhere—written, drawn, or typed out—and available for your reference and editing.

5. Allocate some time to work solely on the one thing you want to create this year. That could take the form of a timeline planning session to set up how you see yourself achieving it or a list of tasks and project phases.

6. Get clarity and the feeling of motivation by visualizing how it'll feel once you've achieved or completed the goal. The clearer you can see, feel, and bring the vision of your goal to mind, the easier it will be to bring it to life.

7. Decide how you will keep this idea front and center daily. If you're a visual person, make a vision board or written plan and put it in plain sight. You might create a plan to check in with your accountability partner(s) to share and hold each other to your respective North Stars.

## TAKEAWAYS

✦ Design *your* vision of success at work (and maybe beyond, too).

✦ Free write to get all your ideas out of your mind so you can sort through them.

✦ Identify the major goal for the next year that you believe will bring you closer to your idea of a meaningful legacy.

✦ Spend time crafting the success plan for your single point of focus this year at work.

✦ List your twenty-five goals and identify the five most important to focus on over the next few years. Remember, you only focus on one at a time until it's complete.

✦ Start a visualization practice to crystalize your vision of your goal and bring it to reality.

✦ Keep your vision in the front of your mind by having it around you as much as possible. This can be any visual or physical form that will remind you of where you're going and what you're meant to be focusing on.

# *Eight*
# Persistence

*"Never give up,*
*for that is just the place and time*
*where the tide will turn."*

—HARRIET BEECHER STOWE

## CORE QUESTION

**"Why is this important to me?"**

Have you ever watched a surfer? Wave after wave, they paddle back out and try to catch the next one. Any past results wash away as they approach the next wave as if it's their first. I love watching this process as it encapsulates this (seemingly) effortless persistence despite past performance or future expectations. Surfers live in the now of the wave they're approaching, and it's what makes it so beautiful. As I write this in Jaco Beach on the coast of Costa Rica, I'm reminded that while persistence might look easy from afar, it's such an inner game practice. It takes strength and resolve, and many of us cop out at the first sniff of failure.

So how do we cultivate the persistence of a surfer on the ocean who knows there's another wave coming? I think that's the first step, knowing there's always another wave. The core of being persistent is knowing you can always try again. It may not look the way you want it to or come exactly when you had planned, but that's the nature of life—it's unpredictable. It's the surfer's job to assess waves as they come and choose which ones to tackle.

Then, you need to mentally prepare for ramping up to catch the next wave. How do you do that if you haven't successfully made it yet? When I first tried surfing in Santa Marta, Colombia, I went through what felt like a washing machine and tumbled back to the coast. I had literally zero successful tries. I never once stood up on the board. Does that mean I'm a miserable failure?

---

### WELL, FAILURE IS MOMENTARY
### AND ONLY THE END RESULT IF I STOP TRYING.

---

I've since tried my hand at surfing in Brazil and Aruba. I'm no pro surfer, but I'm certainly persistent.

We need to know the difference between persistence to achieve a worthy goal and continuing down a path that is no longer meaningful. I think the distinction is in the willingness to put in the effort required to achieve it. To know the difference takes being honest with ourselves. If something isn't in your superpower wheelhouse and you see little return from sustained effort, maybe it's time to pivot. Sustained effort is most days, if not every day for a year, at minimum. Then you can discern if another year of effort is warranted. It all depends on how important something is to you.

So, you need to work out the equation for how long and how many resources you want to dedicate to the success of a given project or initiative. We usually know this inherently, but we often approach matters, especially new skills, driven by emotion. A new endeavor not feeling "right" or "easy" from the get-go could mean you need to put in some more effort. It's up to you to discern the difference, and there's more on that in a later chapter if listening to your instincts feels murky.

Surfing gives us a basic life example, and I can translate this directly to my work. Being an entrepreneur means eternally asking myself to be persistent. If there was one skill I'm cultivating daily, I would, hands down, say it's knowing when to persist and when to let go. With potential clients, potential employees, and even personally, it's all about looking for the next gig and improving current initiatives. Whether you choose to pivot focus or iterate differently, when we keep going, we're learning. That might sound a little too nice and fluffy, but the reality is that if an employer or client turns you down, it isn't a failure—it's a "no" that propels you in another direction.

## Persistence

I've recognized that the biggest thing that helps me persist is when I stop for a little while. Taking pause when things feel insurmountable, whether in prayer, meditation, or a deep breath, is what allows me to see the bigger picture. Then, I can decide to keep going with fresh energy instead of out of exhaustion. Resting and pausing are of utmost importance to cultivate persistence. With the right amount of time away, we can examine our situation from a bird's-eye view, then come back down and keep swimming toward our goals.

## MENTOR'S TABLE

### Chris Voss

When I decided I wanted to start building a multimillion-dollar coaching empire, it felt a little daunting. I looked at coaching authority Tony Robbins and Elon Musk and thought, "I'm not even one percent of the way—so forget it, I'll never get there." While it's a familiar response, it isn't realistic.

> HOW CAN I POSSIBLY GET *ANYWHERE*
> IF I DON'T START?

It's easy to say the first step is the most difficult one—the real kicker—but then what? I call it beginner's bias. And, honestly, it's the reason this book took years to write.

Chris Voss is a successful CEO, author, and speaker, but he was once a hostage negotiator for the FBI. In one of Chris's online videos, he explains how an individual needs to repeat something sixty-four times before it becomes part of their habit system. The number itself is less important than the repetition, but it's a first-tier goal that feels attainable. When I heard that number, I felt forever changed. Ten thousand hours to mastery felt insurmountable, but sixty-four times? I could handle that.

Of course, it still took persistence to open my laptop and start writing this book sixty-four times. Have I mentioned that writing doesn't come naturally to me? "But wait, aren't we supposed to do what we love?" Yes. And I do enjoy writing. Once I start. It's like jumping into a pool. It's never as bad as you think, but the *thought* of that initial cold shock can be torture if you think about it too long.

Voss taught me how to move beyond that first step once you've committed to something. At first, there's discipline in persisting. But the more you repeat it, the more persistence simply becomes another habit. In the beginning, just commit to doing something sixty-four times. Once you get to the sixty-forth repetition, pause to reflect on how far you've come and decide if another round makes sense for you.

## Mel Robbins

In her book *The 5 Second Rule*, Mel Robbins posits that when an individual has an instinct to do something, there's a five-second window before the mind starts actively finding reasons not to. Basically, we stand in our own way when it comes to taking action, and Robbins gives us a method of hijacking our brains so we can avoid procrastination. She says to count down 5-4-3-2-1, and then take an action, any action, to get some momentum.

Being persistent means being great at starting and then re-starting as many times as it takes to achieve your desired result. Combating beginner's bias means starting the thing you're avoiding. I call this my "start process." Use the 5 Second Rule as your start process if you wish or make your own. Create a ritual before you start something you need to do. Stacking actions up can create habit loops that make "eating the frog" (your most difficult task) easier. Robbin's tool can propel you into a desired habit loop.

---

SET UP HABITS AND SYSTEMS TO MAKE PERSISTENCE EASY
INSTEAD OF WAITING FOR YOURSELF TO FEEL MOTIVATED.

---

Once I've started, I look for that feeling of inspiration for the thing I'm currently working on. I find that the quicker I get out of the house in the morning, the better. The moment I'm out, my momentum increases rapidly. I also work better around people, like in a co-working space or café. Some tasks, like editing this book, require me to be alone in a silent room so I can completely focus. Knowing what propels you into action given the task at hand will allow you to build momentum quickly. The crucial step by far is the first, even if it's a small one.

## Milton Erickson

Persistence is related to motivation. However, it's crucial to remember that persistence is the *skill*, and motivation is the *feeling*. The trouble with feelings is that if they aren't there in the moment you need them to be, you're out of luck. If you can connect back to that feeling, though, you're back in business. I learned this from Milton Erickson, a pioneer in the coaching field. His work has undoubtedly made its mark on the industry at large. A core tenet of coaching is about figuring out why something is important to you on an emotional level. Great coaching connects to one's deeper feelings around a topic. Most people head into their first coaching session wanting to make a to-do list, but it's truly about wanting the feeling of confidence, clarity, or preparedness. When we connect to a deeper value, the right action to take will flow as a result.

The core question of this chapter is a way to connect back to that feeling of motivation, and it's one I ask myself daily. Repeatedly asking myself why something is important to me will quickly reinvigorate the feeling of motivation and urgency, and if it doesn't, it gives me a very telling answer. If it isn't important, don't do it. If it is important, then persist through the rough patch. If it's important and not urgent, schedule it. If it's urgent but not important, delegate it.

---

WHEN YOU CLEARLY ARTICULATE
*WHY* SOMETHING IS IMPORTANT TO YOU,
PERSISTENCE IS A NATURAL BY-PRODUCT.

---

By understanding the significance of a matter either for yourself, those around you, your company, or society at large, you will have the fuel to persist through the challenges you face.

## ASK YOURSELF

**What does being "persistent" mean to me?**

**Why is it important?**

**How satisfied am I with the way I persist through the ups and downs of work and life?**

**Would resting and reflecting make sense right now to help me see the bigger picture before diving back in?**

**What in your life is no longer meaningful and needs to be paused or stopped altogether? This might be relationships, projects, hobbies, or habits that you have kept up out of the feeling that you "should" even though they no longer serve your bigger mission or feel meaningful.**

**On a scale of 1 (being low) and 10 (being extremely satisfied), rate your current level of satisfaction with the persistence you bring to your projects:**

1    2    3    4    5    6    7    8    9    10

### Persisting with New Habits

These questions are important to consider when building a new habit and evoking persistence—decide if you're willing to continue with the action even when the initial excitement fades.

- Where might there be room to encourage more persistence in yourself?
- What new habits do you want to introduce into your routine?
- What are you ready to repeat at least sixty-four times to see results?
- What start process might you create to get yourself into the right headspace to act?

## Prioritizing What to Persist With

- What is urgent and important that I would like to bring to the forefront of my list?

- What is urgent and not important that I can delegate or remove?

- What is not urgent and important that I will schedule for later?

- What is not urgent and not important that I can remove from my list?

## Rest

- Remember: persistence requires periods of rest.

- How would you like to incorporate rest and reflection into your life?

- What parts of your life might benefit from a period of rest and reflection?

- What are the stories you tell yourself about rest or "unproductive" time?

- How might you change the way you view it going forward?

## ONE-DEGREE SHIFT

1.  Record the thing you want to make part of your new habit system. Write it down somewhere and do it for the first time before you read on. Whether it's on an old-fashioned sticky note or in your task management system, make sure it's recorded somewhere, and then go do it once now. Then if it makes sense, commit to doing it sixty-four times. Make it a genuine habit.

2.  Create a start process that works for you so you aren't reliant on feeling motivated alone. Feel free to use the 5 Second Rule from Mel or come up with your own to get into action! Maybe it's a few things, hence being a start *process*. Is it waking up, doing meditation, and then taking a walk? What are three or five steps you can stack to ramp you up for the activity you want to do? I find having this in place gives me the space to ease into my day rather than diving straight into emails or work tasks.

3.  Use your "start process." Use it every time you want to work on something important to you. For example, whenever I go to work on this book, I make tea, get a comfy spot in a café or on the couch, grab my laptop, and get writing!

4.  Eliminate what you have decided no longer has space on your plate. That might require shifting your schedule, having a difficult conversation, or delegating some items. Be sure to remove what's no longer necessary so you can persist on what's important to you at this stage.

5.  Make time for rest and reflection in your schedule. Decide what you'll do to fully rest in this time. This might be a good item to commit to with your accountability partner because it's so easy to back out when other things show up on your to-do list.

## TAKEAWAYS

+ Identify new behaviors you want to develop and build them into habits by committing to doing them at least sixty-four times.

+ Beat beginner's bias by creating and using a "start process."

+ Define what areas in your life require rest and reflection before you keep working on them.

+ Cut out projects, people, or habits that are no longer meaningful to you.

# PART TWO

# FULFILLMENT

*"Der Weg ist das Ziel."*
*(The way is the goal.)*

—Confucius

Adapted German Translation

# *Nine*

# Enjoyment

*"When you do things from your soul,*
*you feel a river moving in you, a joy."*
—RUMI

## CORE QUESTION

**"What would make this more enjoyable in the present moment?"**

My grandfather was in the Croatian Army, worked in Germany, came to Canada at forty, and worked in a warehouse until he retired. His work wasn't motivated by feeling "good." He worked to make money, to survive—a noble and necessary goal. And he was a hard worker. He, along with my father, taught me about the value of discipline. "It's about putting in your best effort," my father would say when I was a kid. "Do your best—that's all I expect from you." Again, a noble goal in some respects. And my father is the hardest, most devoted worker I've ever met.

And yet, years later, I found myself working at a law firm, giving it my best shot, and it didn't feel like it was enough. I learned a lot from the position. I had a great manager! It wasn't the $12 per hour I was making, and it certainly wasn't an entitled thought that I deserved "better" that made me long for more. My longing came from knowing that I wanted to put in my best effort, just not into *that* mission. I wanted to put effort into something that *I enjoyed* working for. That was the difference. The feeling started well before I even began working at the firm. I took the job because I knew I should, it was objectively a strong career starting point at a reputable firm, and I was grateful to have the opportunity. I learned a lot there, made friends, and was extremely glad they gave me a chance to prove myself. What I learned was I had to consciously acknowledge when something wasn't enjoyable to me. That takes listening to how we feel on a day-to-day basis to get a read on the prevailing sentiment we have at a given job or environment.

ENJOYMENT IS NOT ABOUT BEING HAPPY ALL THE TIME.
IT'S ABOUT DERIVING A SENSE OF FULFILLMENT FROM
WHAT WE'RE EXPERIENCING IN THE PRESENT MOMENT.

Emotions are like a wave, welling up and then peaking, all to fade into the landscape of our experience until the next one. Ignore them all you want, but they will show up stronger as anger, addiction, guilt, or regret. No matter how rational or logical we aim to be, our minds work this way, and we can either embrace that or work against it. Examining and releasing your thoughts and feelings regarding decisions at work can change the game for you. What if we started acknowledging, analyzing, and using the wave rather than crashing through it?

Our perception impacts our enjoyment and it comes in many forms. Before my time at the law firm, I worked as a bartender and server at a small local pub. It wasn't aligned with my bigger dreams, but it was a lot of fun. I did the job, got people what they needed, and had a genuine smile on my face during most of it—even if my feet were numb after fourteen hours of running around the bar. I think enjoyment has a lot to do with our expectations.

A law firm might be considered a serious environment, but I found it to be inspiring. I didn't necessarily come alive when updating the company's contact list alone in my cubicle, but I loved when I got to interact with my manager, peers, and lawyers at the firm. There are two activities that have remained consistently gratifying for me no matter the job: finding solutions to challenges and collaborating with others. I use creativity to come up with different ways to solve a problem. Then I enjoy figuring out how people's minds work in order to effectively share my ideas and reach a mutual understanding. The idea of finding enjoyment at work is less about the role and more about how you choose to approach it.

## Enjoyment

Your job title and responsibilities will change throughout your career, but the stuff that makes you come alive will likely remain the same. You can also have a few areas of enjoyment—in fact, it's likely you do. As you did with your priorities, I'd suggest ranking them. I love researching and learning. Given the choice, I'll interact with people before I research, but both activities add enjoyment to the way I work.

Fulfillment comes from putting effort into something that satisfies you while doing it. Understanding what makes you come alive is a benefit to yourself, but it also improves your contribution at work. People not only seem to prefer being around those who bring a little life and happiness to a situation, but their enthusiasm spreads amongst the group. If you're performing tasks you enjoy, you're likely to give them more effort and time, which achieves better performance as well.

Stuck identifying exactly what it is that gives you a sense of fulfillment?

Here are a few things you might want to consider:

- Working with others in a team
- Working independently
- Intensive research work
- Data analysis
- Achieving goals or targets
- Building or creating things
- Using your creativity or designing
- Upholding and promoting a cause or a belief
- Helping people
- Teaching or mentoring
- Communicating
- Physical activity
- Strategizing
- Organizing and logistics
- Entertaining

There are many more, and Roadtrip Nation[2] is a great resource for career design if you want more inspiration. Here are the things I enjoy most about my work at this stage of my life, in ranked order. You can expect the ranking to change over the course of your career as your priorities evolve.

1. Communicating: I love sharing stories.

2. Strategizing: I enjoy working out how visions will come to be.

3. Helping People: The core of what motivates me.

4. Teaching/Mentoring: This allows me to share ideas and help people grow.

5. Creating Things: Having a vision and then bringing it to life is exciting!

At the end of this chapter, I'll ask you to do the same, so start thinking about *your* list.

---

2. Roadtrip Nation. https://roadtripnation.com/explore/foundations.

## MENTOR'S TABLE

### God, In Its Many Names and Forms

The true purpose of life is to be in the present moment and cherish the time you have here. Our lives are filled with moments of joy and suffering, and we need to acknowledge all parts of the spectrum. Gratitude and appreciation for where you currently are in life is paramount to fulfillment. Whether you believe you're "spiritual" or not, these are recurring themes in religions and spiritual philosophies. I'd say it's meaningful that revered texts from around the world, written in many different languages and during different time periods, provide similar answers to the same broad questions. Doesn't that say something about the similarity of the human experience? Humans, after all, wrote these texts to encapsulate the idea of purpose and meaning beyond ourselves. I'm not here to debate the merits of various religions or the existence of one or more deities. Your religious beliefs are your own. We'll have to save that for another book.

When I list God as a mentor, I'm speaking of the insight I have gained from interacting with the universal source I have perceived and the teachings from different spiritual and religious texts I've encountered throughout my life. I feel God in my life and within myself every single day. It's a knowing that runs through my veins that I'm held by a force larger than myself. There is such wisdom to be drawn from the texts and philosophies describing this force that's within and around us all.

The teachings of Buddhism speak largely of the impermanence of life and how important it is to be present in every moment. To release suffering, we're meant to be mindfully present in the moment and appreciate the now. While studying Buddhism and mindfulness, I realized how fulfillment stems from being completely present and grateful for the present moment. Impermanence is a strong reminder of how important it is to be present. Whether it's your kids growing up, your parents aging, or your thirties and forties flying by, we need daily reminders that everything is fleeting. If we remember things are perpetually changing and we can't ever recreate a moment in time again, it's a strong reality check to find fulfillment in the here and now.

Hinduism states, "the third purpose of a Hindu's life is to seek *Kama*." In Indian literature, "Kama" is often used to refer to sensual or sexual pleasure or desire, but the concept should be defined more broadly as obtaining enjoyment from life.[3] From the study of Hinduism alongside yogic philosophy, I uncovered that enjoyment brings forth happiness not just for the individual but for the group's energy. We are all considered part of nature and are interconnected. Enjoying your work and your life benefits everyone. In the Western world, we often consider personal enjoyment to be selfish. If we look at it from a collective mindset, fulfilled individuals who enjoy life raise the collective's success.

Taoism speaks of the harmony and flow that encapsulates the human need for action in the concept of *wu wei*. It invites us to act only when needed and in a way that flows like the curves of a river in alignment with the cycles of the world around us. Getting into the state of this flow and oneness with the present and our environment is what brings us pure harmony and enjoyment in our work and lives. This gives another nod to our connectedness with others and the world around us. If I enjoy my day at work, land a new client, or sell another copy of this book and I'm flowing, not forcing those outcomes, everyone wins. I'm not taking anything away from someone else. If we act in flow with enjoyment, we can bring that flow to others by example. The best way to influence or help others, in my opinion, is to show them first and foremost what's possible via what I choose to do and how I choose to act.

With the awareness that we cannot predict the future, consider a core idea that my relationship with God has taught me: We can have a great life if we surrender some of our desire for control and enjoy the ride!

## Mihaly Csikszentmihalyi

Through researching what piques creativity, especially in the workplace, Csikszentmihalyi recognized and named the psychological concept of "flow state"—a highly focused mental state that humans can reach where they achieve ultimate productivity. Many of the people he interviewed during his research described reaching a state of being when their work simply *flowed* out of them without much effort. In Csikszentmihalyi's words, flow is "a state in which people are so involved in an activity that nothing else seems to matter; the experience is so enjoyable that people will continue to

---

3. Khilesh Sivakumar et al., "The Meaning of Life According to Hinduism," Philosophy 1100H Blog, October 12, 2014, https://u.osu.edu/group5/2014/10/12/the-meaning-of-life-according-to -hinduism/comment-page-1/.

do it even at great cost, for the sheer sake of doing it."[4] He determined that flow is not only essential to a productive employee but it's imperative for a contented one.

Have you ever experienced flow? Csikszentmihalyi mentions a few characteristics of flow that will be familiar to most of us who have found ourselves in this state:

1. You have a clear vision of your goal or reward.

2. The passage of time changes. It can appear to pass more quickly or more slowly.

3. The very act of doing the task is rewarding.

4. You feel you're working with ease; there's no struggle

5. There's still a challenge, but you have confidence in your skills to meet it.

6. You're completely focused on your task, both physically and mentally, your mind does not wander, and you don't notice distractions.

7. You have a feeling of being in control.

This is the familiar state of concentration you reach when you're entirely absorbed in a task. It's a state that makes you forget to eat, pee, or sleep, as you entrench yourself into something. You're in the groove; you have found your "flow." Having something that allows me to reach this state regularly is a non-negotiable aspect of my career. It's what brings enjoyment to my time spent working. Spending some (or most) of your working time in this state hugely benefits you and the company or people that receive the fruits of your labor. Mihaly's research on flow shows that there's no substitute for that complete absorption into what you're focused on in the present moment. Flow is something I take into consideration while crafting my career. I take note of the things I get totally lost in for hours, and then I make sure those things are a large part of the time I spend contributing to helping others. Is this project, job, position, or company conducive to me being in flow? No? Then perhaps there's something else that will be a better use of my time.

---

4. Csikszentmihalyi, Mihaly. Essay. *In Flow: The Psychology of Optimal Experience.* New York: HarperPerennial, 2008.

For Csikszentmihalyi, the improved results of working in a state of "flow" are secondary to the individual's enjoyment. He explains: "These examples suggest what one needs to learn to control attention. In principle, any skill or discipline one can master on one's own will serve: meditation and prayer if one is so inclined; exercise, aerobics, martial arts for those who prefer concentrating on physical skills. Any specialization or expertise that one finds enjoyable and where one can improve one's knowledge over time. The important thing, however, is the attitude toward these disciplines. If one prays to be holy, or exercises to develop strong pectoral muscles, or learns to be knowledgeable, then a great deal of the benefit is lost. *The important thing is to enjoy the activity for its own sake,* and to know that what *matters* is not the result, but the *control* one is acquiring over one's attention."[5]

What I continue to put into practice about flow is reminding myself that the process is as critical as the final result. I can't emphasize this enough, from one overachiever to another: the result is only a fraction of the equation.

## Brazilian Culture

*"A joia de viver.*
*Liberdade pra dentro da cabeça.*
*Vai dar certo."*[6]

Every culture has its expressions about what it means to have a good life. While in Brazil, I saw and experienced how to embrace the joy of living. Brazilian culture has truly refined the practice of enjoying the process of things, the very act of existing. Take a walk along a street in the evening, and you'll see people out talking, dancing, and enjoying the night. It's a different pace and prioritization of savoring everyday life.

We all talk about life being short, but let's quantify this and get serious about letting go of the stress and pressure in our daily lives. When we momentarily forget the tight, constricted feeling of deadlines, responsibilities, targets, and timetables, something cool happens. Our faces and bodies relax and we're instantly more attractive to others. People are drawn to others who are enjoying their lives. Sometimes, as a result of the softening and releasing

---

5. Csikszentmihalyi, Mihaly. Essay. *In Flow: The Psychology of Optimal Experience.* New York: HarperPerennial, 2008.

6. English translation: "The joy of living. Freedom inside your mind. It will work out."

of the feelings of martyrdom and burden, those deals, opportunities, or promotions start pouring in.

Most of us want to be around the magic of enjoyment rather than pressure and obligation. My aim is not to take productivity out of the work equation. We can be a balance of both characteristics. We can be dedicated and hardworking but also loosen up a bit and produce even more by bringing some lightheartedness to the table.

I put on a Brazilian song by the band Natiruts while working on this section, and it has changed my entire experience of writing this chapter. I notice my mood when I listen to music versus when I don't. That small switch changes my mood as I do desk work—every time. My state of mind is different, especially depending on the genre and specific song. I find ideas flow faster, and I'm more inspired to write. I am *enjoying* this moment right now—while also achieving something. Throw on music while you work, crack a smile at a meeting, ask someone you have fun with to come on board and help you get a project done, and see what enjoyment can do for your personal performance and bottom line.

A specific mentor who taught me this concept is Neto. No matter what happened during my time in Brazil—whether we got robbed, or our apartment got broken into, or I got Dengue Fever—Neto showed up with complete support and unruly optimism. "*Vai dar certo,*" ("It'll be okay") he would say. A staple Brazilian expression. Although this was tied to a kind of faith, his lighthearted approach was also accompanied by an ability to see solutions that cut through even the most dire of straits. And, when you're hooked up to an IV system in a Brazilian clinic, seeing stars, this type of attitude has a make-it-or-break-it impact on your experience. I deeply appreciate what Neto did for me during my time in Brazil. His outlook on life changed my own and set the benchmark for what enjoyment means to me, both in life and in work. Now I aim to bring a bit of Brazilian love and passion to everything I do.

## Martin Seligman: A Pioneer of Positive Psychology

Thinking positively chemically alters your brain, influencing which hormones are released and which neural pathways you reinforce. Enjoyment literally changes the way your brain works. Martin Seligman is a renowned professor of psychology and the pioneer behind the theory of "learned helplessness." Seligman asserts that, as individuals, we can learn to endure unpleasant experiences *even when it's within our capacity to avoid them.* His work has taught me to recognize and let go of feeling helpless and get myself thinking about possible solutions. He has encouraged me to ask, "How can I?" rather than, "this is so difficult, I'll never solve this issue."

When I find myself in an unpleasant situation, I focus on what's possible and within my control. When I refocus on solutions, I feel capable, and then I start enjoying the situation as a challenge or new adventure. Rather than feeling stuck, helpless, and hopeless, I cultivate faith in the fact that I can find a way out. Then, my brain comes up with answers to the question, "how can I resolve this?" That feeling of capability brings immense enjoyment to the task at hand rather than dread. Obviously, there are situations like excruciating pain that don't lend themselves to this easily, but there is an increasing body of research behind the effectiveness of visualizations and meditations. With pain, there are exercises to visualize the pain going away, which shows we have a lot of power in where we put our focus. For things you desire, like enjoyment at work, visualizing your desired outcome primes your mind to bring that visualization to life.

In Seligman's Theory of Positive Psychology there are three pillars:

1. **Positive experiences**

   We collect experiences along the way and label them as positive when they have either good memories or end outcomes. Either way, these are often subjective and based on our expectations. I've changed the way I set expectations. Rather than try to predict the enjoyment I want to have, I do what I can to remain present and experience the enjoyment the situation has to offer me. This has helped me have more positive experiences because I don't try to control the outcome as it arises.

2. **Positive individual traits**

   We can define traits we deem positive that we'd like to cultivate. The usual suspects—kindness, compassion, patience, and optimism—may show up. It may also mean you choose to focus on something like resourcefulness, resilience, or courage. This goes beyond positive thinking and into traits that benefit your thought process of the second pillar. If we focus on cultivating our positive personality traits, we leave less time and attention for the negative ones to overshadow them.

3. **Positive institutions**

Institutions as a category is an interesting one for me. I take this to mean communities I choose to associate with. This can mean your school, church, government, clubs, community, or place of work. I would also invite you to consider your family unit or extended family and friends. The adage, "you are who you surround yourself with," holds true in this pillar. Take good care in choosing the institutions you associate yourself with both at work and beyond.

Optimizing our enjoyment within the three pillars increases our internal satisfaction and how we experience the world around us. I've found that cultivating these three areas has an exponential effect on how I feel and perform at work.

Harvesting enjoyment in our daily work is about finding deep fulfillment in seemingly small actions. We can do this by using Seligman's PERMA Model for well-being. It is built on five elements: positive emotion, engagement, relationships, meaning, and accomplishments.

1. **Positive emotion**

When Seligman talks about "positive emotions," he means more than simple happiness. He's speaking more broadly about the human experience, which is comprised of hope, love, pride, gratitude, and empathy. These are all positive feelings, and Seligman argues that we can actively cultivate them in our everyday existence. By savoring these positive emotions, we counter negative ones. That doesn't mean you ignore the challenging—it means you set your aim toward the light, not the darkness. You could do this in various ways: engaging in actions you enjoy, spending time with people you love, listening to music, singing, dancing, running, or reflecting on something you're proud of or that makes you feel a sense of gratitude.

Seligman is asking us to take deliberate action to bring more positivity to our lives. The idea makes sense, but the challenge is following through and doing it. I've found that ensuring you bake this into non-negotiable parts of your day is the only way it consistently gets done. For me, my morning walk is imperative because Max, my dog, requires it. I do well to have a yoga practice with a class or group; otherwise, it somehow doesn't happen if I'm alone. It's funny how easily we can deprioritize what we know breeds positive emotion and benefit. Social support is the best way I know how to ensure this isn't the case. Reach out to someone, pet or otherwise, and leverage accountability to motivate positive emotions. This will bring positive momentum to your practice and ultimately allow you to build strong habits in your daily life. More frequent positive emotions equal more enjoyment.

2. **Engagement**

Seligman explained engagement as "becoming one with the music," and in this sense, he comes close to Csikszentmihalyi's idea of "flow state." It's the complete absorption in an activity, being entirely present in the moment and focusing completely on the task at hand. Furthermore, Seligman writes that we're more likely to reach that state when we're engaged in activities that harness our best strengths—things we're *good* at.

There's a lot of talk about skill development in the career coaching space. You can try to become really good at things that don't come to you easily. That may be useful for things like basic accounting or legal knowledge; however, the majority of your focus is meant to be on your "genius zone," as many call it. Engage with the things you're good at because they'll become your calling card. It's great to be known for things you enjoy doing repeatedly. That may have been one of my biggest challenges when I started coaching.

One-on-one work is extremely gratifying, but it doesn't scale well. At some point, you can't take on more clients in this model. Had I asked myself, "Do I want to repeat this forty hours a week, fifty weeks a year for the next ten years?" I may have thought twice about solely focusing on a one-on-one practice. I was learning about my genius zone when I started coaching and quickly realized that teaching concepts to groups in a classroom is where I shine. Do I enjoy one-on-one coaching sessions? Yes, but the next question to ask is how many hours can I dedicate to this so it stays enjoyable? There's always a threshold where efficiency and excitement go over the edge into burnout and frustration. Consider what will keep its intrigue ten years down the road when looking at your strengths. You can be good at something and enjoy engaging with it, too.

3. **Relationships**

Seligman recognizes that humans are social beings and that relationships are crucial to our well-being. Good relationships make an individual feel valued, loved, supported, and heard, but Seligman notes that we need to work on our relationships to achieve this. Positive responses to others like empathy, enthusiasm, interest, and compassion improve relationships. In practice, this means making time for genuine interactions.

It's too easy to be engrossed in our objectives and next task. I've found that it's always the person who takes an extra minute to check in and truly care about how I'm doing that'll change how I perceive them and the relationship. I've learned this lesson when it comes to fully enjoying my marriage. Creating satisfaction in relationships is about being willing to be honest and climb the mountains you encounter together. The deep fulfillment that comes from facing life together is what marriage and friendship is all about.

4. **Meaning**

For Seligman, "meaning" is about purpose, and he acknowledges that this is different for everyone. Your purpose is tied to your values and your sense of worth. It might be a cause, a belief, your community, or a creative endeavor that is your passion. Having a sense of meaning is crucial to finding fulfillment, and it brings focus to your life.

We covered this in *Chapter 2: Purpose*. Impacting something larger than yourself is critically important. When it comes to mixing meaning with enjoyment, it often has to do with *who* is defining the meaning and what *their* definition is. We regularly get caught in the noise of others' definitions of our lives.

There's a concept of internal and external locus of control. Some of us are more driven by internal motivations (internal thoughts, feelings, ideas), while others grasp the external world for reference (winning competitions, awards, being validated by others.) Most of us are naturally somewhere in between, depending on the context. I challenge you to question where you derive your sense of meaning from. Is it mostly internal or external?

For your own sake, eradicate the things you spend time on that don't give you a sense of deep purpose or make you feel meaningless, even if others disagree with you. Find a way to make the things on your plate more meaningful. When work is mainly an obligation, your life will fly by, and enjoyment will take the back seat. Building a meaningful career doesn't denote that every minute will be happy or light-hearted. It's the attitude of showing up and getting the most out of every hour and every day that will allow you to enjoy the process and not just the fruits of your labor.

5. **Accomplishments**

A sense of "accomplishment" doesn't solely come from achieving your ultimate success. It can come from meeting a target, mastering a skill, persevering, or simply taking a small step toward a larger goal. It's a reason to be proud of yourself. A feeling of victory will naturally occur when you've given something your honest effort.

We can invite a sense of accomplishment into our lives by setting ourselves challenges, then recognizing and celebrating our successes, however small they appear. We often use technology and social media to give us a hit of artificial achievement. When we hinge our sense of accomplishment on a flighty or superficial source, we must go back for more with greater frequency. We can substitute this sense of comfort with food, gossip, or addictions. It gives us the feeling we're accomplishing something without producing anything meaningful. This is why all five parts of the PERMA model work in tandem. Set your aim toward accomplishing something that is realistic and attainable, then ensure you celebrate when you hit your mark.

The PERMA model can be used in all aspects of our work. We can approach it with positive emotions. We can identify the activities we do well that get us into a state of flow. We can foster positive relationships with our colleagues, clients, and suppliers. We can find work that gives us purpose and leaves us with a sense of achievement at the end of the day. Use all elements in tandem to create an enjoyable and meaningful project, role, or company structure.

## ASK YOURSELF

**What does "enjoyment" mean to me?**

**Why is it important?**

**How satisfied am I with my level of enjoyment in life?**

**On a scale of 1 (being low) and 10 (being extremely satisfied), rate your current level of satisfaction with enjoying your work and daily life:**

1    2    3    4    5    6    7    8    9    10

- Where in your career might there be room to cultivate more enjoyment?

- What activity are you most likely doing when you reach your flow state?

- What do you obsess or completely nerd out about? How does this relate to your idea of purpose or what you see as your passion?

- What do you enjoy doing?

- Do you *enjoy* what you do most days? Answer honestly, and if the answer is no, then consider finding a way to make a change.

## ONE-DEGREE SHIFT

1. Make a list of positive experiences, traits, and institutions you'd like to bring to life or put more attention on.

2. Build a PERMA model for a project or situation at work and come up with ways you can bring more enjoyment to it.

3. Audit your current work situation with your accountability partner.

   - Rate your level of enjoyment at work on a scale of 1-10.

   - Which parts do you enjoy most?

   - What are you doing when you're most likely in a state of flow?

   - What would you like to enjoy more?

   - What parts will you never enjoy?

   - What are your strengths?

   - How often and when do you use them?

4. Look at the list you've made with your accountability partner and rank the things you've noted in terms of levels of enjoyment (things you love, things you like, and things you dislike).

5. Write down what you enjoyed and spent hours doing as a child.

## TAKEAWAYS

✦ Enjoyment means finding joy in the process of doing your work, not having fun all the time with zero responsibility. It's the feeling of fulfillment derived from work.

✦ Recognize that it's truly possible to really enjoy your work. (Please don't move forward without this clear in your mind.)

✦ List positive experiences, traits, and institutions you'd like to bring into your work and life.

✦ Identify the aspects of work that light you up and reveal your character strengths.

✦ Explore the activities that put you in flow state.

✦ Build a PERMA model about the characteristics of your work or a project you're spending time on.

✦ Audit your current work situation in terms of enjoyment by talking it through with your accountability partner or on your own.

# *Ten*

# Courage

*"To dare is to lose one's footing momentarily.*
*To not dare is to lose oneself."*
—SOREN KIERKEGAARD

## CORE QUESTION

**"What's the best possible choice considering my hopes and fears?"**

I was flying more than 10,000 feet above Paraguay, and the instructor yelled, "Okay, NOW!" I shot backward out of the small plane and fell at what felt like lightspeed. I did this in 2016 while soaring over Iguazu Falls in Argentina. With an instructor and a parachute, I cascaded over the Brazilian border. Skydiving is a simple example of courage. It seemingly takes one instant to be courageous and jump. However, it's important to deconstruct everything it took for me to be on that plane and then fall toward the ground. I made a series of decisions, saying "yes" to multiple propositions.

I said yes at least six times before actually jumping out of the plane.

I said yes to book the skydive.

I said yes to getting in the cab.

I signed a yes on the consent form.

I said yes to putting on the gear and to learning the safety instructions.

Finally, I said yes to getting in the plane.

Not to mention the yes I had to tell myself repeatedly to get over the fear of jumping!

Courage

I believe that courage is about understanding and directing our inner dialogue. Courage is the fuel to navigate the series of yeses and noes we need to build a meaningful legacy. Set a vision, find the courage to say "yes" to it, and take small actions toward that result as many times as possible. Courage is about taking the leap when you know what you need to do, but it feels slightly uncomfortable the moment before you do. Courage is also saying no to the numerous opportunities that may sound great but don't lead you further along the path you want to walk on.

Whether you jump out of the plane or stay standing on the sidelines is dictated by your "courage quotient." Of course, we must address that courage is inherently related to self-advocacy. When your yes is exceptionally clear, you'll instantly know when you need to say no to the extraneous options that don't make sense to you. Courage does not mean saying yes to things that don't fit in with the person you want to be or your vision for your life.

I see being courageous as necessary. Our ancestors wouldn't have made it without this trait. We have numerous examples that those who succeeded once dared to pursue the unknown and took risks in the name of their values.

We often find a way to muster the courage for big moments in life—a loved one's passing, divorce, or a big promotion. I think the everyday moments where we shy away from who we truly want to be are deceptively dangerous. It can be in small things, like sending that email, applying for that job, having that scary meeting, or telling your boss that thing you know they don't want to hear. Those things all take a level of courage and they're easier to avoid.

Anything that makes you uncomfortable requires courage. I had a client who told me her dream was to take her photography to Cambodia but felt daunted by the prospect of going so far from home. The idea of traveling to Cambodia isn't that scary to *me*, but for her, it was a leap that would require courage. The idea of sharing my feelings and the potential of being rejected is scarier than any journey to a faraway country. For her, this idea and desire would be life-changing.

We need to harness fear as an indicator and listen to what it's whispering. It lets us know what we want to move toward or away from. It's interesting to flip fear on its head and ask, is this fear or excitement? Our body responds quite similarly to both signals, so we need to make sure we're naming the sensation correctly. What we need to muster the courage to act depends on our personalities and perceived fears. The key is acknowledging the fear. Check in with yourself to be sure what the feeling is. Name it. Is it truly fear? Or is it excitement about what is possible when you act? If you decide it's some level of excitement and the outcome would be enjoyable, rewarding, worthwhile, or meaningful, then take the plunge! I think we would benefit from this reframe in our daily lives. We automatically see a big opportunity as risky, which elicits fear and, naturally, that means fight, flight, or freeze. It certainly doesn't mean, "yes, I want to do this." That makes sense and forcing ourselves into something like that will lead to reluctant action and suboptimal results. We need to clarify our motivation and be sure we're acting from a positively expectant place. If you can't negotiate with yourself to find the action worthy of taking a leap, perhaps it isn't right for you at this time. Waiting for the right moment to act is wise, an absolute act of courage, and takes patience, too.

A word on balancing courage with recklessness and a personal story about my failure to soften the blow: I was on a ski trip in the Swiss Alps. I was a beginner and quite terrified of skiing. "I'll teach you," my husband said. Perfect.

Out on the slopes, a few children whizzed past me on the almost-flat hill we picked to start. After two hours, I thought, *tomorrow, I'll try the beginner's slope!* So that's what we did. After going down two versions of a beginner's track probably ten times, I was still scared, but getting a lay of the land. I started thinking about how I'd like to be courageous.

"Are you ready for the big slopes?" he asked. My heart said no, but I didn't want to disappoint him.

Two hours into skiing I decided I would go for it. What's the worst that could happen? We went up about two thousand feet into the mountain and were treated to a breathtaking view. Then, I took a glance down that enormous slope and was petrified. Too much. Too soon. I knew I was biting off more than I could chew. But I tried anyway. It resulted in me flat on my face. Luckily, a snowmobile ride helped me descend to the bottom, quickly and comfortably.

The moral of the story? Courage was getting to the top of the beginner's hill and being excited to try it. Biting off too much was being scared and knowing it wasn't the right time which resulted in me falling flat on my face.

Trust your instincts when judging whether it's *only* courage that you need to climb up your mountain. Map out all the steps to reach the top.

Ask yourself how comfortable you feel. What are the risks? Be honest with yourself and admit when you feel you need more time or preparation. Again, what others think or expect is null and void here. You and only you need to live with the results of your decisions.

If you're worrying about whether you'll ever start to climb your mountain, if you find you're spinning your wheels at the bottom, it may be because you don't truly want to climb the mountain in front of you. This is something you must address openly with yourself. Why did you pick *this* mountain? Perhaps you're preparing to climb the wrong mountain for you. If you feel stuck and reluctant to start, I encourage you to get more clear about where you're headed.

If you're spinning at the bottom but *know* you want to get to the top, you might need to work out your roadmap. Get clear on the steps and checkpoints you can create for yourself along the way. They need to be big enough to be true progress toward your goal but not too big that you expect yourself to go from zero to one hundred in one big leap. A decent rule of thumb is to set up three levels—bronze, silver, and gold—and then set up three to five checkpoints at each level. Create your roadmap to be as exciting as reaching the summit. Each checkpoint can bring you that sense of achievement when crafted meaningfully. Then you're employing reasonable amounts of courage without the burnout or overwhelmed feeling that ensures you're biting off more than you can chew.

At the end of the day, goalsetting and any other coaching tool can bring you closer to a clarified understanding of yourself. Your feelings, hopes, dreams, and vision for your life are ones only you can define. If you get halfway up a mountain and decide it isn't the one for you? The only person you need to report to is yourself. No matter who you might disappoint, courage is making the decision you believe is right at this exact point in your journey.

## MENTOR'S TABLE

### My Grandparents

There are many greats in history that I could use to support the notion of courage. I could look at biblical stories or the lives of great politicians and entrepreneurs, but the point hits so much closer to home when I think of my grandparents.

I'm sure there's someone in your family that you grew up hearing stories about. They were courageous, defeating all odds to create something for your wider family and its well-being. All four of my grandparents moved from Croatia to build a better life in Canada. They chased the quintessential "North American Dream." It took extraordinary courage to leave their familiar lives and pursue something new, exciting, and scary. This level of courage and faith inspires me every day. They flew across the world in search of something more for their families, suitcases in hand, without any guarantees.

We often look for certainty in the chaos of life. Whether through routines and lists or using substances and hedonistic pleasures to forget the uncertainty, we often try our hand at controlling chaos and change. But we know change is inevitable and can be out of our control at times. We need to become our own version of courageous to create a better life than the one we're living today.

### Joseph Campbell

Joseph Campbell was a literature professor at Sarah Lawrence College in Yonkers, New York. He's most known for his study of mythology and especially his work *The Hero with a Thousand Faces*. Campbell spent his life studying myths from around the world and outlined the journey of the archetypal hero in his theory, "The Hero's Journey." Campbell's theory is that all "heroes" follow a similar path that takes them from the status quo of their existence into something unknown and new by way of an invitation.

The hero ventures through trials and failures and often has a mentor to guide them. At the halfway point of the journey, the hero faces his darkest hour—a moment of death and rebirth. The rest of the journey sees the hero profoundly changed by the experience. Even when they return to the status quo of their normal existence, they're fundamentally different from the person they were before the journey.

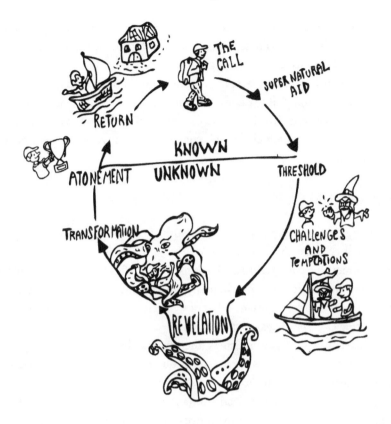

How is this literary theory relevant to your work life?

Make the shift in your mindset and realize that *you* are the hero, and your career is the adventure. Your career will move through cycles like in Campbell's theory. You will choose opportunities or roles that might initially feel daunting. The unknown could be a new company, a new industry, a new skill, a new place, or a new challenge. You'll earn promotions and have many mentors. You'll also inevitably have troubled times when you're called upon to test your character and resources to succeed.

Campbell's theory taught me that, to create a new world, we effectively need the death of who we know ourselves to be in order to face our darkest fears. Courage is the thing that allows us to accept the invitation into the unknown—the first step on the hero's journey. Courage is what helps us accept the "death" of our old selves, or reality, and leap (ham-handedly) into our new metaphorical day. Nothing I've ever created has been without altering myself or something else in my world. People often describe this as a sacrifice. But to me, it's prioritization. If you want a new job, you must be courageous enough to let go of the old (current) one. It's also an act of faith. If you want to build a business, you must have the courage to take risks and bet on your ability to learn how to grow it successfully.

Ideas are in your mind, begging to come out. Having courage gives you the impetus to jump, pull the cord, and take action. Daring to act will bring your ideas to fruition. It's time to consciously embody your version of the "hero" and identify which challenges you're willing to work to overcome on your journey.

## David Hawkins

Our feelings are never final, but we can cultivate them to elevate our experience. Using courage to sit in our fears, recognize them, and move beyond them is something Sir David R. Hawkins, M.D., Ph.D., an internationally renowned spiritual teacher, psychiatrist, physician, researcher, lecturer, and developer of the widely known "Map of Consciousness," writes about in his book *Letting Go: The Pathway of Surrender*.

In his Levels of Consciousness theory, Hawkins explains how some human emotions can act as forces upon our existential state, and we can harness others as powers to extend ourselves into a better place. Fear, along with grief, guilt, and shame, lead humans into states of inactivity. When these emotions hamper us, we can't move or be productive, akin to the fight-flight-freeze response. The first step to moving into the emotions that actively benefit our sense of well-being is feeling courage, which breaks through the negative emotions that hold us back and launches us into a state where we can start being productive.

There's a pervasive idea that if we enjoy our work, it means we're taking it too "lightly" and aren't serious about the outcomes of our endeavors. Here are some of the most common beliefs or fears around the idea that work is something that can and should be enjoyed:

1. We only deserve things through hard work, struggle, and sacrifice.

2. Suffering is good for us.

3. We don't get anything for nothing.

4. Simple things aren't valuable.

# THE LEVELS OF CONSCIOUSNESS

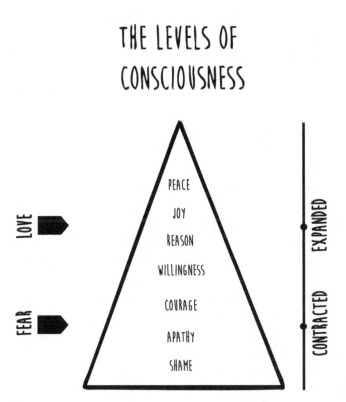

Hawkins's theory shows us how we can overcome these psychological barriers if we build our thoughts and feelings up to the level of feeling courageous. There will always be challenging times in life. Hawkins taught me to remember that my feelings are just that—feelings to be noticed and then released. If we allow ourselves to be governed by our fear, then we will never be in a state to make good decisions. It feels like a big leap to go from scared and apathetic straight to loving and peaceful. It's much more realistic to move up the ladder of emotions.

Here's an example: You hate your job. You don't think you're good at it and feel lost. In this place, you're in no state to make decisions about your next step. Your self-belief is low and you're worried and fearful. What can you do to bring yourself to a place of courage?

You start with changing the dialogue in your head. You acknowledge that you're giving what you can to your work. You acknowledge that you might not like the work, but you can accomplish things when you set your mind to it. You identify areas where you're valuable—perhaps you make contributions in meetings, you meet deadlines, and you see things differently from others. You might feel grateful that your work allows you a good work-life balance, compensation, or the opportunity to challenge yourself. Slowly you invite in these positive emotions, and your situation doesn't seem quite so negative. From this point, you can call on your courage and start moving toward change and progress. Using only statements that you believe are true, you can talk yourself from a place of feeling guilt, apathy, or fear into feelings of courage, willingness, or joy.

Hawkins writes in depth about not attributing feelings to outside causes. Focus within. If a work contract is frustrating me, I take the frustration for what it is, and I do my best not to lay the blame on the work contract as being the cause of it. If a client is "making" me feel frustrated, I take responsibility (see *Chapter 1: Responsibility*), identify the frustration as my own, and let it dissipate with acknowledgment and time.

It's easier to blame things outside of ourselves, but no situation is the cause of our "suffering"—we are. Those are big words to chew on.

As discussed before, feelings are signals. If you notice you're in the lower levels of consciousness, living with fear, irritability, or guilt, pause and find a change of pace. I've been there. Life as an entrepreneur is no easy feat. You get to keep creating and showing up when most of the things you do miss your intended mark. That's why enjoyment of the process is so critical and getting into a courageous headspace is one of the keys to continuing on the path when things get rough. Honestly talk yourself into a courageous state by moving up the emotional ladder, then act from that state of mind.

## Moving Around

As a kid, I moved around a lot—about ten times in ten years. From the age of four, I got used to packing my backpack and being shuttled to my other parent's place. Many of us have experienced the same because of divorce. Not surprisingly, I grew into an adult who has traveled around the world and can make home anywhere. My secret is that it never became easier. Leaving my hometown and going off on an adventure excites me and leaves me choking back tears of sadness. I've learned what courage is by not having a choice. Many times, our safety blankets of life are ripped out from our grip, and we're flying through the unknown, grasping at straws of certainty. The truth is that real certainty comes from focusing on what we do have control over, our thoughts and actions and surrendering the rest.

We often know that no other person is coming to save us, but we wait eagerly for someone or something to save the day in our lives. Cultivating courage isn't a luxury—it's a necessity because life will demand difficult things from us repeatedly until it's over. I wanted to figure out how to harness the same feeling of necessity when working on projects and goals.

After speaking with hundreds of people, the story was the same. Limiting beliefs become some sort of truth in our minds, and then the fear of failure makes daring to act too dangerous, so we don't.

THE TRICK IS DECIDING WHICH FEAR PROPELS YOU.
YOU CAN BE SCARED TO JUMP OUT OF THE PLANE,
BUT WHAT ARE THE CONSEQUENCES OF STAYING INSIDE IT?

The fear of things staying the same and becoming stagnant always trumps the new and foreign for me because of my values. What values are more important to you than the perceived safety of comfort?

Every time we moved, I thought of all the new people, places, and experiences I'd have in a new neighborhood. I didn't want to miss out on that by being upset about the home we left behind. I also didn't have a Plan B—that helped. I couldn't backpedal on the decision. The same rings true for a new job, relationship, or goal. We need to move away from fear, commit fully to our next step, and put faith in the unseen possibilities of the new situation as we make the leap.

## ASK YOURSELF

**What does "courage" mean to me?**

**Why is it important?**

**How satisfied am I with the courageousness I bring to my life?**

**On a scale of 1 (being low) and 10 (being extremely satisfied), rate your current level of satisfaction with the courage you bring to your daily life:**

1    2    3    4    5    6    7    8    9    10

- Where in your career might there be room to cultivate more courage?

- How is your fear keeping you safe?

- How can you create safety while also going after what you want?

- What fears at work are you ready to acknowledge and start to release?

- What are you scared of failing at (and maybe secretly want to try)?

- What's a mountain—a challenge or achievement at work—that you're excited to climb and conquer?

- How does this factor into the one big thing you decided to achieve at the start of the book?

- What would you do at work if you *knew* you'd learn and grow no matter the outcome?

## ONE-DEGREE SHIFT

1. Using your answers from above, write down five things that you wish to approach with more courage. What's one courageous act you can take at work this week? Do it. Report back to your accountability partner(s) and bask in your courageous glory.

2. Take a step toward the ideal vision you have for your life. Say yes to something that brings you closer to your vision in whatever big or small way you can muster up the courage for. Be bold and brave.

3. Define a limiting belief about your work that you're ready to move beyond. Keep yourself in check: Ask your accountability partner(s) to remind you whenever you or they realize you're heading down the same path of succumbing to negative emotions like fear, guilt, and shame.

4. Write out your hero's journey. Having a clear narrative about your life makes it easier to plot out where you're headed. Where are you on your journey so far? What have you learned from the previous parts of your journey? Who have you identified as your mentors? What did they invite and encourage you to do? What steps have taken some courage? What have been your high points? What have been your lowest points? How did you react at both these times?

   Here's my story as an example:

   > Today, I've coached more than five thousand hours with clients in fifty-four countries, but when I started out, I was told I'd never make a dollar doing it. I've hit multiple rock bottoms. Some months I made nothing and needed help to pay my bills. Then, one day at a leadership conference, I learned some new math.
   >
   > How much were my services worth?
   >
   > How many clients would I need to make a profit?
   >
   > I wrote the numbers on a worksheet:
   >
   > $5,000 per person x 10 clients = $50,000
   > *or* $1,500 x 30 = $45,000
   > *or* $10,000 for 10 people = $100,000
   > and something clicked.

*Wow.* I could do this, and it would take ten to twenty people per year signing up to make it work. Out of seven billion people in this world, I can find ten to twenty clients a year. I could totally make this into a viable career. And that was the *"aha!"* moment for me. So, in 2018, I worked diligently and had my first six-figure year. Now at Kickstart Your Work, I have built a network of more than forty coaches, and we're helping people around the world excel at their work.

What's your story? Write it out. Edit as needed.

This will serve you as your career goes through its inevitable peaks and valleys. Creating a cohesive dialogue about your career story is of immense value, as demonstrated by Joseph Campbell's work. It gives you a narrative to follow when you share about your career, and it consolidates the story in your mind, which is important for your identity. It's vital to sort out the story of who you were, are, and want to be so you can act that out in real life with your contributions to the world.

## TAKEAWAYS

✦ Refine the roadmap of your current career mountain.

✦ Set up bronze, silver, and gold goals along with checkpoints along the way to the top.

✦ Define and let go of a limiting belief surrounding courage that no longer works for you.

✦ Open yourself to allowing others to support you in the valleys of life.

✦ Look to your accountability partner(s) for help along the journey to being more courageous in your life.

✦ Write out your own current hero's journey story that you can rely on for your narrative, personal brand, and as a means of communicating clearly with others.

✦ Learn to identify the feeling of being truly ready to take the next step toward your goal.

# *Eleven*

# Curiosity

*"What we know is a drop, what we don't know is an ocean . . ."*
—ISAAC NEWTON

## CORE QUESTION

**"What can I learn here?"**

As I write this section, I'm in a plane flying over Iceland, and the timing couldn't be more perfect because travel has taught me so much about staying curious. Whenever I travel to a new place, it brings a new perspective. I don't have my favorite café or a set route for getting home—my curiosity is piqued about how to integrate myself into my current environment. I believe this, as with most concepts in this book, transcends work and applies to all aspects of life. Curiosity is the skill that lays the groundwork for creativity and contribution.

WHEN WE APPROACH SITUATIONS, ESPECIALLY FAMILIAR ONES,
WITH A MIND THAT REMEMBERS WHAT IT'S LIKE TO BE A BEGINNER,
WE OPEN UP TO NEW PERSPECTIVES AND TRANSCEND COMPLACENCY.

Avoiding monotony to harness your creativity isn't only about keeping life interesting, but it's grounded in the science of how our brains work. We're looking for mental shortcuts constantly. In a known environment like our hometown, we often coast on autopilot, using heuristics (mental shortcuts) to make choices. Travel, or any new environment or experience, forces us out of shortcuts and into a "beginner's mind."

One of my long-standing clients, a director at a tech company managing over $85 billion of assets, came to his first session, where I asked why he got into the work he does. He thought for a second and then said, "Well, I've always been in tech. I've never really thought about it." He's not the only one. Client after client has shared that no one ever asked them what they *wanted* to be doing. When they are asked, the answer usually involves outwardly attractive qualities like money, status, and fame. Anything wrong with that? Nope. Whatever your career path, try ensuring that you actually *like* the work you do, too. He needed to get curious to understand his motivations and areas for growth and improvement. Without questioning why he was in the role he was in, he probably wouldn't have come to the conclusion of leaving his job and starting his own training company.

The best and brightest are constantly innovating and riding the inevitable waves of change. How do you do that successfully? Think like a kid. When you start out in the world of work, you're often naïve, wide-eyed, and open—you're ready to learn. If you're at the beginning of a career path, harness that new feeling and run with it by opening every door and investigating anything that lights you up. Take the feeling of curiosity in the unknown—the beginner's mindset—and think about what you want to create in the world.

Growing up, I was curious until "realistic expectations" and the real world hit me like a ton of bricks. We're supposed to sacrifice the majority of our waking lives to stress and tension for a promised future of retirement? That might sound like a good deal, except as many run toward retirement at the end of the rainbow, a critical question remains: What will you do with your time once you're there? One can only handle so many days relaxing by a pool before boredom ensues. We're built to long for purpose and meaning.

So, get back that child-like wonder and curiosity as we consider the time you have left to dedicate to your career and how you'd like to spend it. Rather than focusing on building a résumé that is full of impressive-sounding job titles, let's change the way we look at this. Instead of the roles you might take on during your career, let's focus on the skills you want to grow and how you want to spend your time. No matter what stage you're at, you'll have time left in your bucket, and how you choose to spend these hours is crucial. This satisfies the logical part of my brain while always knowing I can make a change if a new priority or interest comes up that is more important down the road.

**Let's roughly estimate how many hours you have worked so far:**

Years Worked x 2,000 hours[7] = Hours You've Worked So Far

100,000 – Hours Worked = Rough Amount of Hours Left to Allocate,

i.e., 14 Years Worked x 2,000 = 28,000

100,000 – 24,000 = 72,000 Hours to Allocate

Now that you know the number of hours to allocate, it's time to define how you'd like to spend them. Think back to *Chapter 9: Enjoyment.* What skills are you using or developing when you're in flow?

Identify the areas you'd like to develop and explore. They don't have to be obviously beneficial to your career. They need to be interesting to you and worthy of your precious time. First, list those areas in order of priority. Then, allocate your remaining hours accordingly.

**Here's my example:**

**First identify the skills you would like to develop:**

1. Servant Leadership: leading by example

2. Communication Skills: listening, teaching, negotiating, speaking

3. Strategic Planning: creating an inspiring vision

4. Innovation and Inventing: bringing ideas into the world

5. Analytical Skills: analysis, investing

6. Practical Skills: contracts, finances, and artificial intelligence

---

7. Standard North American Work Hours: 40 hours a week x 50 working weeks a year = 2000 hours (on average, give or take.) As I think about this, I know seventy-five percent of my peers go above and beyond this, especially those that are highly successful in their chosen vocation. That's a *lot* of time.

# 100,000 HOURS

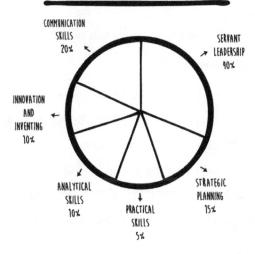

COMMUNICATION
SKILLS
20%

SERVANT
LEADERSHIP
40%

INNOVATION
AND
INVENTING
10%

ANALYTICAL
SKILLS
10%

PRACTICAL
SKILLS
5%

STRATEGIC
PLANNING
15%

# TRANSLATED TO HOURS...

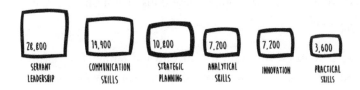

| 28,800 | 14,400 | 10,800 | 7,200 | 7,200 | 3,600 |
| SERVANT LEADERSHIP | COMMUNICATION SKILLS | STRATEGIC PLANNING | ANALYTICAL SKILLS | INNOVATION | PRACTICAL SKILLS |

**Then take the skill areas and create a pie chart with percentages based on the importance of each skill area:**

1. Servant Leadership = 40%

2. Communication Skills = 20%

3. Strategic Planning = 15%

4. Innovation and Inventing = 10%

5. Analytical Skills = 10%

6. Practical Skills = 5%

Now, allocate the hours you have left based on their level of importance.

*Note:* A benchmark number to achieve mastery of a subject or skill is roughly 10,000 hours.

So, I have 72,000 hours to allocate from our example above.

**Based on my priorities:**

1. Servant Leadership = 40% x 72,000 hours = 28,800 hours

2. Communication Skills = 20% x 72,000 hours = 14,400 hours

3. Strategic Planning = 15% x 72,000 hours = 10,800 hours

4. Innovation and Inventing = 10% x 72,000 hours = 7,200 hours

5. Analytical Skills = 10% x 72,000 hours = 7,200 hours

6. Practical Skills = 5% x 72,000 hours = 3,600 hours

This is not a hard and fast rule, nor do you need to keep track of this on an hourly basis unless that's your style. I know many people who get a kick out of spreadsheets and tracking.

The idea is you can easily audit if the time you're spending working is indeed going toward developing these skills or if it's mired by busy work or unrelated tasks.

What skills do you want to cultivate and refine? Test out this pie chart yourself. Use your curiosity about skills to explore what you want to create through the effort you put into your career. It's not enough to get good grades, performance reviews, or have a pat on the back from your peers. Curiosity will point you toward the skills you want to build to change this world for the better.

In the action steps below, you'll set up your buckets related to the skills you want to hone in on. It gives us a sense of the person we're becoming and informs topics for us to pursue. If we know that we want to master performing surgery, our time will be spent differently than if we want to be experts at building things. To maximize the use of our time, flipping the script on who we're becoming on a skill-based level is far more relevant than what titles we've held.

This is especially important as the economy shifts toward a more results-based focus. The dialogue is "we don't care if you're the president or a customer service representative—we care about what you're good at and what you can contribute." With this mentality, it's up to you to pick jobs and companies that afford you the space to get creative in the skills you want to be using and expanding. It's up to you to know what those skills are.

I worked with a chief technical officer at a large company in the post he had held for years. He was comfortable in his role and good at what he did. Events transpired, leading to the company being without a CEO, so the board called up this individual to serve. He had years of experience and a high level of competency as a CTO but less in terms of financial competency or people management. He, understandably, felt daunted and a little out of his depth. Probably a feeling he'd last experienced when he first started his career. He had forgotten that feeling and how he dealt with it at the time—by harnessing his curiosity. This, I told him, was the perfect time to get curious and use the experience he had gained throughout his years as CTO to perform as an equally good CEO. It was his willingness to be a beginner again and ask questions of his team that allowed him to succeed in the new position.

It isn't only learning new skills that requires us to use our curiosity—innovating in any industry or environment requires it. Finding alternative solutions to old problems and challenges or developing solutions to new ones is entirely driven by people looking beyond the way it's always been done. We often repeat the same workday over and over, especially as we become established in our roles. It can be tempting to sit tight and go through our usual routine, use our usual systems and methods, and repeat the process. But what happens to those people when the world moves on? As a results-focused economy, we constantly need to deliver new insights and opportunities to expand growth. If we embrace our curiosity and allow it to open new areas of exploration, we can increase our skillset and produce better results at work.

Curiosity is also a means of crafting an extremely fulfilling career filled with adventures each day. I've found that if we get clear on our ideal day and work to create that, we'll be heading in the right direction. Our careers, after all, are a series of days.

One way to do this is through "idea linking," a process that "entails using aspects of early ideas as input for subsequent ideas in a sequential manner, such that one idea is a stepping stone to the next."[8]

8. Hagtvedt, Lydia Paine, Karyn Dossinger, Spencer H. Harrison, and Li Huang. "Curiosity Made The Cat More Creative: Specific Curiosity As A Driver of Creativity." Organizational Behavior and Human Decision Processes. Academic Press, November 6, 2018. https://www.sciencedirect.com/science /article/abs/pii/S0749597817300559.

It's great because it takes brainstorming, which can feel daunting and unstructured, and makes it more sequential. You start at point A and, through idea stacking, move your way to point Z.

**Here is an example:**

**Topic:** Ideal job

**First Idea:** Being my own boss

**Next Idea:** Where might I be my own boss?

Working from home

**Next:** When will I work from home?

Customized hours

**Next:** What will I customize?

Taking a walk and doing yoga in the morning, then working beginning at noon

**Next:** What will I work on?

Meetings with clients

**Next:** What will I do after my meetings?

Batching different tasks and business activities

You make sure the idea is linked to the idea before it, even loosely. It's sort of like a word association game. My brain often thinks in questions, but you can use images, feelings, or individual words to stack your ideas on top of each other sequentially. You can use this alongside mind mapping to create your ideal day. Then, using your ideas, you expand them to maximize your "everyday" working life.

Another way to go about this is to start with how you'd wake up and walk through your ideal workday in chronological story format all the way to the end of the day. This is another tool I often use with clients when big-picture dreaming about "vision" seems too vague. When you get clarity on the elements of what you want in your daily life, the bigger picture comes together as the aggregate of that.

## MENTOR'S TABLE

### Lucas, Alexa, Kristian, and Children I've Met Along the Way

Children look at everything as if it were the first time because it usually is. In their first six years, my sister and brother Alexa and Lucas were willing to explore without fear of judgment. What I witnessed as they got older was that dancing along to pop songs became "lame" and showing excitement was uncool. Many of us dim our natural curiosity and excitement because of societal expectations and past hurt. It translates into our adult lives and our careers. "I can't share *that* at the meeting because I might sound silly," or "I don't know as much as the VP, so my ideas probably aren't useful." We must ask ourselves if it truly is a case of "can't." Or is it perhaps that you "won't?"

It may seem unusual to see children as professional mentors, but they have so much to teach us. Whenever I spend time with kids, I get a strong reminder to use my sense of curiosity—to ask questions, try something different, see something from another angle, and show interest in something new. It's not enough to get good grades, follow the pack, and keep your head down. Curiosity can guide you on your journey to making a real impact both on your own life and the wider world.

I was once asked in a mentoring session, "Does a baby get frustrated with learning how to walk?" No. They fall and get up dozens of times before they figure it out. I saw it with my brother Kristian. He didn't stop experimenting with different approaches until he understood walking entirely. He explored all facets of crawling, walking sideways, forward, backward, and jumping up and down. That feeds back into our previous chapter about persistence, too, but curiosity drives that first attempt to lift yourself onto your feet. It also makes you explore the full range of movement. Can I do this? How about that? Well, I'm going to try. Curiosity, for its own sake, is paramount.

## Dr. Diane Hamilton and FATE

A well-researched model about curiosity fell into my lap during a Google search I carried out when I wanted to understand more deeply why curiosity matters at work. Dr. Diane Hamilton is the author of several books, including *Cracking the Curiosity Code: The Key to Unlocking Human Potential.* Hamilton identified four roadblocks to creativity and labeled them FATE: fear, assumptions, technology, and environment.

Technology and environment cover the practical constrictions that prevent us from exploring and being curious. Put yourself in an environment that fosters this critical skill. Many companies allow for "innovation time" during the week and have entire departments working on exploring possibilities. Fear, as we've seen, can stop us in our tracks, and we've learned to counter that in *Chapter 10: Courage.* I'd posit that the one roadblock we often overlook is our assumptions. They drive our perception of ourselves, reality, and the world at large. If you take one thing from understanding Hamilton's FATE model, let it be the message to examine your existing assumptions about a topic and ensure they allow you to be curious. The business result of doing that leads to innovation, and that leads to increased profitability over time.

It's no surprise that those who stay curious their whole lives continue to grow, while others who avoid it for reasons of comfort or security fall behind. It's the same for companies and individuals alike. If we aren't regularly changing or exploring new possibilities, then we're being left behind. Curiosity keeps us current.

For me, watching the world deal with a global pandemic reemphasized a reality many of us allowed ourselves to push into the background: that everything is uncertain and always changing. Relying on ways of living that have become comfortable and familiar has merit. However, choosing not to ask questions or experiment with new ways of doing things leads to stagnation, and when the situation changes, you're less ready and willing to adapt. Curiosity is the thing that inoculates us against becoming obsolete, antiquated, and gives us the perspective we need to effectively adapt in our changing world.

## Maria Montessori

Growing up, I attended a Montessori school for many years. They operate based on the teachings and theories of Maria Montessori, whose paradigm for teaching was to harness children's curiosity and translate it into experimentation. Montessori's philosophy comprises the following five principles[9]:

1. **Show children respect.**
   Allow them to engage in focused work without interruptions. This nurtures independence from a young age.

2. **Young minds are ready to learn.**
   Children learn by observation as well as their self-guided exploration within their environments.

3. **Allow children to explore freely in a self-directed manner.**
   Children learn best in an environment equipped with resources and opportunities to actively learn and freely explore in a self-directed manner.

4. **Teachers are observers** watching for moments to support individual learners.

5. **Children can teach themselves through active exploration.**
   Teachers can encourage children to learn and explore by introducing them to new materials.

My experience in a Montessori school directly exposed me to these concepts. We were encouraged to explore topics via project-based learning. I could practice my recorder all day long if I wanted to as long as I completed my other work on time. We had no homework or tests, and the learning was mostly voluntary and extremely diverse. We took two weeks to rehearse for a school play in a theater. We learned French. We played, we researched, and we socialized. For this style of learning, curiosity was at the forefront.

The child-centric model truly empowers any type of learner and capitalizes on the curiosity of the individual as the driver for learning. As adults, this model addresses the four blocks to curiosity outlined by Hamilton: fear, assumptions, technology, and environment.

---

9. Montessori, Maria. *The Montessori Method.* Radford, VA: Wilder Publications, 2008.

1. **Identify and move beyond your fears** about delving into new topics.

2. **List all possible benefits** of exploring the topic for yourself, your career, your colleagues, and the company structure you're in right now.

3. **Give yourself the technology**, resources, or tangible items that support your exploration.

4. **Create an open environment** for yourself to be curious about the things you're interested in exploring.

Being more child-like in our approach to the world by harnessing curiosity can drive human innovation. Our neocortex's ability to imagine and envision is what sets us apart from the machines we've created to carry out work at speed and with efficiency. Let's use our curiosity as the mindset to create new things in our lives and the lives of others.

## Max, my dog

After a childhood of always wanting a dog, I finally took the plunge. I'm writing this in a café in Zürich, listening to Spanish music with Max under the table. Within a few days of dog ownership, I was reinvigorated with the feeling of curiosity. Max approaches everything with inquisitiveness. It's one of the many traits dogs possess that we would do well to emulate in our lives. Their delight when they see you, the way they approach strangers with interest and hope, the loyalty they show, cuddling, and their joyful play. If you ever want to see pure curiosity at work, put a puppy and a toddler in a room together and watch them examine everything within their reach. A word to the wise: the most curious humans are those who understand that we still have so much more to learn. Stay curious like Max, and you'll never be too old or too set in your ways to learn something new.

## ASK YOURSELF

**What does "curiosity" mean to me?**

**Why is it important?**

**How satisfied am I with my level of curiosity in life?**

**On a scale of 1 (being low) and 10 (being extremely satisfied), rate your current level of satisfaction with how you employ curiosity in your work and daily life:**

1    2    3    4    5    6    7    8    9    10

- Where in your career might there be room to cultivate more curiosity?

- As a child, who did you want to be when you "grew up?" This can be a particular profession or the people you admired. What traits or skills did they possess?

- What would the "successful" version of you be doing every day?

- What would you do if you were able to retire tomorrow?

- What are you curious about exploring more of, even if it leads nowhere right away?

- Think of something mundane you feel like you "have" to do every day. Go through the process of that in your mind. Now think of a way you could do that thing differently.

- What are you curious about? It doesn't have to be something that will clearly benefit your career or life.

- What have you always wanted to simply know more about or understand better?

## ONE-DEGREE SHIFT

1. Plot your ideal day. From start to finish, write out all the elements of a great day. This could include your "work" or contribution to the world, taking care of yourself, physical activity, learning, or exploring.

2. Spend a set amount of time weekly (or daily or monthly—make it on a repeated basis) on "creative" time with no set goal. Simply explore a topic or activity you like putting time into. This means time furthering work topics you're curious about and innovating, not a hobby outside of work time—that's different. It's a necessary piece of your work time if you want to grow professionally.

3. Set up your 100,000-hour pie chart. Where do you want to dedicate your remaining hours? What skills do you want to grow and utilize while being curious?

4. Explore the FATE model. Identify where you've stopped looking for opportunities to grow at work (and maybe in your life) and think about which roadblocks might be standing in your way.

5. Take some time to explore a new subject, activity, person, or idea you're interested in this week. Share what you've found with your accountability partner(s).

## TAKEAWAYS

✦ Envision your ideal day, including work and all other activities you enjoy doing.

✦ Define and allocate time to being creative and inviting innovation into your work and other projects.

✦ Set up which skills you've already cultivated and those you'd like to develop over the rest of your 100,000 hours.

✦ Understand the FATE model and use it whenever you feel stuck or blasé about your life to establish and eliminate any roadblocks in your way.

✦ Find something new to get curious about.

# Contribution

*"Happiest are the people*
*Who give most happiness to others."*
—DENIS DIDEROT

**"How can I meaningfully contribute?"**

Contribution is about the legacy we leave as we derive fulfillment from help-ing others. It goes beyond a paycheck and accolades or social status. When we work, we contribute to the economy by providing services and goods. We're familiar with statues dedicated to the achievements of this war hero and that politician, but without that level of notoriety, it's easy to believe *we* don't have to think about the reputation and impact we leave behind.

The concept of contributing to the world on a big scale evaded me for a while. I used to wonder what small actions like loading the dishwasher would change in the grand scheme of things. But if you take anything from this book, understand that the incremental is often what defines the whole. I had to get clear on what my form of contribution would be. I had to ask myself some crucial questions: What was my version of showing up? What did I want to be known for? What did I want to leave people feeling? The answer always came back to love. I want others to feel loved in my presence. I want to fill people's hearts with my words and actions.

I worked with a large U.S. shipping company that wanted to look at its performance management strategy. Executives sought to see if there was a difference between the performance of their contractors and that of their employees to understand how these two groups contributed to the company. They thought it would uncover a clear difference between people who were direct employees versus people hired on a project basis, but executives were surprised to find there was no statistically significant difference between the performance of the two groups. Indeed, many contract staff were more effective than full-time employees. Because we'd researched on an individual level, we realized that basic needs, like money and stability, weren't the major factors in dictating how hard people worked or the effort they put in. Through the individual interviews we conducted, we realized that work ethic and how people felt about their work was the key. Those who felt pride and took ownership of their responsibilities produced more, were more effective, and made a greater contribution. Their peers thought more highly of them, and their managers responded with glowing reports. Their absenteeism was minimal.

Contribution comes from a mindset of taking ownership of our work. There's a reason why so many companies have embraced the slogan, "Made with love." When we do things with care and attention, it shows. And, in turn, it gives us a sense of meaning. If you're giving your effort to something you care about, the time and energy will feel well spent.

My experience has taught me that people's ideas about their contribution change during their lives and careers. In the beginning, our contributions tend to be individual as we learn about the world of work and gain experience. Your contribution is part of the larger team. As an individual matures, their impact becomes wider and more about managing resources and growth. As they reach the final years of their career, many will look to a mentorship or teaching role to share their knowledge with the people who will come after them.

We also make an entirely different set of meaningful contributions outside of our work. We encompass many roles like spouse, parent, sibling, community member, and friend. Deepening our understanding of contribution to mean how we bring our whole selves to the world is a game changer. It's especially relevant for those who see themselves as mainly breadwinners or providers. When we tie our sense of worth to production, it makes us uncomfortable when that changes for any reason. It's vital that our self-concept encompasses all parts of ourselves as we contribute to the world around us.

You're building what you will be known for every day through how you behave, and it's important to be aware of that. I've taken this approach in my personal life as strongly as my professional life. In fact, I'd say there's little divide for me in how I treat personal and professional topics. This wasn't always the case. The more I investigate the careers of others, the more I realize that feeling fulfilled by your contribution is part of what makes you great at it. This is where our fulfillment meets the subject of the final section of this book—impact. Feeling like you're delivering value encourages you to do more and feeds into your sense of purpose. Achievement is one thing, but true contribution is another. Building a legacy you've enjoyed crafting is the difference between being revered solely for your accomplishments or being described as a wonderful mentor and impactful peer. If you only focus on achievements, your legacy will not be the same as someone who poured their knowledge and wisdom into others. Building relationships is a core component of a fulfilling career.

Through my work, I want to leave people feeling like they've just had a hug—often, it'll be a real hug—but even with my remote team meetings, my hope is that whoever I'm interacting with feels uplifted and heard. I want my clients to feel hopeful that whatever they want to create is indeed possible. Keeping this in mind, I can check in with myself to see if my behavior reflects the contribution I want to make in a situation.

Do I fail to contribute at times? Absolutely! I'm not always giving, and we can't do that in perpetuity. We can't *always* be acting for others—as we saw in Part One, we must prioritize ourselves first. If we can't show up as our best selves, our ability to contribute is hampered, and we become less useful in what we can do for others. So remember to check in with yourself if resentment or frustration is showing up. You might need some time to rest and reset.

You know we have roughly 100,000 hours dedicated to work during an average lifetime. How we allocate those hours is up to us. You've done this in a previous chapter regarding the skills you'd like to develop. Now I'd like to invite you to do it in terms of different causes or areas of contribution. What you find in the cross-section of the skills you want to develop and the causes you enjoy will be unique and revelatory if done thoughtfully.

# 100,000 HOURS

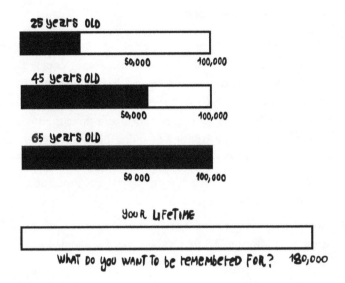

25 years old

50,000        100,000

45 years old

50,000        100,000

65 years old

50 000        100,000

Your lifetime

What do you want to be remembered for?   180,000

\* Note: This image shows someone working 50 years at 2,000 hours per year. We have different phases in life, so this is an approximation.

**Let's try an example:**

Jerry has worked roughly 90,000 hours.

2-year sabbatical to finish a master's degree: 4,000 hours
5 years as a copywriter: 10,000 hours
4 years as a senior copywriter and content manager: 8,500 hours
10 years as a marketing manager: 30,000 hours
15 years as a partner of the firm: 37,500 hours based on 50-hour weeks

What was his contribution in each role?

Let's define his desired contribution areas going forward.

Jerry has 10,000 hours left to dedicate to projects as he spends more time with his grandkids and wife. He knows he would like to mentor more.

It's part of the skills he still wants to develop. So now he must decide what causes would be fulfilling for him to share his wisdom with and how. (You can do this with any amount of hours left.)

**He opts for three main projects:**

1. 6,000 hours to develop and oversee an internal legacy-building program. He will record his virtual mentoring course this year as a pilot. He wants to create a legacy that spans generations at the company, not only for himself but his other partners. He sees his peers struggling to make the transition and share their wisdom with others. He knows this will be a meaningful last project to contribute to a legacy for all the partners that built up the firm.

2. 2,000 hours to write his book on copywriting, marketing, and how to harness our innate creativity.

3. 2,000 hours for a one-on-one mentorship project for any individual at the firm—he decides he wants to mentor people from entry-level to senior marketing managers.

It might feel daunting to map this out if you have 90,000 hours left in your career bucket. But that should not dissuade you from planning out these areas. The time will fly by, and it's important to make sure you prioritize the areas that are meaningful to you. You can look at the list of twenty-five things you want to accomplish that you made using the 25/5 rule from *Chapter 7: Focus* for some inspiration. I suggest allocating some rough amounts of time to the ones that stand out as exciting, meaningful, and impactful.

How much have you contributed already that you might not have fully recognized? Those projects are also part of your contribution to the world and matter as much as anything written on your résumé (if not more.) How can you intentionally make decisions about how the rest of your time is allocated and what you use it for? You might want to dedicate time to charities or volunteering. You might want to help people become healthier, develop a more meaningful and fulfilling work life, or foster better relationships. You might want to help empower women and girls in the workplace. You may wish to become a parent or a mentor.

I visualize a room full of people I've impacted. Whether it's individuals through one-on-one conversations, a group I'm speaking to from a stage, or you reading this book, I'm always asking myself about the legacy I'm leaving behind. What would the group of people in my "legacy room" recall and feel about my contribution? How will I feel knowing I've contributed to their lives? How will I advance my industry?

Your legacy may be different. It may be all the people who work or live in the buildings you've designed. It could be the people you've taught skills to, the people who have benefitted from funds you've raised, or the people who have enjoyed the cookies you've baked. What is it for you? Look to your contribution itself to be fulfilling, not only a pay day. That's why contribution differs from service, which we'll address later. Your contribution is between you and your higher power or intuition. Some people call it a life path or vocation. What do you feel called to change or improve in the world? You might be reluctant to answer the call at first, but I assure you it's worth it when you do.

## MENTOR'S TABLE

### My Parents

My parents are the people whose contributions I benefitted from most growing up. Their impact on me is a part of their legacies. As a young girl, I saw my mom studying for her master's degree and working full-time while also caring for me. On Saturday mornings, I'd go to the shop with my dad and answer the phone. My parents wanted to make sure I knew the value of hard work and was not afraid of it. My grandparents are the same way and passed that down to my parents. Work hard. Do and be your best. Show up. Do something and make it count. Help others. I had it relatively easy and grew up in one of the most privileged parts of the world, but my parents made sure I was no stranger to helping out.

What I learned from the older generations of my family is that humans don't *need* instant gratification to contribute. The act of contributing alone is rewarding enough. They do it because it's the right thing to do and would help a fellow family member or colleague. They feel fulfilled via the act itself. As much as the new digital generation is innovative and individualistic, I think the idea of acting for the simple reward of knowing you have helped isn't always emphasized. There's a notion of "What's in it for me right now?" lingering in our minds. The drawback is that we can fall into a habit of making a risk/reward calculation with all of our actions. Something to remember is that there is a long game when it comes to contributing.

> MOST OF THE TIME,
> THE REWARDS OF CONTRIBUTION ARE NOT INSTANTANEOUS,
> AND MANY TIMES,
> THE KNOWLEDGE THAT YOU'VE HELPED IS REWARD ENOUGH.

We know deep down that the small contributions we make matter. Being ready to contribute is about getting your hands dirty sometimes. The CEO who doesn't balk at the idea of lifting boxes during an office move or helping a team on a tight deadline can be both an inspiration and a morale booster to their staff. When people know they can rely on you to pitch in, it makes them feel you're a team player and trustworthy, and they're more willing to follow your lead.

# Contribution

## Professor Chen-Bo Zhong

Professor Chen-Bo Zhong is a Professor of Organizational Behaviour and Human Resource Management. I took a negotiations course with him during my undergrad, and I heard about his theory of creating win-wins in real business cases. I always thought that, in business, there had to be a winner and a loser. A contract is made based on terms that benefit one side more than the other. Professor Zhong wanted us to think about how to negotiate based on a weighted approach. "Not everyone wants the inside of the orange—maybe one party wants the peel," he said.

I remember my initial thoughts on this statement vividly. "What?! Why? Who in their right mind wants the peel? Come on . . ." But we slowly unraveled where combativity in negotiations could be prohibitive. If one party is fighting for the "fruit" of the orange and the other party doesn't really need it, it's best to use it as a bargaining chip. There's no sense in being difficult and opposing the other party's needs as a tactic. It's much more effective to use the other party's needs and wishes to negotiate for the things that are important to you.

If you come to a negotiation with the idea that you must win, then the process will be harder than if you turn up wanting to find a solution that works for both parties. How does this relate to your contribution? It's about being strategic. If you choose to give based on what's meaningful to you and simultaneously valuable to others, then you're hitting a sweet spot for everyone involved. You gain a sense of fulfillment. They get the impact you've made (explored further in Part Three). This book aims to create a win-win-win for your career. You do this by crafting your contribution with these three questions in mind: What's in it for me? What's in it for them? What's in it for society at large?

## Walter Peterhans

Whenever I meet an entrepreneur, I can see that it's in their blood. A true innovator and business owner is always seeking knowledge and looking for opportunities. Enter Walter Peterhans, my husband's ninety-four-year-old grandfather. Until the end of his life, when Walter was in a restaurant, he would ask to see their whipped cream machine. An odd fascination, you might think. No, he wanted to see if it was one from the factory he had started. Retired for years, he still had an interest in the industry he gave thirty years of his time to. I see this amongst all aligned contributors. They have made their interests (in Walter's case, his various products) their contribution and derived great fulfillment as a result.

Aim to be like Walter. What do you want to still be thinking about and interested in when you're well into your nineties and your working days are "officially" behind you? What can you not stop thinking about, no matter your role? You may be here to contribute to various projects and areas of work. Being deliberate about your contributions will lead to the most meaning and fulfillment for you. Walter's legacy proves that a clear contribution will not only bring you material riches, but the feeling of a life well spent.

## ASK YOURSELF

**What does "contribution" mean to me?**

**Why is it important?**

**How satisfied am I with my level of contribution at work?**

**On a scale of 1 (being low) and 10 (being extremely satisfied), rate your current level of satisfaction with how you contribute to your work and daily life:**[10]

   1    2    3    4    5    6    7    8    9    10

- Where in your career might there be room to contribute differently?

- What do you find yourself doing for others no matter where you go or who you're with?

- Own it: What feelings or impressions do you want to leave others with?

- What are you bringing to the world through your skills and efforts?

- What do you want to be known for?

- If there were no limits, what would your legacy look like?

- What's in it for you?

- What's in it for others?

- What's in it for society as a whole?

- How would I like to describe my contribution to the world when I'm eighty?

---

10. More is not necessarily better. Quality matters most.

## ONE-DEGREE SHIFT

1.  Trust the little voice saying, "that seems unrealistic but super fun and amazing to pursue.

2.  Set up your second set of work buckets.

    ■ What causes or areas do you want to contribute to during your 100,000 hours?

    ■ What topic buckets do you want to create?

    ■ What have you contributed to already?

This is a great chance to take stock and set yourself up to shine in the areas you find fulfilling.

**For example:** I have *72,000 hours* left as established earlier.

Now I want to take those hours and consider what causes I'd like to contribute to.

*20,000 Hours* – Being a Parent
(I'm sure this is a conservative estimate!)

*15,000 Hours* – Podcasting about Leadership Topics, Self-Leadership

*15,000 Hours* – Helping Professionals/Entrepreneurs

*5,000 Hours* – Real Estate Investing

*5,000 Hours* – Passive Income Strategies, Building a Portfolio of Businesses

*5,000 Hours* – Volunteering to Help Young Women/Educational Institutions

*5,000 Hours* – Volunteering with the Elderly

*1,000 Hours* – Hours Caring for Animals

*1,000 Hours* – Service Projects/Retreats

What a wake-up call, right?

Remembering our time is limited is such a great way to get into motion as soon as possible.

3. Sketch out a timeline. How would you prioritize your efforts to these causes? What will you dedicate the next five years to? What will you be contributing to ten years down the road? Whether it's with your accountability partner(s), your best friend, or alone, make a timeline about where these causes could take you. Does the future seem bright? Take one step toward bringing this timeline to life.

4. Write a letter to your future grandchildren or the next generation of adults, sharing about all the amazing things you contributed to throughout your lifetime. If you enjoy writing, this one's for you. Otherwise, you can jot down bullet points, or make a voice note that you transcribe, to gain clarity about causes or areas that would be meaningful to contribute to.

## TAKEAWAYS

✦ Dream about all the different areas you'd like to contribute to in your life.

✦ Define your 100,000 hours in different areas you'd like to contribute to.

✦ Sketch out a timeline for the rest of your career based around this contribution structure.

✦ Act on at least one thing that'll bring you fulfillment via what you contribute.

✦ Visualize yourself at eighty and write a letter to future generations about everything you've contributed to in your amazing lifetime.

# *Thirteen*
# Creativity

*"Life isn't about finding yourself.*
*Life is about creating yourself . . ."*
—GEORGE BERNARD SHAW

## CORE QUESTION

**"What can I take from my mind and bring to life?"**

My former client Nancy is a lawyer, journalist, and photographer. Talk about a diverse skillset. If you asked her if she's creative, she'd initially deny it and say she just "does things." She isn't artsy, she says; she likes taking photographs. Who set the definition of what makes someone creative?

One fundamental misunderstanding seems to be that creativity is something held only by artists. I fundamentally disagree. There are creatives at work in all areas of the world and the global workforce. Nancy is creative when she practices her photography. She's creative when she writes an article for a publication. She's creative in her role within the law. Practicing law doesn't only require training and understanding of complex statutes. A lawyer's role is to develop a compelling argument and deliver it, either in written form or verbally. Nancy shows as much creativity when she has her lawyer hat on as when she has her camera or a pen in her hand. It's time to get over the misconceptions and understand that whatever you do is about building on top of what already exists to create something new.

## WE ALL POSSESS A FORM OF CREATIVITY.

Every design you make, every proposal you write, every member of staff you train and mentor, and every email you write is technically a "creation."

As a child, I'd line up my teddy bears in the living room in front of my mini chalkboard. I'd ramble on and on about who knows what, making sure every teddy was paying attention. I was creating new awareness, learning, and understanding. I was conveying information. I was taking ideas and sharing them with others. What I always wanted to do was find new ways of thinking and doing things. My creativity is in bringing those ideas to reality. That involves communication, persuasion, motivation, explanation, and implementation. All these activities involve a level of creativity. How do you effectively communicate an idea, capture people's imaginations and hearts, and find solutions to things if not through creativity?

It's imperative that you find the mediums that light you up. Your creations at work might be tangible, like designs or products. They might be intangible, such as strategies, communications, or training processes. The point is that creativity is not limited to artistic efforts. Humans are innately inventive, which stems from our creativity and desire to improve our circumstances. We won't be fulfilled if we aren't creating using our gifts. The ways we do that differs from person to person. If you've never thought about yourself as a creative person before, then now is the time to start because the joy you find through creating will lead to fulfillment. For some, it might be creating a space through interior design. Others might find they love creating budgets or plans. Some will find joy in creating a sense of peace or resolution through therapy or yoga. Just acknowledging that you're a creative person can be life-changing, especially for people who've dismissed the idea for many years as they work in what they would define as unartistic industries. Identify the things you do that require creativity, then think about those that spark your fire.

Refusing to identify our creativity can lead to roadblocks in our progress and route to success. As I write this section, I'm on a bus traveling to Lisbon, and I'm considering that this book's biggest roadblock has been me. Writing isn't something that comes easily to me, and I've always identified writing as a form of creativity I didn't excel at. If I couldn't write the perfect book, then why try? The idea of rejection and failure stopped me dead in my tracks until

I reframed it and embraced the idea that I could if I tried. It's also important to note how much of this book I had to cut. The best advice I've received about creating anything is to do it without a filter, at first. The idea is to let all the messiness pour out of you and simply create. Then, you can go back with a fine-toothed comb later and refine what you've produced. There's no use in being judgmental and scrupulous while you're in the beginning stages of creating because you'll produce very little.

Most people who are "overnight" successes in their fields create incessantly for many years. If you create fifty videos, maybe one will be popular. There's a mix of timing, audience, and relatability to factor into the equation when creating to appeal to others. But for our purposes in this chapter, create what you're drawn to, as often as possible, in a variety of areas, because you can always hit the metaphorical "delete button."

Acknowledging and embracing the fact that I *am* a creative person gave me the impetus to begin writing this book and the grit to persevere to the end of the process. I created this for you because the other option was simply to not attempt to communicate these ideas at all. To me, staying silent would have been considerably worse than the possibility of failure. I knew there would be critics and naysayers no matter what I decided to include in this book. But I feel good about the fact that I've done by best to convey what I believe will be useful to you.

## MENTOR'S TABLE

### Beethoven, Adele, and Luke Bryan

You might be surprised that I bring three musical artists to my Mentor's Table having insisted that creativity is not only at home in the arts. But what we can learn from musicians and composers is the practice of presenting and revising our ideas, which is a crucial part of creativity. To be successful, composers need to be willing to produce ideas for a real-world audience, test them out, and rejig them. Like scientists testing hypotheses, if you want to know if an idea of yours will work, you must get it out of your brain and test it in the real world.

Musicians do this by writing and putting their music out there with no guarantee it will be a hit. It's also a nod to how many works an artist needs to create to be a success. Mozart has 626 known compositions. I love how musicians will start writing a song that morphs and changes as it develops and is rewritten. The result can be nearly unrecognizable compared to the original idea. The writing process similarly involves presenting to an audience and revising the piece. That's definitely the case with this book. I've had multiple individuals help me improve it along the way. Creativity involves refinement and revision using feedback from your audience.

### Seth Godin

Structure may seem like an odd thing to add to something as ephemeral as creativity but let me explain. I've coached musicians and writers who've been frustrated with their lack of productivity. They lacked structure and thought they didn't need it to be creative. You don't need to wait for inspiration to strike to hone your creativity, and you won't reliably produce without setting aside time to work at it. Even the most prodigious artists must master their craft and spend time improving. We need to create structure and a process that's enjoyable for us to start being creative regularly and reliably.

Seth Godin has been called "the ultimate entrepreneur for the information age." A former dot-com executive, he has written more than a dozen books on marketing, advertising, business ventures, and leadership. Godin asserts that everyone has the capability of being creative and that it is, in fact, a choice.

For him, creativity is bringing something from your mind to life—into reality. I do this by communicating my ideas and strategies with clients to help them get clear on what they want to change in their lives. I share an idea, a question, or a hypothesis and love the moment when the other person lights up with a spark of inspiration to act. I love helping others spring into action.

What I've learned through Seth's work is that boundaries are imperative to creation. That's why painters have studios and rituals, or writers have set writing days and processes that work for them. Your creativity will benefit from you having processes of your own. Things will take longer than anticipated. You'll get through the process in sporadic moments, and you'll create in increments and within the confines you set. Think about your creative process. What gets you in the flow we talked about earlier?

Without structure, I can assure you that this book would have never been completed. It's too easy to choose to do anything other than sit down and write. That's when you know procrastination is winning, when cleaning your home's baseboards feels more urgent than the projects you're working on. Instead of asking myself to write this book in one sitting, I took the advice of my husband and adopted the Pomodoro Method. It's a system where you commit to twenty-five-minute work sessions with a five-minute break in between. (You can adjust these time intervals to suit your needs.) Many days I didn't feel like it when I started. Other things felt more important. I needed a snack, I wanted to take a walk, or I had to clean before I could open the document to continue writing this book. The one thing that saved me in the creative process was structure. A close second has been accountability to an external force—my lovely editors, Caroline and Sarah. This book would've never been completed if I didn't add another human into my creative process to give me a timeline, formatting rules, and another set of eyes to help clarify my thoughts.

Decide to create using a process and structure that you enjoy, and your creations will be of value. There's something magical about things that come from deliberate intentions, effort, and enjoyment. The way you do things is as important as *what* you do. So, within your creative process, work with love, with excitement, and with care. The world notices even if you think it doesn't.

## Good Will Hunting

It might seem odd to have the 1997 Gus Van Sant movie at my Mentor's Table. Let me explain what I learned from this movie: While structure is imperative to creativity, so is a bit of chaos. You must be willing to play in the chaos and embrace strong emotions. You need to have some level of examination of a known topic coupled with the willingness to rebel against the conventional to create something exceptional. If we all regurgitated what's already known, we wouldn't evolve. It's only when we start experimenting within the sandbox that we build magnificent castles.

Sean teaches us to section off environments, even rather large ones, like "all of the water in the world" or "all of the forests," and work on impacting them. Will's character teaches us to create with our entire hearts, unapologetically and with fire. Once you've defined your creative process and the structure you're working within, let your heart lead and create with all you have. Emotion is a huge part of creativity, even in something logical like mathematics. Strong emotions like love, joy, and courage fuel our hunger to solve problems, build castles, or entertain the crowd. Leverage your strong emotions to create something the world truly needs. Then you'll look back on it with peace and fulfillment, knowing you put your heart and soul into your creation.

## ASK YOURSELF

**What does "creativity" mean to me?**

**Why is it important?**

**How satisfied am I with my level of creativity at work?**

**On a scale of 1 (being low) and 10 (being extremely satisfied), rate your current level of satisfaction with how you harness your creativity in your work and daily life:**

1    2    3    4    5    6    7    8    9    10

- Where in your career might there be room to cultivate your creativity?

- Identify how you're creative. How do you create things already in your work?

- How might your creations help others?

- What do you want to create?

- What did you create as a child?

- Which creators inspire you?

- What's inspiring about them?

## ONE-DEGREE SHIFT

1. Remember your list of 25/5 from *Chapter 7: Focus*? Are the things your mind wanders to in this chapter the same or different from the five goals you decided to focus on?

2. Refine your five goals to fully align with what you want to create in the world.

3. If your previously listed goals aren't related to what you'd like to create whatsoever, make the list again or revise it to have twenty-five things you'd be proud of *creating* throughout your lifetime. Then circle the five most important to focus on now. Don't forget that creating is a never-ending refinement process, so know that these lists aren't set in stone. They're simply tools to help you focus and identify your North Star.

4. Create an implementation timeline for your five most important things to create. Clearly define what you want and come up with a tentative timeline of key milestones and events. Roughly how long will it take? Add an additional six months. This book was supposed to take eighteen months and ended up taking four years! It's always best to give yourself time to refine and get input from trusted sources. Ask your accountability partner(s) to support you to follow through on your timeline.

5. Define at least on action step you're willing to take in relation to each of the top five goals on your list.

6. **Bonus Actions:** Feeling stuck on this? Not feeling the creative juices flowing? That's okay. Set a timer and settle down in a new environment such as a café, park, or anywhere that isn't your usual workplace. Whenever I feel stuck, I put myself in a new environment to stimulate my mind's creativity and resourcefulness. Changing physical locations helps us see the world with new eyes. Take your notebook or note-taking tool and spend twenty-five minutes freewriting whatever pops into your mind. Do this a few times or until some of your twenty-five things emerge from your thoughts. More of a visual person? Create a vision board for yourself. Use magazines and get creative. Make this personal to your tastes so you enjoy the process. I make one yearly. More of a talker? I feel you. Call a friend, set up twenty-five minutes, and talk your list through—better yet, make your lists together.

## TAKEAWAYS

✦ Refine your list of twenty-five things you'd like to accomplish and the five you're focused on now.

✦ Create an implementation timeline for your five focus goals.

✦ Define the habits you'll put in place to focus your creativity.
(i.e., when, where, and how you do your best work.)

✦ Once you've created without judgment, build a structure for the parameters of your creation.
(e.g., an outline, assumptions, success criteria, etc.)

✦ Daydream a little about creativity and what's possible in your life. Most importantly, look at creative solutions to the dreams swirling around in your mind.

✦ Use your eyes, ears, or hands to bring your ideas to life. Make a vision board, talk it out with a friend, or write it on paper.

# *Fourteen*

# Trust

*"All I have seen teaches me*
*to trust the Creator*
*for all I have not seen."*
—RALPH WALDO EMERSON

## CORE QUESTION

**"Have I made the best decision with the information currently at hand?"**

This chapter is near and dear to my heart. It's something I've struggled with extensively in all areas of my life. There are many components to trust, and we'll examine a few ways to be more trusting of situations for your own good.

Trust is not acting nonchalant or "letting everything go." The dictionary definition of trust is "assured reliance on the character, ability, strength, or truth of someone or something." The first people we look to for this are our parents or primary caregivers. The most important person you need to rely on as an adult is yourself. You need to trust that you're there for yourself. That's where the concept of re-parenting comes in, and it's a valuable practice. In a nutshell, give yourself the care, understanding, love, and nurturing you wish your parents had given you as a kid. If more of us did this, I'm certain there would be far fewer issues in the workplace and in adult relationships.

When I started thinking about this book, I had three characteristics of trust in mind. The first part is our inner world—our choices and what we can control. The second is the spiritual aspect of our existence—the part that experiences joy, immense suffering, and fulfillment. For me, it is intrinsically connected to God. It's about surrendering to God what we cannot control while putting in our best effort amidst our circumstances. The third part covers others—people other than ourselves, the wider world, and even human history—and our impact on them through our actions. I view trust through these three prisms. There's a form of trust in yourself, trust in God as the force that governs all things, and trust in others.

## Trusting Ourselves

Trusting myself has been a real process, and I've watched clients go through the same stages to truly trust themselves. It's doing your due diligence in any given scenario, then believing you've done everything you can given the constraints (namely time, resources, and information). It's about knowing your abilities and competencies and understanding your limits. Trust comes from understanding yourself: knowing who you are (values), knowing what you're in control of (responsibility), recognizing your skills and worth (contribution), and understanding your limits (vulnerability and self-advocacy).

Trust in yourself can also be something more visceral than acknowledging our skills and limitations. Your body will give you many signals when you start to listen. Earlier in the book, I asked you to follow your heart. Where did that lead you? I'm now going to ask you to listen to what's often called our second brain—our gut instincts, that knot in our stomachs that shows up when something isn't right.

Let's talk about a dark night walking on an empty street in Seminyak, Indonesia. Two men drove up beside me on a motorcycle and stopped to ask if I was all right. I had my phone in hand to guide me home. We both know how this story ends . . . Did I follow my gut feeling that night? I didn't even check in with it. And the result? I was still lost in Seminyak, and my phone was stolen. Listening to my gut instinct on things is easily the skill I struggle with most. Many of us are very practiced at rationalizing and shutting our instincts down. Cultivating self-awareness which we discussed in *Chapter 6: Self-Advocacy* is one way to get to know your inner voice. We must trust our abilities and selves before anyone else can have a shot. If we doubt ourselves constantly, who else could possibly meet our expectations?

Relate my stolen phone scenario to your career. Perhaps you decide to join a company even though you don't agree with how leadership manages it. You cut corners because no one will know, except your gut tells you it's best to do the job well. The example of a child taking a cookie or treat from the kitchen comes to mind. I have a relative who shall not be named who is notorious for this. Did you have a chocolate bar? "No, I *didn't*," they say with chocolate around the corners of their lips. It's all in good fun in small ways, or so we think. As adults, this manifests in larger and greater untruths as we grow older, and it's because we don't feel safe to tell the truth to ourselves, our parents, or society at large. When we finally begin to listen, our gut feelings have all sorts of valuable knowledge to share with us. Bring in the courage quotient we built up from *Chapter 10: Courage*, and you're on the road to loving what you do daily while acting with integrity.

There has been scientific research that points to how effective and critical gut instincts are. When we make a decision, we consider all the information around us, and it's easy to dismiss the sense that something is "right" as only a feeling. But it isn't. Our gut reaction to things is often based consciously or unconsciously on hundreds if not thousands of criteria we've considered in that split second.

Gerd Gigerenzer, in his book *Gut Feelings*, argues the case for unconscious intelligence. He writes about a study where people were asked about various everyday decisions they made—what to watch on TV, for example. Gigerenzer found that there were two types of decision-makers. "Maximizers" flipped through all the channels, researching the entertainment landscape, and searching for the best option. "Satisfiers" carried out more limited research, quickly finding something that was "good enough" and watching that, settling into a decision much faster. Gigerenzer discovered that "Satisfiers" were likely to be more optimistic and have higher self-esteem and life satisfaction. "Maximizers" tended to be perfectionists and more likely to suffer from depression, regret, and self-blame. The evidence seems to suggest that the rational deliberation of options doesn't lead to happiness and that we should pay closer attention to our gut instinct. It usually leads us in the right direction.

There's another side to having trust in yourself, which involves stress management. Emotional well-being is vital: If you're in an argument with your partner, if your child is sick, or if you're nervous about how a presentation will go, those things can affect how you perform. Performance and results suffer massively if you're off your game. Effectively navigating and dealing with that "off" feeling goes a long way in allowing you to show up at work and beyond. How do we do that consistently at work when stress runs high and pressure is mounting? The crucial thing is that you learn to recognize when a situation is out of your control and release some of that stress. A big way to do that is by practicing self-compassion. Start using the concept of re-parenting I mentioned earlier by directing love and acceptance toward yourself. This will allow you to navigate the stress and expectations others may project onto you with greater ease by asking, "How can I take care of myself in this moment?" If you strengthen your self-parenting muscles, it will deepen the trust you have in yourself.

A study carried out in Germany[11] speaks to the importance of mental health when it comes to effective decision-making. Depression can affect our ability to make great decisions because our emotional intelligence is impaired. This numbing of your gut instinct has been proven to worsen your ability to make adaptive, fast decisions. This makes sense, right? If you're super stressed out, overwhelmed, and not paying attention to your needs, it's easy to miss the signs of a project, relationship, or situation going off the rails. There's a positive correlation between depression and indecisiveness. The moral of the story is to practice listening to your gut feelings because your instincts are considering many variables in the unconscious mind on your behalf.

## The Yerkes-Dodson Law

The Yerkes-Dodson Law was developed by psychologists Robert M. Yerkes and John Dillingham Dodson in 1908. It's as relevant to our lives today as it was then. Dodson and Yerkes explored the relationship between performance and pressure (or stress) in humans and discovered something important. Performance increases with psychological arousal caused by stress but only up to a point. There's a tipping point where *too much* stress or pressure on an individual means their performance disintegrates. They falter and fail. What's important to note is that the tipping point is different for each individual, and we need to be aware of our personal peak.

Represented by a bell curve with stress levels along the bottom and performance along the vertical axis, the Yerkes-Dodson Law can be presented as a series of zones for productivity. Too little pressure and stress and the individual is bored, unengaged, and their performance is poor. Too much and the individual burns out and their performance suffers. We can call

---

11. Remmers, Carina, and Johannes Michalak. "Losing Your Gut Feelings. Intuition in Depression." *Frontiers*, August 23, 2016. https://doi.org/10.3389/fpsyg.2016.01291.

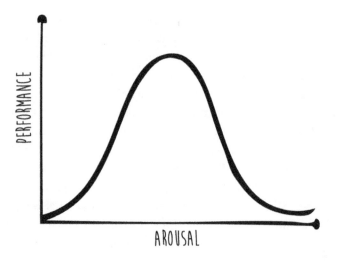

these times "red zones." In moving toward the sweet spot of peak performance between these points, the individual moves to a comfortable level of stress and decent performance. Ramp up the pressure a bit more and the individual reaches peak performance. This is where we stretch and challenge ourselves. We can call these "green hours" of work. Too much pressure and we tip right over the bell curve into decreasing quality of performance, and we're back in the "red."

Think about your typical day. Are you spending most of your hours feeling bored or overwhelmed? Then you're probably in the red zone. Now, what do you do with that information? What can you do to change this? In many situations, we can choose to view the pressure objectively and ask how much of it is under our control. There comes a point when continuing to accept the pressure piling on yourself has diminishing returns. Realizing that there's a limit to the things we have control over is a form of self-trust, and it can help you manage stress levels. I learned this most strongly in occupational therapy after my car accident. We evaluated symptom onset using a traffic light system. Red is many symptoms and extreme discomfort/pain, yellow is moderate symptoms and moderate pain, green is few symptoms, feeling good, no pain. I encourage you to create your own light system with the warning signs from your body or mind that you commonly disregard. It's an easy way to understand your level of stress, hunger, energy, or any emotional symptoms you'd like to manage throughout the day. Trusting ourselves means regularly going inward to hear and listen to what our body whispers to us throughout the day.

## Trusting in God and the Unseen

Trusting God is a huge topic and I recommend reading a variety of religious texts to gather further insight that I can't deliver in such a short space. I'm not talking about a specific religion here, but the feeling, experience, and the knowing that God is within me and around me. I'd like to approach this using a few personal stories to share how I've been learning to trust in that knowing. I was in Australia visiting a friend of a friend in Byron Bay. It was the first time we'd met, and I was sitting in his living room, filled with piles and piles of books. I found myself drawn to one of them—a book on Tibetan rites and rituals—and when I opened it up, the strangest thing happened. I found a map that someone had sketched in pencil on the back of the cover page with the exact streets of the place I was staying in Brisbane (a town hours away by car). Things like that happen to me regularly.

Is it a coincidence? Is it serendipity? Is it magic? Is it fate?

How about a more profound example. After my car accident, I barely traveled for nearly eight months, which was unlike me. I was in physiotherapy, vision therapy, and altitude training. I saw a brain specialist, an audiologist, a hormonal specialist who focused on brain trauma, and a massage therapist to ease the pain. It was devastating in some sense. I questioned why the accident happened. I felt like a "professional" patient, spending twenty hours a week in different therapies. Then, I got a reminder about a wedding I had been invited to in Switzerland. I met Liliana in Bali, and after knowing her for three days, she invited me to her wedding on a Swiss buffalo farm. My friend Emma from Australia (who I met in an equally enchanting story in Argentina) had introduced us and was going to the wedding. "Why not? It'll be fun," she said. Reluctant to travel since my traumatic brain injury, I kept wondering if I should do it. Something inside said, "just go—let yourself be free from these constraints." And so, I did. And that weekend, at a wedding on a little buffalo farm, I met my future husband.

If you're like my husband, you may believe these odd moments are pure coincidence. The message they send me is the firm affirmation that things work out for our Highest Good and that I need to go with the flow. It's a mantra I've carried with me for most of my life, and it's one of the most basic forms of trust I have.

What about suffering? We all have our fair share of challenges in life. Many ask, "If there's a God, why does evil and pain exist in the world?" It's a fair question. My best answer so far is that there's a lot to learn from coming face to face with pain and evil. Sometimes it's our own malevolence we encounter and must reckon with. Everything has a purpose, including the gruesome and horrific, even if we don't always consciously know what it is. That's where faith comes in. Losing a baby is the most emotionally and physically devastating thing I've ever experienced, three times. It goes without saying that trusting there is a purpose for all the pain and grief was difficult to wrap my head around at first. The truth is that I reluctantly learned so much about how powerful and smart my body is, that my "timelines" are more like guidelines, and that there are no guarantees in life. It has humbled me in a way no other experience has. That doesn't mean to abandon free will or that you shouldn't try to improve your situation.

SEEK OUT KNOWLEDGE AND IMPROVEMENT TO THE BEST OF YOUR ABILITIES AND THEN SURRENDER THE OUTCOME OF YOUR EFFORTS TO GOD.

In my darkest days I've found myself trusting in the power of God and forces unseen more than ever to help me through to the other side of suffering. If you're grappling with the suffering of life, looking to God to feel held, rather than vices or other people, might be just the support you've been needing.

It might seem odd to talk about faith, fate, and trust in God when this book is about your contribution to the world. But I think it's vital to balance your head, heart, and faith with planning because you cannot plan and control everything. Finding my ideal balance has allowed me to plan what I can, then go along for the ride to fully experience the things out of my control. The wisdom, as they say, is in knowing the difference.

## Trusting Others

My dad has an admirable sense of trust. He trusts his abilities, has faith that things will have a way of working themselves out, and prioritizes trusting in the abilities and goodness of others. He gives people the benefit of the doubt. What I've learned from watching him work as I was growing up is that you must have trust to allow good things to happen. The opposite is fear—fear that you'll be deceived or manipulated or that others have bad intentions. Sure, malicious people exist, but in my experience, those who seem to win in the career arena all trust in the best of humanity and believe that people are generally good. Those who are stymied by suspicion or distrust or constantly second-guess themselves seem to move much more slowly and with more difficulty. Even when things don't go my dad's way, he doesn't let it get to him—he somehow trusts that it will come together. He has trusted me to make the right decisions for myself since I was a kid. Naturally, he's watched me crash and burn at times, but he's there with open arms, knowing that if I fail, I'll find a way to learn from it. Being there for others in a supportive way when they make mistakes is a huge component of building trusting relationships with others.

A team with high levels of trust can navigate turbulent times much better than one where there is suspicion, rivalry, and distrust. I've seen the difference between teams that trust each other and those that don't. Bringing trust to the table means having faith in your actions. It means that if something doesn't feel right in your gut, you won't ignore the feeling. Something truly isn't right. It's about coming to your relationships with trust in those around you to bring their best. All great leaders have cultivated trust in themselves and built relationships based on trust—it's the magic ingredient in the leadership equation.

## Attachment Theory

I cannot, in good faith, write this chapter without sharing this with you. It's too fundamental to what I believe is the challenge most adults face in both intimate and more collegial relationships. If we understand our attachment style and can communicate our needs more effectively to the people in our lives, the way we trust ourselves and others will skyrocket. If we don't self-advocate effectively, it's difficult to trust. We feel we betray ourselves when we don't share truthfully with others. Building trust starts from securely understanding our thoughts and emotions and then clearly sharing them with the appropriate people in our lives. It's also useful to understand how others view attachments if you're working with them daily.

"There are four patterns of attachment:

1. **Ambivalent attachment:** These children become distressed when a parent leaves. As a result of poor parental availability, these children cannot depend on their primary caregiver to be there when they need them.

2. **Avoidant attachment:** Children with avoidant attachment tend to avoid parents or caregivers, showing no preference between a caregiver and a complete stranger. This attachment style might be a result of abusive or neglectful caregivers. Children who are punished for relying on a caregiver will learn to avoid seeking help in the future.

3. **Disorganized attachment:** These children display a confusing mix of behavior, seeming disoriented, dazed, or confused. They may avoid or resist the parent. Lack of a clear attachment pattern is likely linked to inconsistent caregiver behavior. In such cases, parents may serve as both a source of comfort and fear, leading to disorganized behavior.

4. **Secure attachment:** Children who can depend on their caregivers show distress when separated and joy when reunited. Although the child may be upset, they feel assured that the caregiver will return. When frightened, securely attached children are comfortable seeking reassurance from caregivers."[12]

Figure out which one sounds like you, then consider how this style might impact your relationships today.

Are you distrustful of your colleagues or friends?

Do you resist asking for help when you need it?

Once you know your potential blind spots, you can consciously work on them with your partner, how you approach your boss or colleagues, or with a therapist if you feel you'd like to deepen your work on this topic.

Acknowledging and effectively sharing your emotions with the key people in your life will change the dynamic completely. Look at your close relationships and identify what their style might be. If you're comfortable, have an open conversation about it as well—it creates parameters around a discussion that can be vague and messy without a framework. Knowing the tendencies of those around you makes creating a trusting bond much easier because you notice their wounds and vulnerabilities. I've learned this lesson in marriage, and it extends to managing others and working with clients. If you remind yourself that others' issues are often not about you directly, you'll be less reactive and more focused on resolving the problem at hand. Building trust in others can be a finicky skill, but in recognizing your personal tendencies and having a willingness to understand the other side, you can cultivate strong relationships.

---

12. Cherry, Kendra. "What is Attachment Theory?" *Verywell Mind*, May 2, 2022. https://www.very wellmind.com/what-is-attachment-theory-2795337.

## MENTOR'S TABLE

### Zig Ziglar

An American author and motivational speaker, Ziglar was a guru in selling, and his approach to clients and the art of sales is deeply rooted in building trust. Ziglar believed that objections or questions during the sales process are something salespeople should welcome as it indicates that the potential client has enough interest to make the inquiry. He put forward his Q.U.I.E.T Method for handling these situations.

When you meet an objection or a worry from someone, ask them a question (Q) about their concerns. We need to ask them questions so we can gain an understanding (U) of their worries. Understanding is crucial to overcoming the issue as we cannot identify (I) the heart of the problem until we see it as clearly as the other person. Once we've identified the problem, we can reach the most powerful stage of understanding and empathize (E). Empathy is different than sympathy as we acknowledge that the concern is genuine. In doing this, we can test (T) the concern of the other person and work with them to eliminate it.

For Ziglar, this was the key to being a more successful salesperson, but for me, it has a much further reach. I've used the Q.U.I.E.T Method to handle many other issues and disagreements in my life.

At the center of Ziglar's philosophy is integrity. He categorically rejects the stereotype of the sleazy salesperson and pushes for business to be based more on trust. He recognizes that it's only by being curious, asking questions, and really listening to the answers that can we truly understand the people we're working with, selling to, or buying from. This is vital to building a strong sense of empathy and, as a result, inviting that person to build trust in you. If you employ the Q.U.I.E.T Method when difficult conversations arise, remember to remain solution-focused so you can create the best possible outcome for everyone involved.

## Stephen Bayley and Roger Mavity

My university roommate gave me a copy of *Life's A Pitch: How to Sell Yourself and Your Brilliant Ideas* by Bayley and Mavity, and it changed the way I looked at both business and life. Bayley and Mavity argue that every scenario in society is a sales situation—a chance for us to make a pitch. The crucial aspect is that what we're selling is ourselves, and what we're asking others— our clients—to do is endorse us and our outlook. The book reminds us that business can be emotional and that life can be businesslike.

We're constantly putting ourselves forward for judgment from others, whether we're at work or interacting with society in other ways. We can craft others' perceptions of us by the way we behave. What we put out into the world reflects right back at us through the eyes of others. When we trust them deeply, they'll often rise to the respect we've bestowed on them. We don't need Big Brother watching us all the time to do the right thing. We need to create trusting communities where we expect others to do what's right and make it easy for them to do so.

When it comes to building trust, we're essentially pitching ourselves.

---

### THE ULTIMATE ENDORSEMENT
### SOMEONE CAN GIVE US
### IS THEIR TRUST.

---

This book taught me to be conscious of showing up to all interactions with integrity. Whether it's the customer service person at Costco or a new client, I endeavor to remember that life's a pitch. If we show up with that in mind, we will think twice about what we say and how we say it. It also usually leads to better outcomes. I think you can tell a lot about a person if you watch how they approach the daily elements of life. If you want to know if someone is detail-oriented, don't only look at their résumé—check the emails they send you to follow up and the questions they ask at the interview. We get the best picture of someone else when we consider them holistically and in varied environments. If you approach life's moments as if they're all important, you'll also derive fulfillment from the seemingly mundane and simple things. Trust means being in the present moment fully enough to truly experience it.

## Benjamin Franklin

This man needs no introduction. Not only was he a Founding Father of the United States of America, but he was also a philosopher, a scientist, a writer, and an inventor—a true polymath. There's a story about a letter Franklin sent to his friend Joseph Priestley, an English scientist. Priestley had an important decision to make and he needed advice. Franklin responded in a now-famous letter, explaining that he couldn't advise his friend, which was the right decision to make, but he could suggest that Priestly try something Franklin called "Moral Algebra." Franklin told Priestly to divide a sheet of paper into two columns and set aside three to four days for "consideration," essentially creating a list of pros and cons. Priestley followed his friend's advice and made his decision. He became a renowned figure in the scientific community.

Franklin teaches us that while we can turn to friends and colleagues for advice, the answer often lies within *us*. By creating a pros and cons list, you're turning a decision over in your mind and exploring where your instinct is telling you to go. By giving yourself time to deliberate, the "right" answer will reveal itself one way or another. Sometimes we even find that the "rational" right answer just isn't the one we truly want. Trust in yourself will give you the courage to make the right decisions for you, regardless of what your cons list might look like. There's also something to be said for writing things out on paper for them to be seen. Often our biggest worries feel like jumbled-up thoughts in our minds. When we get them out on paper, we can organize and see them outside ourselves more clearly. This simple list approach has helped me and my clients bring countless big decisions, projects, and ideas to life.

## ASK YOURSELF

**What does "trust" mean to me?**

**Why is it important?**

**How satisfied am I with how you bring trust to my life?**

**On a scale of 1 (being low) and 10 (being extremely satisfied), rate your current level of satisfaction with bringing trust to your work and daily life:**

1    2    3    4    5    6    7    8    9    10

- Where in your career might there be room to cultivate more trust?

- What is your gut feeling about the career situation you're in right now?

- In what parts of your life are you most trusting?

- Where could you trust yourself more?

- What's your attachment style?

- How can you re-parent yourself?

- Where can you show more self-compassion in your life?

- What's your relationship to trusting God and the unseen?

- How do you normally handle things that are out of your control?

## ONE-DEGREE SHIFT

1. Consider researching a spiritual text of some sort. There are traditional books of faith, but there are also yogic philosophies and philosophers like Nietzsche that cover the topic. This could open you up to a new way of thinking about your life's work. Consider the opposing forces of control versus the unknown.

2. Assess which attachment style you are. Decide on at least one thing you can do to re-parent yourself to know you're someone you can rely on.

3. Look at the attachment styles of your partner, closest family, or friends. Perhaps look at the attachment style of your boss and colleagues. How does this help you understand them further? Would it be useful to have a conversation? Journal, talk, research, or explore this as you see fit.

4. Make a list like Benjamin Franklin's Moral Algebra for whatever decision you want to make. Take a few days of consideration and revisit your pros and cons lists at regular intervals. See if the choice reveals itself.

## TAKEAWAYS

✦ Remember that trusting in ourselves and others comes from putting attention and care into the details.

✦ Trusting others is a choice we make in spite of past hurt to lead with love instead of fear.

✦ Contemplate God's role in your life and what you do/don't agree with when it comes to trusting in a higher power.

✦ Explore a religious text to deepen your relationship with God and the unseen.

✦ Consider your attachment style and that of the people around you.

✦ Make a decision using Moral Algebra and consider all of the options available to you.

# PART THREE
# IMPACT

*"The influence of a beautiful, helpful, hopeful character is contagious and may revolutionize a whole town."*

—Eleanor H. Porter

# *Fifteen*
# Discernment

*"There is wisdom of the head,
and there is a wisdom of the heart."*
—Charles Dickens

## CORE QUESTION

**"*Who* am I meant to serve?"**

Over the next three chapters, we will fill in the answers to the statement: "I serve X (people) to solve Y (problem or issue) and bring them to Z (solution)." This first chapter starts by considering the X—who you want to serve and impact through the legacy you're building. We'll also consider how you can be more discerning to improve this skill for yourself as you hone in on your impact.

Discernment is about good judgment, but it also encompasses something bigger. When you use discernment to make decisions, you listen to your instincts—those little whispers that tell you where you feel called to go. Listening to your inner wisdom helps you understand the true nature of a person, situation, or thing. Often it feels like something outside of ourselves is compelling us to move in a certain direction. This voice helps us focus and discern where and how we spend our energy.

Over the years five thousand hours of talking to people about their work, I've come to realize that everyone, at their core, wants to help others somehow. Yet, when I get on a call with a twenty-one-year-old university student and ask, "*Who* do you really want to help?" a blank look often ensues, followed by an admission: "Well, great question. I've never really thought about *that* before."

I've found it's not only Jenn from San Francisco State University that hasn't given this much thought. People take roles and join companies without considering the impact of the company they serve. They often focus on their credentials and skills. "Well, I'm a marketing guy, and Kraft is offering me $400,000 to lead the department, so I guess I'll sell peanut butter," is a common utterance when speaking to clients who see themselves as "realists" of the corporate world. Making decisions regarding our careers is often skewed such that we forget our values and morals when money is at stake. It can feel like we're asking too much to impact the people we care about while also getting paid. A need to "go where the money is" often prevails. It makes sense because it's a survival mentality that keeps us safe. In this book, we're here to elevate out of survival and into meaningful impact, both personally and outwardly.

A crucial piece of the puzzle is who you help via your work. It can feel daunting to completely change careers without experience, especially if that might mean a pay cut at first. An avenue seldom explored fully is volunteering. When I first began coaching, I knew I wanted to help women, especially those who reminded me of a younger version of myself. I knew the pain of feeling like I didn't belong and the lack of self-esteem to take myself and my gifts seriously. I wanted to help girls rise above those feelings. One of my first steps was to start volunteering for Girls Inc., which helps young girls become strong, smart, and bold through afterschool programs and summer camps. Going to some of their events to volunteer and donating to their programs exposed me to my people while I helped them simultaneously. If you want to make an immediate impact on a group of people that you care about, there are ample opportunities to volunteer virtually and in person, serving many different groups of individuals and causes. Want to learn more about construction? You can go on a volunteer project to build a home for a family. Interested in exploring teaching children but not sure teaching is the career path for you? Volunteer at a school or kid's club first. Rather than dreaming about what something might be like in our minds indefinitely, it's imperative we move into action to see if an opportunity is truly like what we have imagined.

I'm not asking you to throw caution to the wind. I'm not asking you to jump ship with no idea where you're going or how you'll get there. I'm asking you to discern who *you* care about impacting at this point in your life. Find ways to make sure that the effort you're putting into the emails, presentations, and designs you create are moving the needle on something that matters to you. This is different than finding your focus. It's about ensuring your personal goals also contribute your energy meaningfully to the people you care about impacting.

I've identified the people *I* want to impact via my work and that's *you*. Because you're reading this book, I'm clear that you're a person who is open to change and willing to consider new viewpoints and ways to operate in the world. Since you've made it this far, you're also committed to the process and appreciate my approach. All these little details point to who *you* are and, thus, who I truly want to serve through the effort I'm putting into writing this book. I also know I mostly support professional women between the ages of twenty-five to fifty-five who feel lost about their purpose in life and want to make more money and feel a deeper sense of meaning.

Considering who or what you want to serve is tied intrinsically to the goals we discussed in *Chapter 7: Focus*. Think about the list of twenty-five aims you created before whittling them down to your top five after we talked about the 25/5 rule. Can you use these aims to identify who you want to impact?

In reading Viktor Frankl's work, *Man's Search for Meaning*, I discovered that we need to direct what we do daily in relation to our broader mission.

---

THE MORE DISCERNING YOU ARE
ABOUT WHO YOUR IDEAL PERSON TO SERVE IS,
THE MORE YOU CAN TARGET THEM AND
IMPACT THEIR LIVES IN A MEANINGFUL WAY.

---

Your judgment will ascertain the difference between using your skills to help billionaires become trillionaires or helping Doctors Without Borders fund more projects effectively. I'm not saying one is better than the other, but I do know that if you continually take opportunities without being consciously discerning, it's far more likely you'll fall into a series of jobs rather than building a legacy with a personally meaningful impact. Deciding who you want to serve is one thing, but *how* you help them is the next step. We'll talk more about that in the upcoming chapters on structure and authenticity.

There are also many small decisions you make throughout your career. Will you commute? Work part-time or full-time? Accept commission or receive a fixed salary? Work for a corporation or stay independent? Being discerning means employing wisdom to decide what makes the most sense for you, your family, and your mission in the current situation. Don't let outside circumstances force you into submission. Listen to your wisdom to decide from an aligned place. You do that by checking in with yourself using the tools we discussed in *Chapter 3: Awareness*. Then discern which option aligns with where your guidance is leading you. We often try to control outcomes because it makes us feel safer, but an expert at discerning their impact will allow it to unfold over a series of small moves leading to a reveal of the big picture. You don't need to know exactly *how* you'll attain your end goals so long as your vision is clear and guided by inner wisdom on the road to your greatness.

Many opportunities will come your way throughout your career and using discernment to hone in on the right next step for you is critical to how you create an impact on the world. I know it's easy for me to get shiny object syndrome and want to say yes to everything. Saying no can feel difficult, ungrateful, or like I'm closing myself off. If you know an opportunity or client is meant for you, the logistics will line up and helping them will feel inevitable. Employing discernment might mean saying no to helping those who would be better served by someone else. In the coaching industry, referrals are a massive business. It helps us when we refer people to a better-suited professional. It shows that we understand ourselves, our skills, and the people we can best help. It also shows we can recognize those things in other professionals.

It might seem easy to find the people you want to serve if you're an immigration lawyer or professional chef. But even with careers like these, it's important to get even clearer. Do you, as an immigration lawyer, want to help young single mothers looking to live in New York for work? How about focusing on recipes and nutrition for pregnant women in your work as a chef? The more specific you can be about who your people are, the better you can tailor your messaging and the easier your people can find you. If you stand for everything, you stand for nothing. Decide who you stand for, and the right people will come knocking.

# MENTOR'S TABLE

## Tim Ferriss

Tim Ferriss is an entrepreneur and author but also an investor in many start-ups. He became famous after writing his book *The 4-Hour Workweek*, where he argues that there's an alternative to the traditional career trajectory—putting in long hours, taking few vacations, and sacrificing decades of time to enjoy life after retirement. The book recalled Tim's realization, which happened when, burned out from working long hours at his company, he took a sabbatical and traveled. After that, he changed his work and lifestyle for the better by automating, systematizing, and delegating.

This experience meant that Ferris knew exactly who he wanted to help by writing his book—people sick of existing on the hamster wheel. Tim looked at what he learned through his experience to work freely and crafted his book to help others emulate his path. Through personal transformation, he identified the people he wanted to serve, and those people looked exactly like his former self. This is a standard mentor-mentee model: This is what I did to get to this place, and here's how you can, too. What better way to connect with and impact people than by identifying the challenges, failures, and successes you've had in the past and using that to teach and guide?

Tim places heavy value on mentors, and this feeds into his writing. We all recognize that we emulate and are influenced by those around us, and he prioritizes learning from a broad range of individuals who have become experts in their fields. Tim has used discernment to take his career into places many wouldn't dare and made the nomadic and automated lifestyle relatively mainstream as a result. He has popularized automating your business by using systems and support to remove yourself from the equation. By speaking to a targeted audience, he has built a devoted community and impacted millions of lives around the world with his writing and ideas. It took sound judgment and cutting away the excess for him to narrow down and judge which opportunities and people to focus on based on his core competencies. If you learn one thing from Tim, it's that specificity is critical. No niche is too narrow if you're clear on who you want to serve. And one way to see who you might serve is to look at who you once were . . .

## Joseph Campbell

Let's return to Campbell's idea of the "Hero's Journey." I've used it to write my personal story and with clients to help them write out their journeys. Campbell's idea allows us to see the younger version of ourselves clearly. That helps us identify others in similar situations. It clarifies whose lives you want to impact and help. I started out with women and students exclusively when I began coaching, using my life experiences as a young professional to help them. As I developed and grew my business, I broadened the scope of who I impact to include all professionals who want more from their careers and are interested in entrepreneurship. Then I took on leaders from Fortunate 500 companies. I imagine the group of people you impact will evolve, as it has for me.

Recognizing and embracing your story and struggles can often point you toward people who will benefit from your learning and experience. If you struggled with something in your past, it might be your calling to support those similarly struggling in the present. You might also realize a cause or group you've been passionate about from childhood or adolescence. This early yearning to help a certain group might guide you toward creating a meaningful legacy.

Campbell's work taught me to recognize the mentor in myself and to identify those I could best help using the lessons learned via my past experiences. It's important to note that this can completely differ from your professional training or past work experience. If you've found a group you'd like to pursue supporting but it's way out of your current professional wheelhouse, remember volunteering is a great place to start getting experience within a certain demographic. Internships and rotation programs at large organizations can also expose you to a variety of clients and industries. It might take a while to transition from helping retirees to becoming a kindergarten teacher, but remain clear about where you're headed and the right decisions will present themselves, one step at a time.

## Your Conscience

Christian faith has a lot to say about discernment. It's framed in the light of "right" and "good" judgment in the eyes of God. The Holy Spirit is what's guiding us when we hear the subtle voice of our conscience moving us in a direction that feels moral and just.

No matter what you believe about a higher power or the universe, we all have an undeniable feeling of "right" and "wrong" from the voice inside our head. We know when things feel like the "right" thing to do. This is a reminder that discerning your impact on others is similar to finding your "calling" or vocation by listening to that voice.

Many career books talk about finding your passion. I like to think a big part of passion comes from finding your *people*. No matter what work you do, it makes a world of difference to pursue your mission around a supportive community. Being clear about who your audience is helps with crafting your offering and communicating with them effectively. That's why your past experiences can influence who you choose to impact and how. But your "calling" can be anywhere you've felt guided to go repeatedly. And our superpowers to help others don't have to feel like they're "super" or extraordinary. It often feels like it's just what we do. As a child, I always asked far too many questions for my mother's liking and didn't take anything at face value. This potentially annoying level of curiosity has stuck with me and makes me a strong coach who gets to the root of the matter in an unwavering fashion.

Your mind generates unique solutions to the challenges you encounter. The journey is finding who you want to "shine your light upon," and that's where discernment comes in. There's always a place you feel most at home. This isn't meant to keep you in your comfort zone but rather to harness your innate knowledge. The thing you see so clearly that others don't seem to "get" as quickly or easily is your inner knowing. I had a client who was so great with animals. She had a sense about what they needed. After some sessions and personal soul searching, she finally allowed herself to get a veterinary degree and found work helping injured stray dogs and cats. Sometimes we need to give ourselves permission to go after the impact we want to have. If you haven't found it yet, use your curiosity and awareness to seek it out. Check in with yourself and give yourself space to explore. We discussed the idea of gut instinct in *Chapter 14: Trust*, and I know you'll have had experiences where your inner voice has told you which way to turn.

Your mission and your niche will shine through when you're rooted in a clear mind and listening to where your conscience tells you to go. I've learned this the hard way. I initially thought I could guide and direct everything from a rational perspective. But it's often the clients, projects, ideas, and opportunities that come out of left field to find me—the unplanned surprises—that are the most successful and fulfilling for me. I realized my work needed to change after my car accident. I knew I wanted to impact more people. I started remembering my days as a child when I would play teacher in front of my teddy bears. I felt guided to expand my team, formulate more courses, and launch my podcast to help more people. By listening to my gut, discerning my best next step, and taking action on a daily basis I've found my new path and people.

I'll forever be discerning the best way to impact others. It's a learning process, as is working on every other skill in this book. But if you harness your conscience as your guide, powered by the Holy Spirit, it will always lead you to wonderful learning experiences. It will tell you what to walk toward based on what's right for you in your personal story. Even when your plans go awry and you diverge from your desired path, following what appears to be the *right* decision in the moment will allow you to serve others with integrity.

## ASK YOURSELF

**What does "discernment" mean to me?**

**Why is it important?**

**How satisfied am I with the discernment I bring to my life choices?**

**On a scale of 1 (being low) and 10 (being extremely satisfied), rate your current level of satisfaction with using discernment to make decisions:**

1    2    3    4    5    6    7    8    9    10

Look at your hero's journey from *Chapter 10: Courage.*

Envision that struggling past version of you.

- Can you identify that person in the people around you?

- How might you help and support them?

- What other groups do you identify with that you would like to impact?

- What group of people really lights you up?

- Who do you find yourself standing up for no matter what?

To illustrate the concept here are a few examples: Someone who had their house burn down may be driven to raise money for a firefighter retirement fund or teach fire safety in schools. Were you fascinated by dolphins as a child? Maybe you'll start a charity to protect them. As a bookworm who's into unicorns, maybe you'll become a fantasy author writing for children. Turning tragedy into purpose, if you've lost a family member you might train as a bereavement counselor to support others in healing.

- Who can I help with my superpowers?

- What group will benefit most from the solutions I create?

- What do I think needs to change in the world, and who needs that change the most?

- Where do I keep finding opportunities to help others without looking for them?

- Who asks me for help?

- What do they ask me for help with?

- What group of people am I drawn to spend time with?

- What does my conscience say?

## ONE-DEGREE SHIFT

1. Who have you helped so far? Write a list of groups you've impacted through formal positions, volunteer opportunities, or side hustles.

2. Think of who or what you cared for immensely as a child, before you became weighed down with societal expectations or your hang-ups about what makes a person successful. It can be pets, older relatives, certain friends or family members, a cause, or something completely different.

3. Write out the demographics of a few groups of people you'd like to help throughout your career.

4. Do you help these people already? What sorts of projects would help you learn more about them?

5. Create an avatar of the key people or group you'd like to impact. What do they want? Need? Fear? Desire? What do they think about? Where do they spend their time? Make this as realistic as possible. Name your avatar(s) and make distinct personalities, like characters in a book.

6. Write a letter to yourself from your conscience. What does it have to say about your work, what you're doing right now, and who you're meant to help?

7. Research and check out opportunities (paid or not) that will allow you to test the waters with new ways to impact your people.

## TAKEAWAYS

✦ Fill in the X portion of your niche statement to define the people you help:

"**I serve X (people)** to solve Y (problem or issue) and bring them to Z (solution)."

✦ Acknowledge your past successes in helping others.

✦ Take a trip down memory lane to remember what you cared about as a child.

✦ Create avatar profiles of the people or causes you will impact.

✦ Check in with your conscience to look at the work you're doing now and who you feel compelled to support.

# *Sixteen*

# Empathy

*"Attract what you expect,*
*reflect what you desire,*
*become what you respect,*
*and mirror what you admire.*
—UNKNOWN

## CORE QUESTION

**"What do others need from me?"**

In all honesty, the months leading up to the publication of this book were some of the most difficult in my life. I lost another baby, moved to Dallas for work, and was completely removed from family and friends. I craved for others to ask, "How can I help?" A few family members and friends rose to the occasion in a way I never would've anticipated. Surprise deliveries in the mail, text messages, jokes, hugs, and endless phone calls to check in. They all knew what I needed without me having to ask. That's one form of empathy—anticipating another's needs. They did it effectively because they asked themselves what I might need given the situation I was in. One stood out from my friend Vanessa. I opened a package that was in the mail, and it said "Sending a hug" on the card. I teared up. This gift was exactly what I needed. It brought me feelings of love and care at a time when I felt sad and deflated. But what about when you don't know exactly what you can do to help someone in need? Well, simply put, just ask them. Or, do a bit of research to see what somebody in their shoes might be going through if you haven't been there yourself.

I've been asking you to think about what *you* want as we worked through the first two parts of this book. Now we're going to think about what others around you might want and need. If we take the idea of giving gifts, we know that to be impactful we must give what the receiver wants or needs, not what we want or think they should want. Let's modify the golden rule of "Treat others as you would like to be treated" and make it more effective.

---

I PROPOSE A GOLDEN RULE 2.0:
"TREAT OTHERS AS *THEY* WISH TO BE TREATED."

---

Appreciate that everyone has *their* working methods, standards, goals, and ideals. We see this in the way we respect different cultures, religions, and traditions. Imposing our views rarely has the desired result. That doesn't mean losing sight of your own values—it means acknowledging and working on the basis that others won't always see things your way. We're often told to treat people as we would like to be treated, but this is a blinkered way of looking at things. Instead of focusing on how *we* want to be treated, we need to focus on the wants of the person we're dealing with. That starts with communicating in a way that best suits them. That's how you can make the biggest impact going forward. It sounds simple, but it takes conscious effort and skill to identify and then act in the best way for others rather than the familiar approach that has always worked for you.

One of our earlier seats at the Mentor's Table was taken by Chris Voss. He writes about what he terms "tactical empathy" and explains that it's a tool that can be used in negotiations. By utilizing empathy, we can put ourselves in the other person's shoes and truly understand what they need. It's easy to ascertain what someone needs from us when they ask us for a favor directly, but when the message is less clear, we need to ask questions to establish their expectations. By making their needs the focus, we take our empathy to the next level. Instead of asking, "What would I need if I were them?" we ask ourselves, "What are they *showing* me they need directly or through non-verbal communication or body language?" If possible, be sure to clarify rather than assume, especially if it's a high stakes scenario.

How does this relate to work? Let's look at some common examples. If you're interviewing someone, give them details, information, and questions you think they'd find useful based on what you know about them already and the job at hand. Or, to help them prepare in advance, by setting up a "Frequently Asked Questions" section based on what you've found others have asked in the past. If you're signing up a new client, observe how they communicate and relate to you or the way they relate to others in their lives—something you can ascertain from the stories or examples they give. Observe and mirror their behavior. Effective communication comes when our message is not only received but understood and welcomed. Backtracking specific words is a coaching concept that helps the person at the other end of the table know you're on the same page. You do this by repeating the exact words or phrases they've emphasized.

**For example:**

> "I would like to increase profit by ten percent next month because we're planning to build a new product line next quarter."

Using backtracking, you'd reply,

> "A new product line? Tell me more . . ."

You can also use it to clarify what's being proposed:

> "You would like to increase profit by ten percent next month, is that right?"

By repeating exactly what they've said, it gives them a chance to hear it and consider the information for a second time.

This strategy is much more effective than paraphrasing:

> "Oh, so you want to make more money and launch another item?"

which can lead to misunderstandings. It's important to use the exact words the speaker said to get the benefits of backtracking.

Another way to get clarity on what your people need is to chat with them directly. Consumer needs and the subsequent building of solutions is a huge topic, but let's start with a few main questions you need to answer. Customer interviews are a great way to structure an information gathering meeting. When in an interview, the key rule is to not talk about what *you* think would solve someone's issue but rather allow their ideas to shine.

Investigate these core questions using empathy and curiosity:

1. **What's your biggest issue with [topic/situation]?**

   This will inform you of the challenges and problems they're facing in your area of interest. You'll see the areas that are priorities to them and what they don't care about. Both are equally useful.

2. **What have you tried so far to solve [issue]?**

   Asking this will help you to learn their pain points and what's currently prevalent in the industry. It might inform that your approach to solving the problem is either tried and true or more unique and novel. This will give you a lot of language to communicate your product or service down the line.

3. **What is the ideal solution?**

   This gets the person to visualize exactly what they'd want to see a solution provide. Use backtracking and get as many details as possible. This is informing you of their needs, wants, wishes, and ultimately the product or service you're building.

4. **How urgently do you need to find a solution?**

   By getting curious about your people's urgency to solve a problem, you'll understand how important it is to them and what they're willing to pay or change to achieve their desired solution.

After interviewing multiple people and understanding what their needs are, you will be well equipped to decide which problem of theirs you want to solve.

To get the most out of customer interviews and interactions with others in general, let's think about the effectiveness of your communication style. What is the purpose of your message? How adept are you at actively listening to both verbal and non-verbal cues? How effectively can you craft messages? Ask yourself questions before you communicate. Is this simply to get something off your chest, or could you be communicating a more constructive message that will be heard with more welcoming ears? When you do it forcefully or try to deceive people, it often comes back to bite you. If you show up with empathy and a desire to serve, you'll succeed no matter what challenges come your way.

It's difficult to empathize with people we don't like. It's especially hard if it seems like the other person has zero empathy for our side. When I reach the end of my rope with someone, I imagine that person as a child. I don't do this to demean them. In doing so, I consider their deep hurts, challenges, and what has motivated them to act the way they are. Often a prickly response is the result of our defensive spikes going up to protect a soft, vulnerable part of ourselves.

My first major assumption is that people are doing the best they can. I open myself up to trusting others, which we explored in *Chapter 14: Trust*. When I start from there, I remind myself that their hostility is likely not about me but about something else happening in their lives. Do your best to see how they're simply trying to do *their* best, protect themselves, or fight for a cause they believe in. It's even better if you can go a step further and be curious about where they're coming from—ask questions and encourage them to open up to you. When I do this with a person I'm having trouble communicating with, I see them with new, more empathetic eyes. I can see their vulnerabilities. This is often the last thing you notice when someone annoys you—their vulnerability.

Opening the door to vulnerabilities and acknowledging their existence and impact is what gets to the root of many matters. Anything else is like a placebo. I liken it to taking painkillers for a headache, which will solve the problem for a while, but if the root cause of the situation is dehydration, things won't really improve until you start drinking more water. Resentment is anger retained for too long, and anger is often inflamed fear. Once you understand that, vulnerability becomes less formidable to move through. When we approach situations with empathy, we're less likely to return anger with anger. Instead, we exude compassion, understanding, and love. It's tough to argue when you're the only one upset. At some point, their anger will dissipate, and you can get to the bottom of the underlying issue.

I recently gave a talk to an audience of young girls at the high school I attended. I was honest and laid out my experience of feeling like I did not fit in at school and how I used that feeling to learn to trust myself and my judgment. The talk led to an open, frank discussion about bullying and other experiences where empathy is often lacking. Because I opened up, the girls felt they could be honest with me, each other, and themselves. We can't expect others to be truthful with us when we aren't showing up that way ourselves. Embracing and acknowledging our vulnerabilities invites others to do the same. We see this with true leaders who embody the notion of leading by their own example.

Naturally, there's a balance between empathy and self-advocacy. It's one thing to seek to understand your clients, friends, and family by being empathetic. If someone's behavior crosses a personal boundary, it may be time to speak up and stand up for your needs. If you have a boss who repeatedly shoots you down and bullies you or a client who is disrespectful, then the time has come for you to use your self-advocacy skills. That might involve being upfront or potentially the crucial ability to walk away.

When you've reached your "empathy limit," take a break and some space. Having time away from connecting with others is restorative, even for self-proclaimed extroverts. This can be for a day or simply for a few minutes, depending on the time immediately available to you. I have always felt better after a nap or some time away from a strained relationship to clear my head.

Another potential pitfall with the quality of empathy is getting into a victim-savior relationship with people. Sometimes it makes us feel good and important to be the savior or, surprisingly, the victim. That's why we allow the dynamic to perpetuate, because it gives us a sense of importance. There's a better way to get that feeling, and it's through true connection with others from a loving place and being in service, which we'll get to shortly. It's vital to remember that if something or someone is draining your empathy or compassion, it's a signal to take a closer look at the situation and walk away if necessary. Like a gas tank, if you run on empathy fumes too long, it can blow your engine. The right use of empathy is showing compassion for others and considering their needs in the way we interact with them. It's not meant to lead to martyrdom, resentment, or regularly coming to the rescue.

There's something to learn about yourself from the relationships that prove to be difficult. When you pause and consider what's going on, you reach realizations you wouldn't have discovered if you had stayed in the fray. In these situations, take any time you can afford to head back into yourself. There, you can understand why you feel hardened or closed off to the topic or person you're dealing with.

Many of us have been taught to deal with stress in a strong-handed manner. At these times, we can lose our perspective, making it impossible to empathize effectively. Feeling a lack of empathy for the cutest puppy or child is a clear sign that we need a break of our own to recalibrate. So think about it like a math equation, the left side must equal the right side. What we give out must balance with the energy we take in. We're more likely to recognize and engage with people who we can help when *we're* taken care of. Our ability to extend empathy and kindness to others multiplies when our gas tank is full. Knowing when you need to put the focus back on yourself is an important part of building a sustainable impact through your work. So, if you feel like you're running on empty, your best bet is to head back to Part One to fill up your tank. I'd encourage you to check in with yourself about this giving equation regularly. If empathizing with your clients, or partner, or kids is becoming a task filled with resentment, it's not the time to be making an external impact—it's time to be stepping inward.

## MENTOR'S TABLE

When allocating the seats at your Mentor's Table, remember that the people you choose will have a significant impact on both you and your career. I know that when I started working, I admired many professionals. And then I recognized one simple but pivotal thing: if you take advice or learn from watching someone, you'll become more like them over time. So, it's important to make a conscious choice when it comes to mentors rather than relying on whoever happens to be your colleague or your superior.

The history of career design has abundant evidence for the prevalence of the apprentice model.

"My father is a banker, so I'll be a banker and follow in his footsteps."

"We're a family of doctors, so that's what I'll do."

"My boss does it that way, so if I want to be successful, I should too."

So much of this that still occurs, and it isn't surprising. Having a parent, family member, or boss as a mentor truly gives us a leg up on the competition. They can help us avoid beginner's errors and pave the way for further success with a shorter learning curve.

But what about those of us who define success differently from our parents? Well, given how many courses, seminars, and self-proclaimed gurus and influencers exist, we have our fair share of options to choose from. My first mentors in the coaching industry are phenomenal individuals. They taught me about being open-hearted in business and showed me that coaching could be both a fulfilling career and profitable for many, not only a select few. That being said, in those early days, I didn't ask myself if I wanted to build the same business they had. Did I want to emulate how they were making money?

It took me many months to realize that our ideas about the type of businesses we wanted to run were different. Figuring out that your views differ from those you've learned from is a big moment. You can admire a hugely successful person, but it doesn't mean you want to replicate their approach in your career. My life started to change when I focused on the business projects I was taking on, as well as the people I allowed to influence my choices. You can be mentored and influenced by many people during your life and career, so remember to be mindful of who you have sitting at the table.

Empathy is deeply personal. It depends on one individual trying to understand and relate to another. So, now that we've reached Part Three, I'd like to use this section to invite you to put together your *own* Mentor's

Table filled with the people you admire. This will help you consciously assemble the podcasts, authors, entrepreneurs, family, friends, and colleagues influencing your life on a regular basis. It's valuable to clarify what you're gathering from those around you. Then you can determine how you'd like to mentor others and the way you serve through your work. Have you been following someone else's approach to impacting the world? Who do you want to emulate going forward? What's the type of impact and business model that'll best serve your audience? Finding aligned mentors will help you discover meaningful answers. Here are some pointers to get you started based on what I've learned so far:

1. **Identify a few individuals.**

   No one is an expert at everything, so have focused mentors for different areas of your career and life. I have mentors who are my go-to for finance, real estate, business growth, online advertising, marriage, and many other personal elements of my life in health, spirituality, and wellness.

   As mentioned, you don't need to know the mentor *personally* to benefit from their experiences and expertise. Make your list broad, and ensure you have different philosophies to consider. I've had great personal success interacting with a variety of people I admire via social channels. We're lucky to live in a time when people are highly accessible. The worst case is they don't get back to you. It's worth the effort to craft a thoughtful, useful message to someone you admire. Many times, you'll receive a note back. The key thing if you do reach out is to deliver some sort of value or shared interest to the person. It's a great moment to practice empathy and understanding for what they value and deliver something useful during a first interaction. You do that by asking yourself:

   - What kind of help might they need in their work?

   - What might their day-to-day worries or problems be?

   - What is of interest to them?

   - How can I help them improve?

   - What can I do/provide that would be meaningful to them?

These questions may seem difficult to answer at first, but think through them with empathy for who your mentor is and what they find important. I'm sure you'll discover at least one way you can be useful and provide value based on your areas of knowledge. It could be something as simple as sharing what part of their recent blog post was valuable to you and why. This lets them know you appreciate their work while simultaneously informing them of where to focus based on what is helping their audience.

2. **Pick deliberately.**

Be mindful of the idea that you will be looking to these people for advice, whether it's given directly or by their example. You want to make sure you trust their judgment enough to implement their ideas in your own life. Check that you're aligned with their values and *modus operandi* in their area of expertise. If they're in your mind because you listen to their podcast or because you're around them every day they have the capacity to influence your thoughts just the same. This might mean removing some current mentors in order to make space for more aligned sources of inspiration and knowledge.

3. **Understand that this is an evolving process.**

As I said, my mentors at the beginning of my career were not the same as they are now. As I've grown and developed, both in my career and as a person, I've had different areas that I'm focused on improving. Just because I found inspiration and supportive ideas from one individual doesn't mean I must emulate how they conduct *all* of the aspects of their life. It's normal to outgrow a mentor and seek different teachers throughout your life as you grow.

Pick mentors who give you what you need to move into your defined version of success from Part One. If you know them personally, make sure they're asking you what you need from them and exuding a quality of empathy in the way they interact with you. You can often have an informal mentorship relationship with those you admire, but be sure to ask focused questions and keep track of what you learn. The dynamic is informal and convenient for them, but you're responsible for capturing their wisdom.

4.  **Be a mentor for others.**

When considering who you view as mentors, it's just as important to consider the impact and power you have in mentoring others. I've supported young women in a variety of programs like Girls Inc., the Rotman School of Management's Alumni Mentorship Program, and via online internships through FLIK. Actively taking on the role of a mentor can be a life-changing way to impact others. I've had the most wonderful experiences coaching young women as they explore their career options. One intern, Katarina, sticks out in my mind. She always gave her all and was extremely independent and resourceful. I know my mentoring impacted her because she said so, and she took an extra step to buy me both a wedding gift and parting present when her internship was complete to thank me. She wrote me a message that brought me to tears with its thoughtfulness. My hope is that our bond is lifelong and that her experience interning at Chiefly was as life-changing for her as it was for me. When I visualize my impact on the world, I hope it looks like a stadium full of Katarinas who feel I've given them a new way of looking at the world and have supported their dreams in life.

Being a mentor is one of the most meaningful and fulfilling forms of impact, in my opinion. If you aren't doing this already, formally or informally, I highly recommend it. It will cultivate your empathy for others, and you'll learn a lot from the relationships, too.

## ASK YOURSELF

What does "empathy" mean to me?

Why is it important?

How confident am I in the way I empathize with others?

On a scale of 1 (being low) and 10 (being extremely satisfied), rate your current level of satisfaction with your ability to empathize with others:

1   2   3   4   5   6   7   8   9   10

- What problems did my people share with me?

- What solutions do they want for their problem?

- Do they seem willing to pay? If so, how much?

- Which of the problems they shared am I interested in solving?

- How do the people around me—my colleagues, my clients, my friends and family, my children—want to be treated?

- What do they need?

- How do they communicate with me?

- How might I emulate their approach so they're more open to my communication?

- Who might I check in with personally to understand them and their needs better?

- Who inspires me as a potential mentor?

- What qualities do they have that inspire me?

## ONE-DEGREE SHIFT

1. Run customer interviews. Whether you're moving toward a career change or tweaking your current path, it's time to get to know your audience better. Use the questions from above or some listed below to understand their needs, wants, problems, thought processes, and priorities. Find answers to the question: "What problems are my people facing that they urgently need solved?" Record the answers in your note-taking tool. Work for a company and not client-facing? You can still run informal informational interviews with colleagues from different internal departments or any stakeholders who are impacted by your work. This will help you understand their challenges and how you can deliver the most value through the work you do in your role.

   - What is your biggest challenge with (a particular area/situation/thing)?

   - What is the most frustrating part of the problem?

   - How big of a problem is this for you?

   - How have you tried to solve this problem in the past?

   - Why didn't the solution work?

   - What is the ideal solution?

   - How would (what they say the ideal solution is) help you?

   - How would the solution fix the problem?

   - Is this problem important for you to solve?

   - How much money would you spend if you could solve the problem right now? (Take this one with a grain of salt—people don't often know exactly what they're willing to pay, especially if you've created a novel solution.)

2. Make a list of all the problems they shared with you and look out for any trends.

   - Which challenges came up repeatedly?

   - What requests and desires did people in your audience have in common?

- If you're working with an audience that resembles your past self, what problems do you wish you had support solving back then?

- If you work with existing products, consider which of the problems (if any) your product addresses with its features and capabilities.

3. Choose the core problem you'd like to solve for your people.

   In looking at all the problems you've laid out, which ones are you interested in solving?

   Decide which one you'd like to address based on your interests, skills, and your audience's needs and wants.

4. Add the Y part to your niche statement:

   "I serve X (people) to **solve Y (problem or issue)** and bring them to Z (solution)."

5. Brainstorm three ways you want to bring more empathy to your work. Maybe you want to understand your vendor's delivery cycle better or find ways to acknowledge your team regularly for continuing to deliver great work.

6. List three to five things you can do to anticipate your boss's, clients', or other peoples' needs to make their day a bit easier. If you're unsure, ask them and follow through on their request if possible. If not, aim to find a middle ground.

7. Carry out an empathy audit. Consider journaling or talking through what gives you energy and what drains your empathy. What situations leave you feeling full of empathy and understanding? What situations leave you feeling like your tank is running on empty? What can you learn about yourself from this?

8. Practice empathy by asking a client, a friend, or a co-worker this question: "What can I do to be a better _____ to you?" i.e., manager, friend, service provider, parent, lawyer, etc. Use backtracking to confirm you're both on the same page and you understand their feedback.

## TAKEAWAYS

✦ Run customer interviews to understand what problems your audience is facing that they urgently need solved.

✦ Build upon your niche statement to define the problem:

"I serve X (people) to **solve Y (problem or issue)** and bring them to Z (solution)."

✦ Consider who is currently sitting at your own Mentor's Table.

✦ Create a new Mentor's Table with individuals aligned with your goals and values.

✦ Brainstorm how to be more empathetic in daily situations.

✦ Show more empathy to those around you by asking them directly or anticipating their needs.

✦ Complete an empathy audit to better understand what drains and refills your energy.

✦ Ask someone for feedback and use backtracking to ensure you're on the same page.

✦ Empathize with yourself when you realize you're running on empty and take time to pause.

# Structure

*"Good order is the foundation of all things."*
—EDMUND BURKE

## CORE QUESTION

**"What structure can I put in place to create my desired result?"**

On another adventure, I showed up to Chiang Mai, Thailand, in the middle of the night after a twenty-four-hour journey. I was exhausted. I had never visited before and had no knowledge of the place. Oh, and I was there to lead the first on-site, two-week retreat I had ever hosted.

I had prepared months in advance. Although I had vendors responsible for the logistics, I had worked hard to consider all the variables, and I thought I had prepared comprehensively. This retreat was my creation, and I was determined make it a success.

What I *wasn't* prepared for was the extent of the unknown: multiple small implosions and disasters. First, *I* had arrived safely in Chiang Mai, but my luggage had not. For the first week of the retreat, my luggage was missing, so I had to quickly run off to buy new clothes to greet my attendees. Content partners turned up without fully prepared content. Some of the attendees quickly came down with a stomach bug which eventually came my way and left me struggling with sickness for most of the first week. My carefully planned event had become a bit of a nightmare.

Did this mean the retreat was a failure? No. Did the attendees get what they needed and came for? From the feedback I was given, I believe so. Even though most of the mishaps were outside of my control, it was hard not to look at my own preparation and see what I had missed. What could I have done to support and ensure an even more successful delivery? The truth is that no amount of preparation could have avoided lost luggage, the let-down of collaborators, or a rather nasty stomach bug. But I could've had professional outfits in my carry on, content to substitute in the event that a collaborator wasn't prepared, and further event support so that I wasn't required to perform every day if something came up. Thankfully, my preparation *had* ensured there was a solid structure for the core event and it could withstand a few knocks and still deliver what I intended to.

Let's start by putting the final piece of the puzzle into place for your niche statement: "I serve X (people) to solve Y (problem or issue) and **bring them to Z (solution)**." As you learned in my Chiang Mai story, having the perfect solution mapped out isn't the goal here. The aim of structuring what you offer to the world is to ensure it's grounded in your defined focus from Part One, relates to the contribution you want to make from Part Two, and addresses the problems your people are having from *Chapter 16: Empathy*. We'll deal with delivery in the next chapter about service. So what solution will you provide?

**Let's take my example:**

I serve professional women to help them leave unfulfilling jobs and start their own businesses to build a meaningful legacy via their work.

So why is my solution "start their own businesses to build a meaningful legacy via their work?" When I consider my personal focus on entrepreneurship, I know I want to help people who have similar career goals and aspirations. That doesn't mean this book or other offers I have don't help a wider audience, it's just that my niche statement, and therefore the impact I want to make on the world, focuses on that solution in particular. I want women to find financial and time freedom from starting their own company.

When it comes to contribution, I know I enjoy teaching, mentoring, and helping others. Helping women to start businesses gives me the opportunity to teach them skills that will help them have ownership and leave a legacy through their work. It gives them creative control. The journey of self-employment is one of building all the qualities we've discussed in this book. It's exhilarating.

And how does it relate to my audience's problems? Well, I spoke with many women in corporate positions, and a big issue they were having is not knowing where to start, feeling unsure they could replace their corporate income, and wanting a structure and community to help them take the leap. Bingo. This was exactly what I was envisioning to create.

Once you have this sentence completed, the journey begins to co-create the transformational process with your customer. If you already know what path you're taking your audience on, be ready to list it out at the end of the chapter. If you're unsure, get back in touch with them directly to get clearer on the vision they have for an ideal solution.

A high-level example of a process digital marketers take their audience on is:

*Transformation:* We are going to help you go from no one knowing your name to everyone in the Tristate Area calling you when they need a plumber.

*Process:*

1. **Strategy Call**
   We will map out your specific goals for a campaign, go over any questions you might have, and discuss the budget and Key Performance Indicators.

2. **Audit**
   We will review any existing campaigns you have run in the past.

3. **Campaign Creation**
   We will research your target audience, competitors, and past campaigns and create mock-ups for you to evaluate.

4. **Campaign Launch**
   We go live on the chosen campaign and start tracking Key Performance Indicators that we agreed upon in the strategy call.

5. **Weekly Calls**
   We review campaign progress with the client weekly.

6. **Revision or Overhaul of Campaigns**
   We will make changes as needed based on the results we're seeing.

If you share your process with your potential clients, or boss if you're employed, and they still have questions, that's a good thing. It's an opportunity to add more features to the offer, take away estraneous elements they don't value, or affirm that you're heading in the right direction. Baking in continuous feedback measures with your people will ensure your process continues to improve and become even more effective at delivering the Point A to Point B transformation you're offering to them.

Remember, you don't have to be the one running interviews in the long run. If you're starting your own business, you may need to begin by doing most things. However as you grow, find competent team members to take on the daily tasks of the business. If you're in a large organization, loop in the appropriate team to help you on the initiative you're working to bring to life.

---

MAP OUT A PATH TO ACHIEVING YOUR GOALS.
HAVING A PLAN MAKES SUCCESS MORE LIKELY,
EVEN THOUGH YOU'LL PROBABLY TAKE A FEW DETOURS.

---

The same goes for any program or product you want to sell to your audience. It needs to be well thought out and structured to deliver on your promised value. Many people don't know where to start.

Let's look at a way of creating structure for any given goal or project—big or small:

1. **Define your objectives.**

   Start with the end in mind. What do you want the result to be? How will you know when you get there? What will be different? What is the transformation you're seeking to provide? Another way to look at this is to clarify your client's starting point—Point A—and then to define the attributes of the end point—Point B—you are going to help them get to. What are the exact steps you're going to help them take to reach Point B? It's important to lay out all the major milestones you guide clients through to parse out what the phases along the way will be. Whether it's buying your dream home or building your business, it's important to imagine what the perfect end result will be. The same goes for the solution you provide to your people. Map out the steps of the journey you're going to take them on. Companies do this for products as well. Even something as seemingly simple as selling a T-shirt has a story of who you'll be when you wear it. Be clear on the journey you're taking people on if they use your solution.

2. **Set meaningful and clear metrics for success.**

If your clear goal is revenue, then don't measure success solely by the number of clients you engage. If you're aiming for actual attendees at an event, you can't measure success by the number of people signing up for your newsletter. If your objective is to ensure you have an effective, efficient team, you need to define what effective and efficient means in terms of daily tasks. Ensuring ownership of tasks is critical too.

3. **Outline realistic and precise expectations.**

On this point, I'm talking to you overachievers reading this as well as the self-proclaimed procrastinators and slackers. I can relate to both tendencies depending on the day or task at hand. Ask yourself, what is a realistic and successful outcome for the role, project, or client, and make that your goal. Then add a buffer for the inevitable twists and turns that will come around right before a major deadline. Be sure to define what your audience can expect from you throughout the journey you're taking them on. Whether you're selling meat as a butcher or building houses, setting clear expectations about what you're offering is vital to building trust and having repeat customers.

4. **Communicate all major expectations with key stakeholders.**

Make sure your plan and expectations of the results are mutually agreed upon with your client or whoever you're working with. Whether you're an employee or working on a contract, confirm that the way you're measuring success is clear and defined for all parties. This will help reduce the odds of the project scope creeping into undefined territory and manage your time well. It's important for everyone involved to know and agree upon key milestones, dates, and success criteria in advance.

5. **Establish milestones along your timeline to completion.**

What will the deliverables, touchpoints for meetings, or useful points of contact be as you journey toward the conclusion? How long will successful delivery take? Remember that buffer you've put in place for any delays with suppliers, team members, decision makers, or clients.

6. **Track all pertinent details.**

Structure is built upon timelines, budgets, staffing, marketing, and communicating what your successful delivery will look like to your client. Represent the details of your structured plans using whatever software tools or written templates you feel comfortable with, but make sure they exist. If you think through possible contingency plans ahead of time, your client will be happy, and you'll be better off knowing where you need to devote your energy. Making sure all tasks are assigned and described clearly is a big one here.

Structure is about keeping your end goal—the successful delivery—in view as you navigate the present moment. Measuring success also involves appraising ourselves honestly. We often shy away from doing this because it's easier to ignore the times when we're not making progress. If I've learned anything from my experience creating a start-up, it's that a big fat zero staring you in the face, week after week, is the most sobering wake-up call. It's a sign that you need to get laser-focused and start forming structure around your success metrics. Tracking things with honesty means you can see a true lay of the land and make meaningful changes to how you're approaching your goals. Knowing and accepting that something isn't going in the intended direction is far better than pretending the problem doesn't exist.

When we create a structure for our work—what our objectives are and how we get there—we (businesses and individuals alike) can focus on the quality of what we deliver. Building teams with good structure means everyone is on the same page and working toward the same goal. When unforeseen problems come up, everyone can do their part to get the team back on track to the main objective.

My retreat to Chiang Mai might have had some unexpected events, but it was overall a valuable experience for the attendees. By preparing a structure, I knew the core elements of what I needed to provide. When your clients know you'll deliver what you promise, they'll return to you again and again. They'll trust you. It gives your working relationships stability.

Allow the way you create structure in your life to be influenced by your personal approach. Some of us are all about the details and others prefer big-picture thinking, so do what you can to create a framework that aligns with your needs. Remember your strengths and ensure you enlist the support you require to cover all your bases. If you don't like structuring a budget or timelines, get in touch with someone who does, and you'll have a much better result than pretending you don't need help. If there's something you're avoiding addressing and shoving under the rug, then think about how you can best deal with it. In some cases, the most effective choice may be to get support from an expert.

It's well-worn advice that you can count on a Swiss-made watch. My husband is Swiss, and during my time spent there, I can tell you that in addition to their exquisite timepieces, you can also rely on their train system. There was a lot to learn when I landed for the first time in the land of milk and honey. After spending time in Brazil, I was used to a lax approach to timekeeping, deadlines, and regulations. Switzerland introduced me to the flipside—a culture based on order and structure. There is a time for going with the flow and seeing where the moment takes you, but the road to success also needs structure. The Swiss train system is a perfect embodiment of how smoothly and reliably things can run to deliver client needs. Knowing that I can almost infallibly rely on my transport to be on time means that the stress of worrying about making meetings or getting where I need to be is taken off my shoulders. When we do this for clients or the people we work with, through structuring our delivery, we show them that we can be relied on.

When it comes to career building, structure is vital as well. If we approach our career trajectories with no structure, they'll develop without our conscious intent. Experiencing the differing cultural environments of Brazil and Switzerland enabled me to discover the balance of chaos and order I was most happy with. On the one side, there's mutability and state of chaos with less of an emphasis on structure and rules. At the other end is pure order, but here, the structure becomes so rigid it doesn't move and bend with change—especially unforeseen change. The most effective form of structure is both strong and focused on our end goal but not inflexible. There's a happy, productive middle state between these two that we can all find. For some, it might be closer to the exhilaration of chaos. For others, it might be further down the line of working with predictable order. Where are you on the continuum when it comes to work? And where are you when it comes to your life overall?

For me, approaching a career path plan without structure is like anything else in life: Without a plan, you're meandering. When you're starting out, this might initially seem like a decent option. It's definitely where I started. But I can tell you that, without a long-term vision or plan, there's also no aim—no clear goal—and without that, there can be no measurable "success." The benefit to having no target is that you'll never really "fail" to hit the mark. The downside is that you'll have a harder time achieving your aims if you don't set any.

If you're not high on the conscientiousness scale and structure seems synonymous with boredom and routine, I promise you I've been of the same mind at times. I used to approach looking at the budgets and systems inside my business reluctantly. Having structure in your work not only delivers good results for those you're serving but, ultimately, delivers results for you too. Creating a system that works can take what might feel messy and cluttered and give it order and purpose. Systems allow us to make a bigger impact in the way we do business and in our personal efforts.

## MENTOR'S TABLE

### Mark Bunten

"Okay, class, I'm going to do a fifteen-minute presentation. You'll then have twenty-five minutes to prepare your ideas. You'll have five minutes to present those to the class and then we'll switch groups for the last twenty minutes to share ideas about what we've learned."

Mark Bunten was a high school teacher of mine. In his class, we knew what to expect, what we needed to know for the test, and what was required of us. Most importantly, we knew exactly how Mr. Bunten would show up—time and time again—at every lesson. He was consistent and delivered no matter what because of his structured approach.

He was a consistent source of support in high school. Like a lot of kids, I never quite felt I fit in, and his office was always open for questions or a chat. In and outside the classroom, he set clear, transparent, reasonable expectations for his students. I believe this is crucial for a learning environment, and it continues to be something we seek out and crave long after we leave school. We want to know what to expect. We want to know what is expected of us. We want to know when it's due. We want to know what we'll be tested on. In later years, this continues. We want to know when the meeting will start. We want to know what the deadline is. We want to know what sales figures are expected. We want to know when something will be delivered. We're looking for certainty at every turn.

Teachers are experts on structure. Every lesson needs to deliver a piece of knowledge or understanding to their students, and teachers have a finite amount of time to do that. I'm predisposed to resisting that rigidity, so I get it if you aren't the first on board for a tight minute-by-minute itinerary. It has its place, and every individual needs to decide what level is right for them depending on the environment.

Make structure work for you. Maybe you thrive in timed, boxed work periods of three hours on one topic. If so, you might find a detailed timetable keeps you on track. Perhaps you function better by measuring your progress through projects and goals rather than time. If so, you might like setting timelines for each goal or listing out daily and weekly aims. The most important thing is setting up a structure that inspires you. It's meant to help you untangle all the moving parts of your projects to see the progress you're making and keep sight of your end goal. Build your structure in a way that makes you most effective.

## Dave Ramsey

We can't talk about structure at work without addressing money in the form of the income you generate and your expenses. This may or may not be your least favorite part of the book, but laying this out in your own way will create structure in your financial life which is imperative if you want to build wealth and manage your money effectively.

Dave Ramsey is the founder of Ramsey Solutions, one of the U.S.'s best-known debt solutions services. The average American owes around $6,000 in debt, and it's Dave's mission to end the American people's reliance on credit. From his perspective, debt is bad, cash is king, and we can change our relationship with money by taking responsibility for where we spend it.

Ramsey speaks from experience. In his early twenties, he had a wildly successful career in real estate, and on paper he was a millionaire. But he relied heavily on credit. At the age of twenty-six, after a change in banking regulations, he found his credit sources cut off. They wanted their money back, and he found himself declaring bankruptcy. With a wife and young children to support, he was at rock-bottom. But rather than give up, Ramsey swore he would never again allow himself to get into that situation. He began offering financial counseling and self-published his first book, *Financial Peace*. Today, Ramsey Solutions has a multi-million-dollar annual revenue, and Dave's radio show has more than fifteen million regular listeners.

Ramsey's method to money management and eliminating debts is a set of "Baby Steps:"

**Baby Step 1:** Save $1,000 for your starter emergency fund.

**Baby Step 2:** Pay off all debt (except the house) using the debt snowball.

**Baby Step 3:** Save three to six months of expenses in a fully funded emergency fund.

**Baby Step 4:** Invest fifteen percent of your household income in retirement.

**Baby Step 5:** Save for your children's college fund.

**Baby Step 6:** Pay off your home early.

**Baby Step 7:** Build wealth and give.

You follow these steps and create a budget where every dollar has a purpose and is allocated. Essentially, his advice is to give your finances a structure and retain control of it. That involves being honest about your income and your career plans while also being realistic about your expectations. Money is a major source of worry for most people, but it's also the one they're the least likely to want to spend time addressing in detail. You can't just ignore it and make the math magically transform—believe me, I've tried. The math isn't going to budge until you change your actions.

Knowing avoidance is one of the biggest challenges regarding money, we need to utilize structure and systems to create wealth. So I'd like to give you the opportunity to look under the rug and evaluate current structures you have in place when it comes to your finances. In this section, we'll do an overview of all the income you generate. Print out credit card statements, bank account statements, and audit yourself. I find having pens and paper help me feel like things are real, but use whatever medium you like. The key here is to have an honest look at what you're earning, spending, saving, and investing. There are tons of free budgeting tools within bank accounts or apps, so find one you like and map out where your money is going. In my experience, it takes doing this consistently for at least a year to get a grip on your financial budget. It might be variable, especially if you're an entrepreneur, get paid in big chunks, or have an income based on performance. It won't always go as expected, but the point is to have clarity, not perfection. Life can get messy. The point is to be honest with yourself and create a structure that supports you to reach your financial goals.

We can probably agree that some level of success is about the ability to provide for our needs and that requires structure. Even if you're the person who wants to live off the grid, grow your own crops, and become self-sufficient, you'll still need an inventory of your crops to ensure you're well-stocked and have enough to barter for the essentials you can't grow. You still need to have the seeds to plant for next year, stock that can carry you through a hurricane or drought, and enough for the future when you, perhaps, can't work as hard on your land as you once did.

Even when we take ourselves outside the capitalist model, we're all consumers and producers. So you need to give careful thought to what you're bringing in (earnings) and sending out (expenditure).

Any great financial advisor will tell you that what you make is not nearly as important as what you keep when it comes to wealth creation. If you make $100,000 and spend $99,999 then you're not necessarily better off at the end of the day. Make sure to pay into a separate jar of your own first and invest in your present and future financial security.

There are two main models you can use in terms of your finances: increase your income or decrease your expenses.

For the purposes of this book, we'll look at how your income progression is structured in your chosen vocation, both your current work and your ideal career path. It's important to see where your career earning potential is headed and what opportunities are available to you. That's what drew me to entrepreneurship. The potential is unlimited.

Some questions to ask yourself at this point are:

- What does your current income growth trajectory look like in your career advancement opportunities at work?

- What about in ten years?

- Consider your boss, their boss, and maybe three bosses up, depending on how big of an organization you're in. What do they make? Is that appealing to you?

- How do they spend their time on an average day? Do you like the idea of spending your time that way, day in and day out?

- What's your ideal money growth trajectory?

- How can you make that happen with your chosen contribution to the world?

There are some careers that we have been able to trust when it comes to earning a decent income, like lawyers, accountants, and doctors. However, there are new tech jobs being created at a rapid pace and more freelancers than ever. There's also a lot of automation happening in law, medicine, and accounting that's changing the landscape of what we once relied upon. Knowing how you'll create enough income for your needs over the course of your career while contributing to humankind is something to consider, no matter how many hours you've put in thus far.

As mentioned, income is one part of the equation, but making your money work for you is the next. If you increase your income, you should increase the amount you're investing in generating passive income. I'm not a financial advisor, but as an entrepreneur, saving for retirement is up to me. Regardless of the occupation you hold, your money is your responsibility, even if you delegate the management of it to someone else for the time being. Some of the things I've investigated are contributing to tax-free savings and investment options like a Tax-Free Savings Account or Roth IRA. Consider building a portfolio outside of whatever employer program you might be a part of. Of course, it should go without saying that speaking with someone you trust or vetting a few financial advisors is critical when it comes to making long term decisions with your money. Some other options include having an investment portfolio or real estate. If this all sounds foreign, look up Mr. Money Moustache and the Financial Independence Retire Early (FIRE) movement to get a further grasp on this material to build wealth.

## STEPS TO STRUCTURE YOUR MONEY:

1. **Make Money:** Look at your earning potential to maximize your income (active or passive) and delegate what you can (structure tasks clearly to do so).

2. **Manage Expenses:** Track what you spend in a budget and use Dave Ramsey's baby steps to reduce debt.

3. **Invest:** Allocate a percentage of what you make to investments you understand and feel comfortable with (Ramsey says fifteen percent, while Mr. Money Moustache, Peter Adeney, and FIRE say as much as possible to achieve your freedom number. Adeney saved half of his income for years to be able to retire by thirty).

There's power in compound interest, so the sooner you get started investing, the better—if you understand what you're putting your money into. There are risks to any investment, and I know many who have been burned by following trends without doing their due diligence, myself included. One avenue to consider is Exchange-Traded Funds (ETFs) for low management fees and funds that mimic the S&P 500 (the five hundred biggest companies in the U.S.). Dave Ramsey uses mutual funds and recommends growth, growth and income, growth aggressive, and international funds. I use that structure but incorporate ETFs because of the similar performance with lower management fees. Always speak to a financial professional about your personal situation. This is just what I do and what I've learned from my research and experience. Financial freedom isn't everything, but it's certainly a huge relief when other challenges, like health or emotional struggles, come knocking. Structure your earning trajectory and money so you know where it's going, and it'll pay off.

## Twyla Tharp

"Shut up and do what you love,"[13] is a quote from a 2019 interview with the next person at our Mentor's Table. A New Yorker through and through, Twyla Tharp is a firecracker of a lady who I admire. She's also one of the most successful dance choreographers on the planet. Choreography is a pure form of structure. It's a blueprint for movement and energy, and the result is a piece of creative art. Like a canvas, an excel spreadsheet, or a software program, a piece of choreography offers a structural home for your creative work. Tharp has things to teach us about structure outside of work. She embodies the idea that structure can be a creative means of bringing things together and a foundation that allows creativity to flourish. She doesn't allow society to impose that structure upon her but creates her own to fit her creative process. She taught me that we need to think twice about the societal structures we adhere to.

Now in her eighties, she brings positive, targeted structure to her everyday life in her daily rituals and philosophy. She's vocal about society's limiting ideas and expectations surrounding aging and the potential people have to make change and work into their later years. As a multiple award-winner, she has already reached the top of her career but refuses to rest on her laurels and has, instead, restructured her purpose around a new reality of continuing to teach others.

She believes that results are all about what you do every day and is keen to evolve her approach to work and life as she ages.

Tharp reminds me that when I structure my work, I can let my creativity flow. The legacy she has created reminds me that my structure will change as I reach goals and stretch for new ones. Anyone who says structure is limiting does not understand that structure is constantly evolving and can be personally formulated. What are the structural dimensions you're working with in your career? Have you perhaps outgrown them? Where can they be changed to get you on the path to where you want to be?

---

13. *Why Twyla Tharp Wants Us to 'Shut Up' and Do What We Love.* YouTube, 2019. https://www.you tube.com/watch?v=XjJ4JHKs60E.

## Herbert A. Simon

Herbert Simon was an economist, political scientist, psychologist, and Nobel Memorial Prize winner. He introduced the world to an idea of "design thinking" in his 1969 book, *Sciences of the Artificial,* which was introduced to me by my husband. The book and the ideas it contains have changed the way I approach any challenge. It allowed me to see how I could apply structure to my decision-making and solution-finding process.

Design thinking is made up of a series of stages:

1. **Empathize:** Develop a deep sense of understanding of the challenge at hand. Who is affected and involved and will be impacted by a solution?

2. **Define:** Clearly articulate the problem you want to solve.

3. **Ideate:** Brainstorm potential solutions.

4. **Prototype:** Design a prototype or formulate a solution to test.

5. **Test:** Start continuous short-cycle tests to improve your design.

The idea is that you use a structure to form your process that allows for adaptations and flexibility as you learn more and develop. A common saying of entrepreneurs is that you need to "Build the plane as you fly it," and I think that's exactly what this way of thinking supports. You can use design thinking to build a company, a new product or service, or to approach a challenge in your life. I've found it useful during product planning for Chiefly's app as well as helping me make life decisions, like where I want to live and how I want my relationships to work. There is no such thing as failure with this method because you continuously test it. It's an ideal form of structure for entrepreneurs and creatives alike. If you're willing to keep testing, you'll always find a possible next step to continue improving your solutions and processes. Use this any time you feel you need a bit of structure for your project.

## ASK YOURSELF

**What does "structure" mean to me?**

**Why is it important?**

**How satisfied am I with the level of structure I bring to my work and life?**

**On a scale of 1 (being low) and 10 (being extremely satisfied), rate your current level of satisfaction with how much structure you have in your life:**

1     2     3     4     5     6     7     8     9     10

**What Solution Do You Provide Via Your Offer?**

- Based on the details about structuring your offer, what solution do you want to provide to your people?

- If you work in a corporate environment, what structure do you want to put in place to provide better solutions to the recipients of your work?

- What is your personal philosophy toward the problem you want to solve for others?

- Is that incorporated in your offering?

- What is the transformation you're giving your audience? What is the Point A? What is the Point B? What happens each step along the way?

- What is the unique process you utilize to take people on the journey from your Point A to Point B?

- What could go wrong along the way?

## Goal Setting and Work Structure

Ask yourself and your key stakeholders (your boss, team members, partner, or potential client) what it will take for this engagement, project, or company to be a success. Then set a realistic goal which can be measured by a primary and secondary metric to track your progress. Add in a timeline so you have a date in the future to aim for.

- What sort of structure have you been using at work so far? Does it still work?

- What's missing or bothers you about your current workflow structure?

- What sort of changes might you make to the structure you use at work going forward?

## Creating Financial Structure

- What's your financial structure?

- What needs improvement (income, expenses, investing, passive income, or financial independence)?

- What have you been avoiding?

- How would your future-self counsel you to implement it?

## Structure and Boundaries in Relationships

- What new expectations might you set with co-workers, managers, and even friends and family about the structures you're implementing?

- What might their questions and concerns be?

- How can you address them while still maintaining the boundaries you're setting?

People around us can be the first ones to tempt us back into old habits and what we're familiar with. Ask the people close to you to support your new work structure, whether it's working new hours, finding new office space, or supporting the new business you want to start. If you find them reluctant, don't let anyone's opinions, fears, or worries stop you from something you have in your heart. As long as *you* feel aligned with your proposed plans, go ahead and learn from them.

## ONE-DEGREE SHIFT

The elements of this chapter can be some of the most formidable things to address with honesty—I get that. Start by tackling at least one part of it today.

1.  Reflect on and write about your insights regarding what changes you'd like to make to the structures in your life. This might be at work, with your finances, the way you manage your time, or something else. Communicate all of your proposed changes with the key stakeholders i.e., your boss, your partner, your parents, your friends.

2.  Do your budget using the Ramsey method:

    Money In – Money Out = 0.

    Your investing, saving, and any other goals you have go into the "money out" category, so you should end up with zero funds to be allocated at the end of the month.

    - What are you earning and what channels are those earnings coming from?

    - What are your main expenses?

    - Where is the leftover money going?

    - If you don't have any investable income, how might you find a way to increase income or decrease expenses to ensure you have some to invest in your future?

    If you have a business, look at it as well. Structure your money coming in and going out. Make sure your outgoings don't outweigh or over-whelm your earnings. Of course a start-up might have some months of losses, but if it's an ongoing trend and not a typical ramp up timeline for your industry, it might be time to take a look at how you're operating.

3.  Finalize your niche statement by defining your solution:

    "I serve X (people) to solve Y (problem or issue) and **bring them to Z (solution).**"

4.  Use the design thinking structure or your own devised structure to map out the process you'll use to deliver your solution to your customers.

Here is my personal example:

i.  **Empathize:** Corporate employees might feel like cogs in a wheel with no purpose to their work. Entrepreneurs can feel alone and struggle to earn enough income via their projects. Students meander and accept positions based on who they know or what they think they should be doing rather than knowing what they deeply value or who they want to help. Corporate leaders struggle with work-life balance and crafting a meaningful legacy via their careers.

ii.  **Define:** People struggle to intentionally earn money and build a meaningful legacy through their work.

iii.  **Ideate:**

- Start a podcast
- Write a book
- Speak at events or online
- Start a blog
- Coach people one on one
- Coach in groups

iv.  **Prototype:**
First Prototype: Write a book to be accessible to all groups at an affordable price point.

v.  **Test:**

- Test #1: Run pre-sale campaign with book outline.
  *Result:* Sold more than five hundred copies with more than forty publishers interested.

- Test #2: Write out part one of the book, and send to publishers to gauge interest.
  *Result:* Forty-four publishers interested in publishing the manuscript.

- Test #3: Send a few chapters to readers of pre-sale and gauge response.
  *Result:* 100% positive email replies.

- Test #4: Send manuscript to editor for review.
  *Result:* Approved and book publishing agreement signed.

## TAKEAWAYS

✦ Complete your niche statement by defining your solution:

"I serve X (people) to solve Y (problem or issue) and **bring them to Z (solution)**."

✦ Outline the transformation you're taking your customers through by writing out your process step by step.

✦ Set up a structure for how you successfully want to approach your projects, role, or business.

✦ Communicate any new expectations and structures to the people involved in your work so that you're on the same page.

✦ Audit your financial situation including all money that comes in and goes out.

# Eighteen
## Service

*"Remember that when you leave this earth,*
*you can take with you nothing that you have received—*
*only what you have given: a full heart,*
*enriched by honest service, love, sacrifice, and courage."*
—SAINT FRANCIS OF ASSISI

## CORE QUESTION

**"How can I create the most value?"**

I had a client named Greg, who had worked in corporate finance for years. "I was bringing hundreds of millions of dollars into the organization with the investment decisions I was making," he told me. "Sure, I lost some of it, but the profits were still mind-blowing. I was coming home with over a hundred grand, and I should have felt happy. I should have felt like a success, but I couldn't shake the thought that I wasn't really helping anyone. I was just bringing in money for the company and getting a fraction of it back for my effort."

Greg wasn't the first person I'd heard these sentiments from. And at times, I had experienced that feeling of futility Greg had about his work. One of the major goals of this book is to get you to think about whether you feel your work makes a meaningful difference. Often that feeling comes from being genuinely in service to others with what you do every day. There's gratification in knowing that by leading the team, or building the mall, you're serving humanity and the world.

In my opinion, one of the core attributes entrepreneurs share is a higher-than-average tolerance for risk. They often don't settle for the safe option, which can be exciting and fun. With big risks can come big rewards—and losses. We know there's a cost-benefit analysis to everything in life. The predictability of income that we get from working at a large organization trades off for less freedom to choose what we do and when we do it. So whether you're self-employed or an employee, the important thing to remember in this chapter is that you've got to be valued and feel valued for what you're producing. One way we often determine if we're being valued is compensation, but respecting your manager, being on a great team, and enjoying the work you do play a large role as well. It's a cyclical concept: the more you serve, the more valued you feel; the more valued you feel, the better you serve.

No matter what you do, people notice when you show up with that extra level of service and care. You'll find that the work you put out is markedly more valued, and that feeds back into your sense of worth and, ultimately, into your impact on the world. As for Greg, he left that job and has become a top independent financial advisor where he helps his clients earn money on their investments. He also tripled his take-home pay, which stands for more than money—it's the feeling of being respected for what he brings to the table. Greg sees the impact on the families he's helping. He feels his efforts are valued with a performance-based compensation model, and he's now incentivized to give his clients the best level of service possible with the goal of creating a win-win for everyone involved.

Let me give you another example of being grounded in serving others. I had a photoshoot in Zadar, Croatia. I needed some new headshots and professional images for my website. The photographer was completely professional and competent, but the session was special to me because she went above and beyond the core offer of taking my photo X number of times. She began by getting curious and learning about me. We connected. She wanted to know what my business involved and what I wanted the images for. More than that, she talked with me about what I wanted to convey with the images. She directly asked what would make the work she was doing of maximum impact and value for me. Her genuine desire to provide the results that would help me most wasn't part of the price tag. It was part of the higher level of service she brought to her work. She was there to genuinely serve me with her creative skills and talent. As a result, I'm more than likely to return to her in the future, and she will be who I recommend if I'm ever asked for recommendations in the area.

What I'd like to help you embody is being in service beyond the price of a transaction. Serving someone else is a specific exchange of energy. I take simple joy in feeding and walking my dog, Max, each day. In turn, I find the routine and the breaks from my desk are invaluable. Of course, we don't pay each other, so the simple joy we get from the exchange fulfills us both. It satisfies a need in us. To truly serve well, we must know how to receive well.

This concept is also related to your reputation. It's asking yourself what you want to be known for. To delve into the meaning of this, ask yourself:

- How do you bring your values to the work you do or the product or service you deliver?

- What is your personal brand promise or slogan?

- Does it align with the values or the slogan of your current employer?

- What companies or individuals do you admire regarding the services they offer and how they provide them?

- What can you take from their approach to service that would work well with your own personal brand?

When he was in his corporate finance role, Greg was decently compensated for the work he did. His deficit was in the respect he was given and the value he felt he created by doing that work. He didn't feel like his compensation matched his contribution. On top of that, he didn't tangibly see that his work had any real impact on the world, so he wasn't turning up with a sense of service. That not only affected the way he felt about his work but also how he performed. Without the feeling of making an impact on others, it's difficult to see the real reason we're showing up to the office month after month.

That's where defining how we want to serve the world matters. When we show up ready to be of service to our people from *Chapter 15: Discernment*, the results are drastically different. Ensuring we deliver our product or serve our clients with that little bit of extra care and attention means we're more likely to be recognized as someone *worth* paying for or *worth* working with or *worth* hiring. What level of service do you bring to your clients with your work? Are you fairly compensated for the added value you deliver every day?

Let's look at how you package what you want to offer to the world. How do you secure that new client or persuade your boss that you're worthy of that raise? Using the skills from previous chapters, you've discerned who you're serving and what problem you're solving with your solution. In the rest of the chapter, we'll focus on how you're delivering your solution—the metaphorical packaging. It's about the extra polish that makes what you offer unique and worth paying for.

I'm the first to admit I haven't perfected the art of being in service. I've been refining it my entire life. We're perpetually putting ourselves forward and pitching for the things we want in life, and serving others is no different.

---

SERVICE DOESN'T MEAN USING THE RIGHT WORDS
OR MAKING ATTRACTIVE PROMISES;
IT MEANS DELIVERING WITH INTEGRITY
AND GOING THAT EXTRA MILE TO SHOW YOU CARE.

---

This is what gives you an edge. The competitive advantage is often found in simple changes to how you interact with a customer and finding ways to make it more personalized. Showing up in service doesn't mean you have all the answers or solutions—it means showing up with the willingness to help to the best of your ability.

## MENTOR'S TABLE

### Evan Luthra

I met Evan at a club in Miami. We chatted and I learned about his business, never expecting to see him again. Evan is an entrepreneur working with innovative technologies, like cryptocurrencies. He told me he had made his first million by the age of eighteen. One short interaction with him had a big impact on me, and it took only a few seconds. He said that all you need to do to become a millionaire is build something that will help a million people for the price of $1 or something that will help a thousand people for a price of $1,000.

It was the first time I'd heard impact conceptualized so clearly. A lightbulb went on in my consciousness. When he said that, my whole understanding of monetizing how we serve changed. Success didn't directly correlate to long hours toiling away, "hard" work, suffering, or sacrifice. That wasn't the key. The key was creating something of value, not only to you but to those you serve. Service means creating value. The name of the game was to show up in service. People pay millions for things that take minutes and dollars for things that take days—think about trading stocks versus the wine industry. Neither one is superior to or more successful than the other. Both work because they provide something—a service or a product—for someone who values it enough to pay for it. Value in what you do for others often isn't tied to the amount of time or effort you put in. You can impart something of value to people around you in many ways.

Go back to the notes you made in *Chapter 15: Discernment*, where we looked at who you want to serve with the work you do. Think about the statement from Evan and whether you want to serve ten people or ten thousand people or maybe a million people. By defining your market, you can monetize the value of the service (or product) you bring. It is an eye-opening way of looking at things.

Instead of living by the paradigm that "hard" work is valuable, let's think about delivering value instead. People pay for what they think is "worth it" to them. What you charge (as a product, service, or your annual salary) needs to be based on the value delivered, not the time spent. If you can provide a solution in ten minutes but it saves the person thousands of dollars, then what is the value of that work? Price your impact based on value creation rather than time going forward. Release your mind from the old model as swiftly as you can. You and your stress levels will be glad you did.

## Grace Lever

Grace coaches female entrepreneurs on how to automate and scale their businesses by working smarter not harder. An Aussie with real charisma, I found her when I was just starting out and took a few online courses with her. One thing that applies no matter what business you're in is the concept of The Value Ladder. It is a well-known idea, and I'm grateful for Grace's re-introduction.

The Value Ladder approach involves creating a structure to your offerings based on their price. It helps you to convey the value of the different solutions you offer your audience. The idea is to have an ascending range of products or services that increase in value and, therefore, in price. We're already used to this kind of structure as it's used by businesses like spas, yoga studios, and restaurants. This applies no matter what work you do because you can have different price points for whatever project you're working on. If you're an employee, use this to consider all of your projects and how each one impacts the bottom line of the company. Researching other similar roles, projects, or companies will serve you well if your role feels more creative. You can use your hourly rate, salary, or other compensation to discern if you're quantifying your value fairly.

**An example of a value ladder for coaching services might look like this:**

| |
|---|
| One on One Coaching Program: $9,997 |
| Group Program: $4,997 |
| Online Course: $1,997 |
| Online Three Hour Workshop: $97 |
| Book: $35 |
| Free Resource/Webinar: As a lead magnet to add the person to your email list |

Here's one for a senior copywriter at an ad agency with an $85,000 salary:

### Three Ad Campaigns per Quarter for Major Clients:
(Editing, Researching, Writing)

20 hours per week, $42,500 per year, ~$3,542 per campaign

- How much are these clients paying per campaign?

- How much value are you personally delivering in terms of each campaign?

- How much would you charge per hour if you were doing this independently?

### Developing Pitch Concepts:

~10 hours per week, $21,250 per year

*Note:* This is outside of the compensated forty hours that need to be delivered every week because you're spending time generating ideas for the work you're doing. You're generating *uncompensated* value. Showing an explanation like this to your supervisor might help them see that reducing time in meetings or allocating you a part-time assistant for emails might be worthwhile so you can deliver more value based on your skillset and expertise.

### Team Meetings/One-on-Ones to Develop Ad Campaigns:

~10 hours per week, $21,250 per year

I imagine some of these are more meaningful than others.

- Do you need to be in all the meetings?

- Where can you get time back and focus on delivering value based on your interests and zone of genius?

### Attending Company Events, Industry Conferences, Photoshoots, Casting, etc.:

~24 hours per month, $12,240

This is purely the time you spend at each of these events. This doesn't factor in the value generated from the ways you might be improving a photoshoot or the client you helped to bring in via your networking at an industry event.

**Answering Emails/Admin Time:**

~5 hours per week, $10,625, just by taking the time to answer emails!

That's what it's costing your company based on the time you spend let alone the intangible value you might be creating via your communications.

*Note:* The above is an $85,000 salary broken down into projects and key responsibilities to put a more tangible figure on an employee's projects. $42.50/hour is the hourly rate based on $85,000/50 weeks worked/year and divided by 40 hours/week of working hours.

- Does the hourly rate you see compare to the industry standard?
- Where might you be delivering more value than your hourly rate?

When I walk people through these calculations for their jobs, it often blows their minds. As an employee, I'm not promising that your boss will increase your salary because of this list, but it will certainly give you more transparency on where you add the most value and where there might be room for negotiation. It's a game changer to provide visible service at each level. Remember to price these out in a way that honors what Evan says about how many people you want to help and the value derived for the end user. If you're an employee, this can be different pay grades or bonuses you receive based on your results. I know advertising agencies that take a monthly retainer and add a profit-sharing bonus that is contingent upon sales performance. Real estate agents take a percentage of sales. Many salespeople get commissions on their contracts and referral fees. Maybe there's an option for a commission structure or bonus based on performance that your boss might be open to.

What if you could add on ancillary services as an independent contractor outside of your work? Even if it's not conventional in your industry, employers are often open to creating more financial incentives if it improves their bottom line and creates a measurable impact for the organization. This approach can be seen as selfish or untoward if you're working at a charity or not-for-profit, but I think we need to remember that when we're valued, we can create more value for others. I've been seeing charities also looking at creative ways to compensate their core team and volunteers for the value team members bring to their mission.

Some compensation options include base salary, hourly overtime, commission performance-based pay, referral or affiliate fees, project-based pay, milestone-based pay, annual bonuses, signing bonuses, monthly retainers, and profit sharing.

Think about your industry and model and consider if you can package the value you deliver in an innovative way using this method. If you're an entrepreneur, design what you offer using a Value Ladder. As an employee, estimate the value you bring through the different projects or initiatives you're working on. Feel free to look at compensation for similar roles at other companies. The goal of the above concepts is to illustrate that there are many ways to deliver and clarify value. You are the one responsible for ensuring your client, boss, or business partner is clear on what you're delivering through your effort. Using the ladder above will support you in explaining what you bring to the table in an effective manner to have everyone on the same page.

## Rabbi Daniel Lapin

Daniel Lapin has been dubbed America's Rabbi. He's a speaker, a writer of best-selling books, a noted scholar, and a TV host. Lapin has a lot to say about life, faith, and fulfillment, but he has a seat at my Mentor's Table on the subject of service because of the insights from his book *Thou Shall Prosper*. Lapin is insistent that, for work to have meaning and purpose, you must be working for yourself. "Be in business for yourself," is one of his key phrases.

Lapin isn't suggesting that everyone should be a self-employed entrepreneur—he's asking us to value what we do regardless of whether we're an employee or a business owner. Our ability to produce valuable work is dependent on ourselves as individuals. We, therefore, need to value ourselves as the producer to provide service that is recognized as valuable. You can tell when someone takes ownership in their craft. It's in bringing the care and attention of an "owner" that we serve best.

A lot of employees, especially in larger companies, easily fall into the trap of feeling that their individual contribution doesn't really matter. I often hear some variation of, "I just don't see how what I'm doing is moving the needle." At the end of the day, it means they ultimately don't take responsibility for the work they do. They don't give their energy as they would if it was their own company. When we take ownership and realize that every task matters, the energy we bring to it is different. Our work becomes infused with care and attention. For me, being in service to others is encapsulated perfectly in the phrase, "there is no task too small."

Lapin asks his audience to recognize that all the work we do is part of building our reputation and, ultimately, our legacy. Every project, every email, every meeting, every sale, every effort we make builds into the impact we have on the world through our work. It doesn't matter if you're working alone or as part of a huge company's team, every action you take in your work is stamped with your own brand, and you get to decide what that brand looks like. Bringing an attitude of service to our work—be it with passion, care, attention, or something else—reveals our unique brand to the people we're serving. It shows them what they can expect and brings them back through the door for years to come.

It's apparent when I work with top performers in organizations that most of them bring an unparalleled sense of duty and service to the work they do. They consistently get great ratings from bosses and clients, not because they schmooze, but because they deliver true value. That's also why many of them get approached by competitors, attract new clients, or receive promotions. The secret is that they see the personal service they provide as their responsibility and deliver a unique experience to the receiver of their efforts. Even a software developer coding an app has their own way of setting up systems and code that other developers either admire or curse. To cultivate the skill of true service, bring your A-game and provide something extraordinary that you'll be known for.

## ASK YOURSELF

**What does "service" mean to me?**

**Why is it important?**

**How satisfied am I with the level of service I bring to my work?**

**What is unique about the way I deliver my offer?**

**What can I do to enhance my level of service?**

**What are other people missing in the way they approach this problem or group of people?**

**How can I stand apart in my delivery?**

**On a scale of 1 (being low) and 10 (being extremely satisfied), rate your current level of satisfaction with how you serve others in your life:**

1   2   3   4   5   6   7   8   9   10

### Serving Others

- What values are most important to you when it comes to serving others?

- What value do you create in the work you do right now?
  - For your company
  - For your end user or client
  - For yourself
  - For others (e.g., broader families, community, stakeholders, etc.)

- Who am I (either yourself or the company you work for) providing service to?

- How large is your target market? Do you want to serve many or few?

## Packaging Your Contribution

- What is your multi-million-dollar service to the world?

  (Remember, quantity of time does not equal quality of service.)

- What is your time worth in terms of the returns it generates?

  This can be hourly or in package terms (forty hours per week is worth
  _____; five sessions are worth_____).

- Are you being truthful with yourself about the best way to offer your service to the world?

- What would be the most exciting possible outcome?

- How can you map out a way to reach that income level?

  For coaching services and entrepreneurs, there's a per unit or per sale approach.

  For someone in a company, maybe you need to start your own, or maybe it's consulting versus being an employee, which is tried and true.

## ONE-DEGREE SHIFT

1.  Define your work on a personal values basis. What are the words that guide how you bring an attitude of true service to your work?

2.  Write out your personal brand mission or slogan to let your people know what kind of service they can expect from you.

3.  How much value are you bringing to your organization? Is it time for a raise? A new role? Your own company?

4.  Define your prices based on the value being delivered to the end user and/or organization. If you're working hourly or on a salary, think big about how valuable your time is to you because it's finite. Consider how many people are served because of your contribution.

5.  Build your Value Ladder: Take your service or product offering and create prices/values and what's included at each level to maximize your efforts and give people multiple ways to derive value from your work.

## TAKEAWAYS

✦ Define what your personal approach to providing service is.

✦ Craft your personal or business brand promise or slogan.

✦ Quantify the value you bring to others via your work.

✦ Build your value ladder.

# *Nineteen*
# **Authenticity**

*"What comes from the heart goes to the heart."*
—SAMUEL TAYLOR COLERIDGE

## CORE QUESTION

**"How can I truthfully share what I think/know/feel/believe with the world?"**

You've clarified the path you're on in Part One, Part Two asked you to go deeper to consider true fulfillment, now let's narrow the scope to how you're going to share your solutions with your audience. This chapter is about learning to be authentic in how you communicate your mission to others. It's much easier to hide in plain sight than share our hearts with the world. Authenticity means being a reliable or accurate representation, and in this context, we're talking about a reliable representation of your true nature. This dictates how we show up and communicate with others. We can learn a lot from children in this regard. They have none of the built-in filters we develop as we grow into adults. As a result, children often tell it like it is, sometimes to their parents' embarrassment. Children will dance anywhere, sing loudly, and generally follow their instincts without caring what the world thinks of them. They exist in a state that comes before we're aware of societal expectations, the opinions of others, or our own doubts. As we move toward and into adulthood, we become aware of the eyes watching and judging us. We become conscious of what other's expectations are and how we appear to them. Our lives become more filled with performing as we stretch and bend to fit those ideals, either our own or in response to what we think society expects of us. This chapter serves as an homage to my inner four-year-old who wants others to remember what existing in that state was like and to reconnect with what they really care about to be able to share it with others.

Authenticity is messy. It isn't perfect and it doesn't always follow the norm or reasoning, but it's vital and it's satisfying.

---

AUTHENTICITY IS WHAT ALLOWS YOU TO SLEEP WELL AT NIGHT
KNOWING YOU'RE BEING TRUE TO YOURSELF.

---

There's immense value in social norms, fitting in, and ensuring that you belong within communities and societal constructs. I'm the first person to advocate for the importance of humanity's deep need to belong. What I'm saying is that you can choose where to belong and which community to name as your own. In high school, we drift into cliques and the same happens in society on a broader scale. Make sure you put yourself in the arena you genuinely want to be in, not what appears to be the cool kids' group to put on a show for others. You've started to do this by selecting the audience you want to serve in *Chapter 15: Discernment* and updating who gets a seat at your Mentor's Table in *Chapter 16: Empathy*.

We must use self-awareness as the precursor tool to authenticity. If we don't know what we truly feel or want or take the space to listen to our inner voice, then it's difficult to behave in a way that exudes authenticity. There will be times when you need to consider self-preservation over sharing what you believe to be true, especially if your beliefs aren't mainstream or accepted by society. Being authentic is not for the faint of heart and requires courage too. When it comes down to it, you must weigh the cost of not living in an authentic way with the benefit of sharing your heart with the world. There's a bigger burden and a deadening of the soul that happens when we refuse to show important parts of ourselves.

As with every quality in this book, there's a continuum, and it's up to you to decide whether you're living and sharing from a place of authenticity that feels right for you. Being aware is noticing what's true in the present moment. Being authentic with others comes when you act consistently in line with what you know to be true.

So how do you share your mission and goals from Part One with the people you identified you want to serve? It starts with authenticity and humanizing ourselves. Sure, do deceptive people win at times? Yes. But the long-term game never pays off. Being disingenuous with clients or the people we work with never ends favorably. Doing what you say you will do and operating with integrity is a core component of being authentic and true to your word.

Humanistic psychologists would say that, by definition, authentic people possess several common characteristics that show they're psychologically mature and fully functioning as human beings. In general, people who have high levels of authenticity in their approach:

- Have realistic perceptions of reality

- Are accepting of themselves and of other people

- Are thoughtful

- Have a non-hostile sense of humor

- Can express their emotions freely and clearly

- Are open to learning from their mistakes

- Understand their motivations

We're going to use authenticity, inquiry, and a touch of that childlike wonder to craft how you'll communicate about the problem you're solving for your people. This differs from empathy, which is about understanding what others want or need. Even if you mostly work with technology and want as little to do with humans as possible, you benefit from communicating effectively with peers or key decision-makers. As long as humans exist, conveying your message will matter as much as having a good idea to convey in the first place.

## MENTOR'S TABLE

The mentors in this section have helped me show up more authentically with others and share what problems I'm here to help solve in the world. You'll find more aligned people to serve when you communicate about the problem and the way you solve it in a way that's authentic to you. You can use these strategies to help you communicate your niche statement of "I serve X (people) with Y (problem) and bring them to Z (solution)" with your audience.

## Indrani Singh

When we think about communication, it's easy to think about talking. But a crucial skill is learning to listen more than you speak. Indrani was one of my elementary school teachers when I was in Montessori school. As a teacher who was meant to convey information, I was enthralled by how many questions she asked me. She always wanted to know what we thought and how we'd approach the topic or problem. This approach to teaching harnessed the authenticity in her students to bring out their innate capabilities. Communication is about your ability to understand where the other person is coming from so you can communicate appropriately for your audience.

The concept of active listening is taught across disciplines. I've interviewed and worked with more than 150 coaches while building my business, and I can tell you that the best coaches are those who employ active listening to engage with clients. This is a skill I believe everyone needs, regardless of workplace aspirations. If you can truly listen while someone talks, the information you will gain is invaluable. You get to know their actual desires and needs. It's especially useful if you can put yourself in a beginner's mind-set and presume you can learn something from the person speaking. Using active listening doesn't end with customer interviews—this is something you need to continuously do in order to stay in tune with your people.

Showing up authentically means making the space for others to do the same. Then, you can show yourself to them knowing who's on the other side of the table. Indrani didn't change who she was, at her core, dependent on the student she was teaching. She changed her tone of voice or the words she used. She has a strong resolve that what is in her heart is worth sharing and will be received by others with respect. She treats others as she would like to be treated. She is clear on what being "Indrani" means. And she is even more crystal clear on who Indrani the teacher is, her teaching philosophy, and what her standards and values are. Her authenticity shone through regardless of the situation or learner, and that's what I strive for in my business interactions and life. You do this by maintaining a clear focus and mission for why you're offering what you are to your audience.

## Paul Ekman, Amy Cuddy, Chris Voss, and Joe Navarro

The names above are some of the greats when it comes to studying body language and facial expressions. I'd be remiss if I didn't mention non-verbal communication. A significant percentage of our communication comes through our body language, our attitude, and our non-verbal cues. My close friends have often teased me for my insistence on the importance of non-verbal communication. No matter if you're on the phone, in a video meeting, or in person, it's often more revealing than what people choose to say to us. We can ascertain more about a person's true intentions from reading this kind of communication, especially when they aren't being open in what they say. More often than not, you "feel" that someone is being disingenuous. It's that gut feeling we talked about earlier that says something isn't right about what they're telling you. Our eyes send signals to the brain where we pick up on stimuli from the environment and that's what makes our gut contract: "I've seen this before, it's dangerous." Likewise, others can read your non-verbal cues when you're being less than authentic. We have a human way of showing when we're uncomfortable, when we're not being honest, and when we're not being our true selves—and other humans are conditioned to hone in on it. So, when you approach situations with authenticity it will show in both your verbal and non-verbal communication. You'll be more convincing and more magnetic to others. They will be drawn to you. You will immediately feel like someone they can trust. This is something many of my coaching clients have come to sessions about. They regularly ask about how they can exude more confidence, be more compelling, and influence decision-makers. It starts with believing in what you say, and then authentically sharing your message in your own way. If you try to put on a show, people will know.

When it comes to non-verbal communication some key areas to think about are:

## FACIAL EXPRESSIONS

Our faces say a lot about what we feel. Paul Eckman is an expert researcher on the topic, and I've learned a lot from his work. It's hard to hide our true feelings about a topic, even if we show our truth for a flash of a second in what are called micro-expressions. Look out for the core emotions of happiness, fear, sadness, disgust, and surprise as a start.

## EYE MOVEMENTS

If you pay attention to where someone's eyes are looking, that'll also give you insight into what they're focused upon, thinking about, or valuing. Looking up often means visualizing one's thoughts. If we look up and to the right, it's engaging our imagination so often people point to that being a sign of lying. It can also be "coming up with the best answer" so using this in conjunction with other indicators is important. It's a holistic picture. Looking down can be showing respect, submission, or feelings of guilt. Again, it's important to discern the context of the situation before making a snap judgment. Looking away or staring can show where someone's focus is.

## SHOULDERS AND UPPER BODY POSITIONING

Broad shoulders with an open heart space signal confidence, openness, and a readiness to tackle a situation. Conversely rounded shoulders can convey dejection, a lack of confidence, or wanting to be "smaller" to avoid attack or attention.

## HANDS

Open palms signal openness whereas fists signal anger or frustration. If we hide our hands, it can mean we're hiding something. If we put our fingers over our mouths in a "shh" gesture with our fingers over our lips, we're likely wanting the other party to stop talking. Hand gestures are especially communicative if you're making a presentation or having an important meeting with a client. Public speakers are often advised to maintain a ninety-degree angle with their elbows so they form a box around their torso. This can be somewhat useful as it's an "open" posture. Remember though, the goal is to be authentic to build meaningful and trusting relationships. Anything robotic or forced will take you further from your intended result.

### SPACING

It's notable to consider how closely people stand to each other. Closer relationships will stand closer and newer acquaintances will stand further apart as a general rule.

### LOWER BODY

Similar to the shoulders, we either take an open stance with our feet apart or we cower and cover our stomachs and pelvic region with our hands or hide ourselves behind something like a chair, podium, coat, or bag when we feel defensive.

### FEET

Interestingly, they lead the way. You can tell if someone is itching to leave the room if their feet point toward the door. Remember, it could mean they need to go to the bathroom or are late to an appointment, so it isn't always necessary to take this personally. That goes for any non-verbal cues. In this case, it might open you up to ask a useful question like, "Would it be better to pick this up later?"

A rule of thumb would be to open up your posture and smile if you're hoping to invite connection with the other person. If you're looking to quietly get out of a situation without verbalizing it to the room, maybe point your body toward the door and move in that direction. Humans instinctively pick up on these cues whether or not they consciously name them.

For most of us, the aim is to leave a positive impact on people around us, and that can be achieved through virtues like honesty and integrity. The legacy of your career is built upon your ability to speak and act with integrity. This is a lesson I learned after many years of trying to find an "easier" way of doing things. When you cut corners, it'll come back to bite you one way or another. This holds true for any marketing or written communications you create. Write and speak the way you would to a friend, even if it's an email marketing campaign. It'll change the tone of your writing and that'll help your intentions shine through authentically. Likewise, when people around you know they can trust your word, they're more ready to listen. It's not only about being honest about what you can deliver but about being honest when you can't.

Understanding how to recognize authenticity in others also makes it easier to recognize inauthenticity. It makes it easier to note the moments when information is being withheld or manipulated.

I've learned some key things from these communication experts regarding dealing with inauthenticity from others:

- Lies or mistruths don't necessarily tell you the whole story. If you feel someone is being dishonest, consider what they might be concealing and why.

- Trust your instincts (this goes back to *Chapter 14: Trust*). If it feels shady, have a second look. Ask a follow-up question.

- Emotions have universal definitions, but people's baseline of emotion looks different. Really tune into the person you're with and actively listen to them—both their verbal and non-verbal communication. No "formula" works all the time when it comes to reading people, we all have individual traits and tendencies.

A key takeaway from this chapter is to bring authenticity forward in yourself to attract potential clients or business associates. Make sure your actions and communications align with what you know to be right for yourself. The second part is to remember that others may have multiple motives for being inauthentic and you can do your best to support them by actively listening and giving them a chance to share their true selves with you. If they don't want to share, reading their body language can give you valuable clues into what they might actually be needing so you can adjust your approach accordingly. That might look like asking more questions or giving them some space. Show up with your true self and look for authenticity from others—that will give you a strong base to start from every time.

## The Book of Proverbs

Being authentic doesn't mean saying whatever you think, and it certainly doesn't mean saying it without first thoughtfully crafting your message to your audience. There's a line from this book of the Bible that reads as follows: "The words of the reckless pierce like swords but the tongue of the wise brings healing."[14] Our baser emotions like anger and fear (which we explored in *Chapter 10: Courage*) can lead us to take reckless actions that aren't in line with our authentic selves. I've found that the more I refine

---

14. "Proverbs 12:18." New International Version (NIV). https://www.bible.com/bible/111/pro.12.18.niv.

my messaging and think about what's authentic versus impulsive, the more useful, helpful, and wise my responses are. If your boss says something nasty, is it worth the quick reply or the behind-the-back bashing at happy hour? It might feel good in the moment, but it usually only lasts for as long as the words remain in the air because it can and often does come back to bite you. Same thing goes with email policy—think twice before you click send on that customer response. Being silent and thinking your response through, along with the consequences of it, is always a good idea. It doesn't mean you can't be authentic—it means that you consider the repercussions of the way you deliver your message before you share it.

Ask yourself in every situation, what is driving your response? Is it a reactive feeling like anger or frustration? See if you can work through that feeling before you craft your reply. Even when you're reacting to something that has come from another's anger or fear, a well-considered answer is always more productive than returning the sentiment in kind. You want to be truthful in your reaction but as close to an accurate representation of your values as possible.

Your reactionary instinct might be to say, "I hate you because you passed me over for a promotion." After taking a moment to let your anger fade into the background, your response might evolve to something more constructive: "Naturally, I'm disappointed about the outcome of this decision. What can I do to stand out next time? What do you believe I could be doing better?" There are ways of dealing with anger and disappointment in a healthy way. I'd recommend *Anger: Cooling the Flames* by Thich Nhat Hanh or *Letting Go* by David Hawkins for further work on letting go and releasing anger before communicating your message.

Authenticity is about living and acting from our hearts. When we follow the guidance of our hearts, we won't respond from a place of anger. The greatest learning process for me has been understanding that the wise speak with authenticity and voice concerns in a fashion that is diplomatic and thoughtful. As the saying goes, someone else's emergency doesn't have to constitute one on your part. Craft your messages respectfully and as you see fit.

## The Book of Ecclesiastes

Sometimes our hearts don't seem to have the answer. We need to look beyond ourselves to find what is true and authentic. After my car accident, life didn't make sense. I struggled to find the meaning or purpose of the situation. When tragedy and challenges affect our lives, we inevitably find that our sense of self is eroded and we question our purpose. At these points, it's important to recognize that trauma affects us profoundly and to deal with it authentically. Honestly, I felt defeated. I couldn't pretend to be fine but I vowed to show up. As time went on, what I could give slowly increased. It was a matter of showing up for physical therapy on good and bad days with whatever strength I could muster. I had to rely on forces greater than myself to guide me along my path during my recovery. I had to look to God to see what was true.

I remember my first walk outside in the snow after the accident. I was scared because my balance was still off and I didn't want to fall on the ice. I kept hearing, "one step at a time," and that kept me going. I felt powerless and like all of my control had been taken away. By allowing forces greater than myself to guide me I could open myself up to the recovery process. I realized that what I was giving was *enough* and that I didn't have to face the road to recovery alone. Recovering meant allowing nature to take the wheel and for me to figure out what my part in the process was. Trying to control everything wasn't authentic. This was my great lesson in learning when something is not mine and gave me the wisdom to know the difference.

Our responsibility is to show up with our best for that day. Being kind to ourselves allows us to relate better to those we serve as well. We're all fallible and go through challenges. Be authentic with your boss if you need time, space, longer schedules, more feedback, or even a sabbatical. Share with your partner and manager that being a stay-at-home parent instead of working is your priority for the next couple of years. Manage your business from home and scale back your efforts when your aging parents need you around. Again, remember to frame your communications with respect, but don't avoid sharing the most important things that are closest to your heart. Find a way that feels right to share with those who matter so you can craft a work life that supports you fully, including a paycheck. Allow authenticity to mean giving your best while simultaneously reaching for help from others and from the universe.

## The Book of Job

From these Bible passages I gathered that being humble about your knowledge allows you to communicate better. Less assumptions and less entitlement make authentic communication from all parties easier. Don't come to a conversation thinking you have all the answers. Being humble means acknowledging that people know what's best for them. That should be apparent in any communications you share with your clients or colleagues. What works is understanding what you know to be true in your area of expertise and what skills and services you know you can bring, then presenting them in a truthful and humble way. Wisdom and authentic communication come from a sense of humility—the knowing that no one person has all the answers and we can only speak the truth that we know with our current state of knowledge and experience. Communicate with the humility of being aware that you know only a fraction of what's out there. That's why I created the Mentor's Table section of this book. The wisdom that has been gathered before and around me is so vast, and I'd be foolish and inauthentic to say that I came up with it all myself. The value of this book is the unique compilation of the expertise and wisdom of others communicated through the lens of my experiences.

Bring humility to the way you impact others by remembering that they know what's best for them given where they are. You can serve as a support of their process and as a guide given your area of expertise. This will also absolve you of anything that doesn't go their way. You aren't responsible for your client's successes or failures. You can only give what you know and do your best to fulfill your promises. If you can't, share why and do what you can to make amends. If you've been fully authentic about your approach and humble in what you say you can provide, you'll always overdeliver and bring meaningful impact to the work you do for others.

## ASK YOURSELF

**What does being "authentic" mean to me?**

**Why is it important?**

**How satisfied am I with the level of authenticity I bring to my interactions with others?**

**On a scale of 1 (being low) and 10 (being extremely satisfied), rate your current level of satisfaction with your level of authenticity with yourself and others:**

1    2    3    4    5    6    7    8    9    10

**What is the message you want to get across to your people about what you offer?**

- How can you humbly serve your target audience?

- What is your heart authentically telling you to share?

- What medium aligns with your personal vision and offer to best share with your people? It could be a blog, photos, videos, short-form written content, a social group, an offline community group, one-on-one- interactions, an email newsletter, or personalized email marketing.

- How often would you like to communicate directly with your target audience?

- What sort of communication would be best before, during, and after the delivery of your product or service?

- What do you truly think, feel, or believe about the situation you have at hand? What can you do to share that in a manner that will be well-received by your audience? (You can only do your best here. It's unrealistic to think everyone will always agree with you.)

## Define Your Four P's of Marketing: Product, Price, Place and Promotion

### PRODUCT

- What solution are you offering to satisfy your customer's needs or wants?
- What differentiates your product from the competition?

### PRICE

- What is your pricing model based on your target market?
- Are you selling a high- or low-price service or product?
- What does your consumer expect to pay for your offer?
- What is your Value Ladder?
- What can you uniquely offer at increasing price points?

### PLACE

- Where is the best place to reach your people?
- How would you like to share about your offer to attract customers?
- What are the best distribution channels for my product or service?

### PROMOTION

- What is your service slogan?
- How might you relate it back to your personal values defined in Part One: Choice?
- What features or benefits set you apart from others?
- Which part of the target audience would I like to engage?

## ONE-DEGREE SHIFT

1. Develop a marketing plan to authentically address your audience. Use the 4 P's of marketing: product, price, place, and promotion to structure your thinking.

   The key components of a marketing plan are:

   - Market research (You have done this via customer interviews in *Chapter 16: Empathy*. You can look back at your notes to draw upon the priorities of your people for inspiration.)

   - Tailored messaging to the different types of people within your target audience.

   - Choosing the right platforms/medium to share your message.

   - Using metrics to measure the success of your efforts. Are you on the right track? Are you reaching the right people with your message? Are they responding to your efforts positively?

   Be sure to answer:

   - Who is each message geared toward? Which subset of your target group?

   - What medium do you enjoy communicating on?

   - Where are your people spending their time (online or offline)?

   - How often do you want to be in conversation with your audience?

   - What details will you share about your product or service?

   - What stories or examples can you share to bring the transformation you provide to life?

   - What metrics will let you know your marketing efforts are successful?

2. Journal about:

   - What would showing up authentically at work be like?

   - What is your "brand" of authenticity?

   This connects to your values which we explored in *Chapter 7: Focus* with your priority octopus. Living in congruence with your values (what's important to you) means living authentically.

3. Bring a new idea or dream to life by sharing it with the world. This could mean sharing verbally, via visual means, or by kinesthetically creating something. You could try out a new outfit or accessory you normally wouldn't wear but have always wanted to. Share some of the creative work you've been hiding away. Devise a new recipe for a meal. Share an idea at a meeting that seems risky, but your heart wants you to share. Authenticity is a muscle—it needs training and practice to strengthen along with a good dose of courage.

4. Think about yourself as a child—how did you authentically communicate? Were you auditory, visual, or kinesthetic? This will help you define how you can best communicate your ideas to others.

5. Consider if there's a place in your life where you haven't given yourself permission to be authentic. What might you do to bring more authenticity to that part of your world?

## TAKEAWAYS

✦ Define authenticity for yourself and how you want to bring authenticity into your life.

✦ Explore the 4 P's of marketing: Product, Price, Place, and Promotion

✦ Create the plan of how you'll share about your offer with the world.

✦ Identify your communication style as auditory, visual, or kinesthetic.

✦ Take the leap to share something authentically with a trusted person.

✦ Bring a creation to life using authenticity as your guide to do so from the heart.

# _Twenty_
# Adaptability

_"There can be no life without change,_
_and to be afraid of what is different or unfamiliar_
_is to be afraid of life."_
—THEODORE ROOSEVELT

## CORE QUESTION

**"How can I update my plans given the new information at hand?"**

Adapting our plans to important new information we receive is critical to successfully navigating life's twists and turns. Driving in a '93 Chevy down the New Jersey Turnpike, I had a conversation that changed how I view running a business. I was talking to a trusted business advisor about how to approach a yoga company regarding offering coaching services. I wanted to see how we might collaborate. I felt unsure whether my coaching could help and wanted his input on how we might work with them. At first glance, I wasn't necessarily their "ideal" service provider . . . or was I? During that conversation, we brainstormed all sorts of ideas for ancillary offerings to yoga. We discussed consulting, psychological services, and online mindset and meditation classes, to name a few. We thought about what people who practice yoga would value as additional benefits in the studio. During that conversation, I realized that it's limiting to define a business by what the sign on the door says. I recognized that we sometimes fall into the habit of defining ourselves solely by our job titles or self-imposed limitations when, in fact, our impact is made up of the many ways we can change the lives of others.

We realized that people who practice yoga in big cities also have careers they need support with. We agreed to run workshops in collaboration with the yoga studios, expanded our offering to a new industry, and adapted our offering to serve yogis. Through this experience, I learned that we can open up possibilities by adapting our offering to suit our audience. I think entrepreneurs are particularly good at this. They rarely turn down opportunities, often say yes to contracts, and figure out how to deliver along the way. If we consider beyond the confines of what we think we *should* be doing and move into thinking about what we *could* be doing, then we invite a whole range of possible solutions to the table.

The digital revolution has seen changes in consumer preferences and new regulations as well as evolving cultures, environmental opportunities, and social norms. We can learn a lot about adaptability when we look at notable entrepreneurs like Steve Jobs or Jeff Bezos. They are exceptional as they didn't solely move with changes in market and culture—they shaped them. Their adaptability changed the world we live in. Bezos grew Amazon from an online book retailer to a marketplace of whatever physical products the company could deliver, completely innovating supply chain management. The company later led the way into the new world of e-books and online entertainment streaming. Digital technology clearly moves fast with products updating and older versions dying out every year. We live in a world where, if you can't adapt, you get left behind.

So, what do we do to ensure we remain relevant, effective, and valuable in the work we do? As individuals, we need to adapt both outwardly and inwardly to succeed.

### Outwardly consider:

- The changing environment of your industry (competitors, regulators, suppliers, adjacent companies). Research industry innovations to remain current on relevant improvements that are being made.

- The needs and wants of the people we serve (current clients, new client groups, clients from related industries or competitors). You can use customer interviews from *Chapter 16: Empathy* to get insight in this area.

- The technology or systems you utilize to provide your product or service (think suppliers, ingredients, supply chain, software).

**Inwardly consider:**

- Your mindset on what's possible in your work (evaluate and maximize your goals by magnifying your original vision by ten times, pivot when necessary, and review your thought process to look for opportunities and limiting beliefs).

- Have an idea journal or other method where you can note ideas or new possibilities that come up, no matter how unrealistic or undeveloped the ideas are.

- Prepare contingency plans or alternate possibilities. Create a plan A, plan B, and plan C. Consider what you'll do if everything doesn't go to plan.

- Create buffers for when things inevitably shift: time buffers if schedules slip; budgetary buffers in the form of saved funds or access to funds; or emotional, physical, or mental buffers if your energy levels take a hit.

I think recognizing that things are constantly shifting is the first step to being adaptable. It's easy to become complacent and fall into familiar habits and ways of doing things. I worked with a client in the fashion industry. Her passion was make-up rather than clothes, which was her employer's major focus. She also suffered from eczema, which meant she struggled to find products that didn't irritate her skin. She began posting on social media about the issue and found that many shared her struggle. She had found her audience—the people she could serve. She went on to develop her own brand of make-up using only naturally sourced ingredients, adapting what she had learned about the industry to fill a need for her specific customer base. The world hadn't changed—those customers had always been there. What she'd done was identify them, work out how to serve them, and used her existing skills and experience to build a business that helped her niche.

Being adaptable is about large and small shifts. We can either choose to or be compelled to adapt. I advocate for filling our days with small adaptations. If we remain open-minded in our approach to our work, we can move with the times and find ways to serve our audience better. The more open and willing we are, the more likely we are to end up in surprising places we never imagined we would.

## Adaptability

One way I've adapted  is evolving to serve businesses when my initial focus was on coaching individuals. My first clients were mainly young women—students and professionals who had entrepreneurial ambitions. I eventually reached a point where I wanted my audience and impact to grow. I asked myself how I could take what I knew about coaching individuals and serve a wider pool of people. The answer was right in front of me: talk to *groups* of individuals about how collectively improving will make the entirety of their organization better. I began by changing my packages, taking what I'd learned and developed during my years working with individuals one-on-one and working out how I could deliver that service for teams, departments, and even entire companies. I retained the core purpose of my coaching business, but I widened the scope of who I could reach by adapting my offering.

Another way I worked out how and where to adapt my business was by listening to my clients. At this point, I've conducted more than five thousand hours of coaching sessions and have a decent understanding of client needs. People will *tell* you what they want and need if you listen. Listening sometimes means reading between the lines and understanding pain points to craft solutions yet to be devised. Being adaptable means taking in new information and creating an offering accordingly. From the start, at my software company, Chiefly, we've built our product guided by consumer direction. Our first Minimum Viable Product (MVP) was based on what our biggest client said they *needed* us to deliver. As a start-up, we could be flexible and take the client's needs to heart. By inviting constant feedback, we have the raw material to know what we need to adapt.

Lots of tech companies provide beautiful examples of this approach to customer service. Slack, a messaging tool for teams, regularly offers new clients sandbox environments where they can test out and give feedback on tools. Salesforce builds a product from a basic version into a highly customized Customer Relationship Management tool for your company's needs. Even non-tech companies thrive when they listen and adapt to customers' wants—think of Domino's Pizza allowing you to choose any topping you like for your pizza. No company is too big or too successful for this type of approach. The best companies are customer-focused and continually adapt. They identify and anticipate the user's needs and develop solutions accordingly. What are *your* clients or users telling you they want and need? Remember those interviews you did in *Chapter 16: Empathy*. That's what you must deliver, packaged with your own unique take on their request, and serving them to the best of your abilities.

I resonate with the saying, "It is a rising tide that raises all ships." Our environment is always changing like the tide, and it's important that we can move with it. It can be about recognizing change and working out how you bring your skillset to a new set of circumstances. It might be about getting curious and questioning the status quo. Or it can be about looking for ways to improve things.

ADAPTABILITY IS ABOUT EMBRACING CHANGE
RATHER THAN RESISTING IT.

It's my belief that so long as you're one of the people helping to raise the tide where you are, you'll be compensated for that one way or another. Use adaptability to respond to new information and enhance what you can offer to the world.

BEING ADAPTABLE MEANS PUTTING MY GOAL
ABOVE MY PLAN.

What I mean by that is that I keep my focus on my endpoint—my North Star—but if my journey doesn't go exactly as I thought it would, that's all right. I allow the tide that carries me to ebb and flow as it wills. If you feel connected to God, it would be His will. This doesn't mean leaving your core values or compromising your authenticity. Serving your clients is not meant to feel like sacrificing your soul. It's meant to feel invigorating. Keep your goals and boundaries in sight. If a client, employer, or partner's request feels like you must give up your soul to oblige, it isn't worth the return, in my opinion. Let's approach our daily activity with adaptability to remain curious and flex with the new information and situations that pop up in the present moment.

## MENTOR'S TABLE

### Bill Gates

Although he's controversial, there's no doubt Gates has adapted and evolved to shape countless industries. Though entrepreneurs are known for being multi-passionate, I'm not saying you should aim to be a chameleon that doesn't specialize in anything. What I've learned from watching Gates is that you can diversify into multiple niches if you do it strategically, over time, and with the right support.

As an entrepreneur, adaptability has served me well over the course of my life. I use it to navigate my way through challenging scenarios. Yesterday, I used my limited legal skills to review a patent before submitting it to my lawyer. I needed to work with my team to build the application from a template. As someone with little knowledge of machine learning, adapting in this case meant leaning on a data scientist with the expertise to help me write the technical aspects of the patent. While I was responsible for sharing the vision and conceptualizing the invention, they could write out the technical details that the patent needed to explain our product fully. Adapting can mean knowing when to ask for help when something is out of your scope of expertise.

The reason Gates can be involved in so many industries, projects, and companies is because of his willingness to take in new information, assimilate it into his plans, and then get help on the aspects he can't or doesn't want to do himself. It's wiser to know what you *don't* know, than to try and be a jack of all trades. You can adjust to new situations by knowing when you need to pick up the phone and call someone who can do it in half the time and produce a better result. It's important to remember not to try to be everything to everyone or else you'll not be known for anything in particular. Gates put a stake in the ground initially as to his core mission. He only diversified once he mastered the computer software space and, even more importantly, put the systems and people in place to manage the operation without his hourly or daily input. Gates's approach taught me to keep a firm focus on my area of expertise, then use adaptability to source the right people for the job as new needs and challenges arise.

## Travel

Being a traveler is part of my identity and every trip I take teaches me something. As we explore a new place we've already defined that it opens up the quality of curiosity. I'd be remiss if I didn't discuss how travel teaches us to be adaptable. You can absolutely learn the core skills of adaptability in other ways, but this has been an effective teacher for me. When flying, especially if you go standby, you're setting yourself up for changing plans and uncertain timelines. One of the best trips of my life happened because I was willing to standby on a plane to Hong Kong. The skills I've gathered from traveling around the world have helped me to become adaptable across all areas of my life.

I'd say adaptability boils down to three key areas:

1.  **Problem Solving Skills**

    From losing luggage on countless occasions to delayed itineraries and missed connections travel asks you to loosen up and be willing to solve challenges as they crop up. This involves strategic thinking and creativity.

    *What creative solutions can you bring to the table to solve your challenge?*

2.  **Communication Skills**

    Flight attendants, hotel managers, fellow travelers and locals at your destination will all require you to adapt your communication style. Similarly at work we all know the feeling of tailoring our message to our audience.

    *How can you refine your message to ensure it's received by your audience?*

3.  **Teamwork Skills**

    Travelling with others definitely reveals a lot about their adaptability. Better yet, think about the dynamic of sharing the elbow room with a stranger you've just met. Figuring out how to work with others is paramount to being adaptable in life. We all have different timelines, preferences and styles. Add in conflict resolution and cultural differences to really spice up a team dynamic. Your adaptability will be called into question with all relationships you have in your life.

    *How can you effectively partner with the person across the table?*

## George

George was the father of a high school friend. When I was younger, I spent time at their house on weekends and regularly chatted with him in their dining room. He was a huge influence on me while I was an impressionable, stubborn, rebellious teen, and he continued to act as a trusted advisor when I began finding my way in the world.

George was adopted and had experienced a challenging childhood. As an adult, he worked his way to success in the manufacturing space in Canada. George taught me to question things, strategize, and gather basic acumen in areas like law, accounting, finance, and investing. George always knew how to adapt to his audience and the current circumstances to get the best outcome in any given situation. It wasn't about manipulation—it was about pure strategy. He was a great chess player and tried to teach me about the strategies it took to win. He told me to constantly look as many moves ahead as I could and analyze the different potential outcomes before making a move.

"Don't let yourself feel trapped in a corner—there's always a next move," George would say. When a company I joined for a part-time summer job wouldn't let me out of the agreement and claimed damages for trying to exit the position when school resumed, George helped me draft a letter arguing my case. The company was persuaded to let me out of the agreement because of his logical reasoning and approach. Even though I felt trapped, he knew a way out. I regularly went to George if I needed advice on how to deal with a challenging situation, whether it was work related or my Friday night date.

He taught me that adaptability means anticipating and being prepared for change. It means mapping out the possibilities and adjusting your strategy so that you're always aimed toward your desired end result. George saw life as a game of sorts. When I reach a challenging situation and need to be adaptable, I think of him and how he would examine the options. Always consider where different decisions will lead you and think four moves ahead. Then, when one of the potential outcomes becomes a reality, you will have already considered the next possible moves to make.

## ASK YOURSELF

**What does "adaptability" mean to me?**

**Why is it important?**

**How satisfied am I with my level of adaptability?**

**On a scale of 1 (being low) and 10 (being extremely satisfied), rate your current level of satisfaction with adapting to situations at work and in life:**

1    2    3    4    5    6    7    8    9    10

- Where in your career might there be room to cultivate more adaptability?

- How can you adapt based on what your clients, co-workers, boss, or market are telling you they want and/or need?

- Where can you find opportunities to connect with the people you impact?

- What are some ways to improve your offering by adapting your approach?

- Where might you be adapting *too much* for others and going off course with your vision and goals?

- What would it be like to think four steps ahead?

## ONE-DEGREE SHIFT

1. Think of a time you successfully adapted to a challenging situation. What did it take? How did you successfully navigate through it?

2. Make a list of parts of your job or role that could use a refresh. Consider processes or systems that are outdated or technology you use that could be upgraded or removed altogether. Is there something you do manually that would be better off delegated or automated?

3. Let's talk about your personal brand. When's the last time you did headshots or updated your personal website and LinkedIn? Is it up to date? Now's the time to adapt your brand colors, tagline, or copy to reflect your current priorities. It's good to revitalize any messaging about yourself professionally any time something new comes up and ideally every year so you can catch any glaring holes or things that seem outdated and no longer important.

4. Think about the structure of your ideal day from *Chapter 11: Curiosity*. How might you make some small changes to adapt your usual routine to something more fulfilling or exciting? What new information in this book or things you're noticing would you like to act on? Now's the time!

5. Let's look at the big picture. What's one thing that you know is out-dated about the way you work that needs to change? This could be a certification you want to get, working remotely, organizing more vacation time, or delegating more of your work to your team members. This is something glaringly obvious that you know is overdue to change but you've been putting on the back burner. Take the first step forward and make a shift.

6. Think four steps ahead. Map them out by making a list or drawing them. What do you need to adapt to anticipate potential roadblocks or opportunities you might be approaching?

## TAKEAWAYS

- ✦ Create a strategy of how you successfully adapt to situations.

- ✦ Make a list of areas of your career that could use an update.

- ✦ Complete a personal brand update to refresh what you're showing the world about your work.

- ✦ Adapt your daily routine to incorporate more fulfilling activities.

- ✦ Make a change (however small) to something you've wanted to improve for a while regarding your work.

- ✦ Plan four steps ahead and map out your options.

# Resourcefulness

*"Either I will find a way, or I will make one . . ."*
—Philip Sidney

## CORE QUESTION

**"What do I already have to help me in this situation?"**

This chapter aims to look at how you harness your internal and external resources to overcome challenges along the path of building your legacy. Internal resources are your creativity, mindset, and vitality. External resources are energy, like money, time, and your relationships. Making an impact means finding solutions in scenarios that manifest beyond your wildest imagination.

What's the weirdest scenario you've ever been in? Popping into my mind is the memory of biting off the head of a lemon-flavored ant in the middle of the Amazon rainforest. Or there was the time I found myself on the top of the Hollywood sign at sunset with no cell service as the sky grew dark. I hitched a ride home in an Uber with a family of seven that happened to be passing on their way back from recording an episode of "Family Feud." And the time I crashed a work team rooftop party in New York with my mom, got hired for a job over pizza and wine, then flew to Washington, D.C. the next week, putting all my other projects on the sidelines while I worked with them on a new start-up that eventually crashed and burned.

Life regularly throws up the unexpected. How can you harness the weird, the unexpected, and the stuff that comes from left field to build your legacy?

Not every scenario will be a slam dunk for you, but at least you show up and find a way through it, around it, over it, or teleport your way out of it.

I view these unexpected moments—where my ship veers off course in a direction I'd never imagined—as learning experiences. Each one is a chance for me to challenge my resourcefulness. They're opportunities to harness our creativity and persistence to develop a level of resourcefulness that's superhuman. There's a lot to be said for experiences where you find it's a case of "do or die." If you have no other option but to find a way, you certainly will.

Sometimes these situations can be at your own invitation. For me, writing this book was something I knew would be challenging. I wasn't sure I could do it. So I announced to the world, through an online campaign, that I was writing a book. I burned the bridges, you might say, and gave myself no room to go back. I *had* to do it. And so here I am writing it to the best of my ability with the resources I have.

Use unexpected situations where you suddenly find yourself out of your depth as opportunities to learn. Invite them in and welcome the situations that challenge you. Your resourcefulness improves as you practice embodying it, and you'll surprise yourself by what you can do when the situation demands it. For me, all big projects need to be a case of "do or die."

When I *must* to find a way through, I see possibilities that I didn't see before, and I get solution-focused because there's no other way.

---

WHERE IN YOUR LIFE DO YOU NEED TO
"BURN THE BRIDGES" TO GET YOURSELF MOVING?

---

Unexpected and tricky situations can be scary, I know. In a moment where you might feel panicked and out of your depth, it can be easy to feel that you simply don't have the resources to deal with it. Resourcefulness is about arming yourself with tools and strategies, so you're prepared for those tricky situations or times when you find yourself in unfamiliar territory.

Here's a tool that I use when I find myself faced with a tough scenario. I call it "Pause, Research, Respond" (PRR.) Here's how it works:

1. **Pause:** Take a beat to view the entire situation. What's happening here? What is this person's or group's true intention and motivation? What needs to happen right away (if anything)?

2. **Research:** Is what I'm being told correct? What are the facts? Who can help me? What do I need to find out to respond or feel fully informed about this?

3. **Respond:** Based on your assessment of the situation, figure out your response. If your response is in written form, read it twice or more before sending.

This process uses some of the skills from this book in tandem. We harness our patience to take a breath and pause rather than leap into premature action. We use our skills of focus, curiosity, and perspective to view the situation in the research stage. There's authenticity, self-advocacy, trust, and sometimes courage baked into your response to a difficult situation. Getting your inner and outer resources in order is at the core of this technique.

I want to stress that the final stage—response—can sometimes mean *not* responding. At this stage, always ask yourself whether a response is warranted, useful, or deserved. If someone says or does something out of spite, ignorance, or anger, it doesn't necessarily mean you should sling anything back at them. It's the smart choice sometimes to do nothing and stay silent.

I'm the first one to admit that I struggle to employ this tool when the stakes are high. It takes practice and consideration of the long-term consequences to bring this habit into your life fully. It has allowed me to avoid responding to many situations from a place of high emotion. Let's consider a scenario I faced with a contractor. I had a deadline with a client and had entrusted a contractor with the Search Engine Optimization website audit. It was nine in the morning on a Friday, and I promised to get it to the client by end of week. I checked our file-sharing tool to get the report, and there was nothing to be found. Had the contractor forgotten? Was it incomplete? How was I supposed to review it? I panicked internally for a moment. Then I stopped and changed my environment. I got up from my desk to take my pause away from my laptop and phone so I couldn't rattle off an emotional reply. Physically moving away from the situation works wonders for me. I assessed the viability of the threat and considered all points and potential consequences of any response I might make. Should I tell the client? No. Should I send a nasty message to the contractor? Probably not if I wanted to see that report anytime soon. I did some swift research by checking other folders and looking at version history. Still nothing. So, I decided to call the contractor directly. I didn't want to send an email and have things miscon-strued. My blood was boiling a bit because I felt the pressure to get my hands on this report so I could review it in time. No answer to my call. Great. So, I drafted an email, asking for the report, respectfully reminding the contractor that we had a deadline that day. Still nothing. I was challenged to create spaciousness here. I decided to give it an hour and go for a walk. When I returned? Magically a missed call and link to the document was in my inbox. Live and learn right?

Not every situation resolves so smoothly and quickly. Some issues can take days, weeks, or longer to come to a resolution, especially with legal matters, for example. But the core premise remains.

Pausing and assessing a situation rather than acting from fear or emo-tion allows you to dip into your pool of resources, gather more information, and make a clear-headed decision about how you respond.

What if you're face-to-face with someone—perhaps in a meeting—and feel that you can't pause before responding? I think there's nothing wrong with needing and asking for more time. The right people and opportunities won't cut you loose for saying you need a moment to consider. I experienced this at a pitch competition for Chiefly. We had one minute to pitch our companies, then investors were invited to ask follow on questions. One investor asked a technical question about how we developed our machine learning technology. It wasn't a question I had anticipated, and I didn't have an answer prepared. I could have riffed a response but, instead, I said: "That's a great question and something I don't take lightly. Do you mind if I get back to you with a full explanation of how we developed that?" He agreed. I answered his question in detail via email later that day and that got me another meeting with him privately. Being resourceful means finding a way to create enough space no matter what your time frame, so you can respond effectively.

## MENTOR'S TABLE

### The Tools by Phil Stutz and Barry Michels

Stutz was a prison psychologist on Rikers Island in New York and Michels was a lawyer turned psychotherapist. Together, they co-wrote *The Tools*. They employ visualization to increase our inner resourcefulness. If you haven't actively tried to visualize things before, it might feel odd at first, but I assure you it is a powerful perspective shift. These five tools are for when you feel the need to muster your inner resources to tackle a challenge at hand. They have helped me be more resourceful in a plethora of situations from public speaking to my marriage. If you utilize them daily, you can change your life.

1. **The Reversal of Desire**

   *Use when you're fearing or avoiding pain or difficulty*

   This visualization tool asks you to feel the desire for pain, to become one with it, and to ultimately release it. You visualize the pain as a cloud. Tell yourself "BRING IT ON" repeatedly as you cultivate the willingness to move toward and into the cloud.

   Scream "I LOVE PAIN!" as you go into the cloud of pain and become one with it. This part is important as you are accepting the feeling as it is.

   As you reach the peak of emotion, you will feel thrown out of the cloud and into pure light. Tell yourself "PAIN SETS ME FREE!" Notice as you release the pent-up fear and emotions. You will feel lighter and more willing to tackle the task at hand.

2. **Active Love**

   *Use when you're feeling angry or frustrated toward someone or something*

   This tool is asking you to transmute your anger into love. It resembles the feeling you get when you look at someone you love. Just seeing them melts away any anger you have. I feel this way toward my dog, Max, even after he's chewed up my favorite sandals. You use the tool by imagining that you're surrounded by infinite love in the form of warm liquid light. It might feel like standing outside on a warm summer day. Expand your heart so it fills up with all of this love around you. Let it pour into your heart. Bring your heart back into your chest to a normal size and feel yourself wanting to give this overflow of love away.

Release it toward the person or thing in mind, and visualize it coming out of your chest and into their solar plexus. Focusing on feeling them receiving this love is vital because it unifies you with them. Once you have sent them what they need, allow yourself to go back to the feeling of infinite love. Let yourself to be replenished with everything you gave away. A sense of peace and oneness will wash over you.

3. **Inner Authority**
   *Use when you want to regain your voice*

This one helped me a lot with this book and when I doubt myself about what I share on my podcast. You visualize yourself on stage in front of an audience. Then you visualize your shadow self, the scared, imperfect, nervous part of you that you normally hide from others, off to the side of the stage. It might look scary, funny, inhuman, but it's part of you. Invite your shadow self to stand beside you. Turn toward them and look them in the eye. Accept them as part of you by holding hands. Then, both of you turn to the audience and shout "LISTEN TO ME!" Say this as many times as needed to feel a sense of unity, confidence, and excitement. As you open your eyes, notice the relief of unifying these two parts of yourself and giving the shadow a voice.

4. **Grateful Flow**
   *Use when you're feeling down or comparing yourself to others*

This one is useful to help you remember that there are good things in your life, no matter what you're facing. You're going to make a list in your mind. This takes about thirty seconds, and intentionally feeling grateful or even lucky for each item is critical to harnessing the power of this tool.

Start by thinking of one thing you're grateful for. Allow your heart to feel warm as you think of this one thing. It might be someone you care about, the fact that you have a roof over your head, or something good that happened recently. Think of another one and feel the importance of it. Think of three more. Take your time. If you flippantly list five things, you won't feel the emotions that come with truly acknowledging what you have, so ensure you slow down and feel each one separately.

As you have the five listed, you'll feel the gratitude emanating out of your heart upward to the sky. The feeling will linger beyond you listing any further items. That's your connection to God, the source.

## 5. Jeopardy

*Use when you're procrastinating*

Imagine yourself on your death-bed to activate a sense of urgency. As you visualize, be sure to explore the scene to have it feel as real as possible. Notice your future self getting out of the bed to tell your present day self to use your time wisely and not squander your precious life. Take the time to feel the sense of importance this message brings you. It gives you a feeling of pressure to act now to make the most of this moment. As you open your eyes, leverage that feeling of urgency to take your next step.

## Luke Skywalker, Harry Potter, Khaleesi, and Other Fictional Beings

I would never proclaim myself a "fantasy fan," but there is much to be gleaned about the real world through art. The heroes of the sci-fi films and fantasy adventures that we love so much are great examples of resourcefulness. They are determined, listen to their instincts, and follow what they believe to be the next best move. Are they always right? No. But they try different approaches until they find the right move to beat the villain, escape the trap, or complete the quest. Sometimes their actions might look reckless, but they prevail because they're willing to try.

All epic tales have that moment where the hero or heroine faces the ultimate challenge and wants to quit. As they hang off their metaphorical cliff, what do they do in the final hour that stops them from admitting defeat? They get resourceful. They look around for options. They see a ladder, a wand, a dragon, or a shovel and they figure it out. When I'm in a tight spot, I sometimes imagine my life as a movie. And I ask, how would I, as the heroine of my life, respond to this real-life scenario? Picturing yourself as the hero in a film gives you a boost and the larger-than-life faith in yourself to know that there must be a way—you just have to find that ladder and see that solution. No matter the challenge or unfamiliarity of a task or situation, channel your favorite fantasy hero and trust yourself to harness your inner resources to find a solution that fits your values.

## Mike Ackerman

Many cultures see negotiation as a core part of buying anything. In Brazil or Thailand, if you don't negotiate, you're shopping incorrectly. On the flip side, haggling in Switzerland is seen as awkward and borderline rude, depending on the situation. Regardless of your cultural background, there are high stakes scenarios when taking the first offer is not wise or making use of all the resources at your disposal. Strategically negotiating your salary or the purchase price of your house is a worthwhile endeavour to bring resourcefulness to.

Chris Voss's book *Never Split the Difference: Negotiating As If Your Life Depended on It* introduced me to a strategy called "Ackerman Bargaining." As a former FBI negotiator, he learned this strategy from Mike Ackerman, a CIA operative. Both Ackerman, and later, Voss, used this process to successfully negotiate with international kidnapping rings—and if there's any situation where resourcefulness is required, I think we can agree that a hostage situation is one of them.

While I've thankfully never faced down kidnappers, I've used this strategy for hundreds of difficult negotiations, from renting apartments to negotiating vendor deals for software. Being prepared with a tactical negotiation framework has been a great resource to employ that ensures both parties get a fair resolution.

Here is how Ackerman's strategy works:

**"Remember: 65-85-95-100**

- Set your target price or preferred outcome (your goal) in your mind.

- Communicate your first offer at 65% of your target price.

- Calculate three raises of increasing increments: 85%, 95%, and 100% of your target price.

- Use lots of empathy and different ways of saying 'No' to get the other side to counter before you increase your offer.

- When calculating the final amount, use precise, non-round numbers like $37,893 rather than $38,000. It gives the number credibility and weight.

- On your final number, throw in a non-monetary item (that they probably don't want) to show you're at your limit."[15]

---

15. Voss, Chris, and Tahl, Raz. *Never Split the Difference: Negotiating As If Your Life Depended On It.* London: Random House Business Books, 2017.

Ackerman's strategy works when you're negotiating from the other side and selling something too:

- Establish your asking price or preferred outcome (goal) in your mind.
- Communicate your first offer at 135% of what you'd accept.
- Negotiate down to 115%, 105%, and finally 100% of the original amount.

This strategy might seem too rigid or calculating, but I assure you it works. The strategy is grounded in psychological principles like anchoring and allows you to negotiate consciously. It's especially useful when the stakes are high and it's critical that you put your best foot forward. If you're interested in more on this, I highly recommend Voss's book or a negotiation course to learn the basics and practice more frameworks. I've had clients say strategizing or negotiating in this way feels manipulative or calculating. I think your intent behind using the tool matters immensely. I would also offer a reframe of being strategic and well-prepared. You are looking out for your best interest and using negotiation tools to communicate them as effectively as possible. Having mental models and established strategies in your playbook for important business or life situations will increase your resourcefulness tenfold because you'll have effective tools to rely on.

## Anyone Who Runs a Business

I could have put any number of renowned names at my Mentor's Table on resourcefulness: Henry Ford, Albert Einstein, or Walt Disney. But if you want to see real examples of resourcefulness, take a walk in your local neighborhood. Look at the owners of a boutique clothing store who started an online option to widen their market. Look at the people who morphed their business from internet cafés to co-working spaces for an increasingly nomadic workforce. Speak to people who work in competitive fields. I had a conversation with the owner of a nail salon in Lake Como who told me about the ways she promotes her business in a busy tourist spot with lots of local competition. Chat with small charities about how they attract funding and raise money. Talk to any business owner who has had to close their doors during an economic downturn. Listen and learn about how they got things back on track, kept things moving, and grew as a result of the difficult experience.

If you're going through a tough work or life situation and feel like you don't know where to turn, your best bet will always be to turn to those around you who have made it through challenges themselves. If you're having trouble with a client or with increasing revenue, call upon mentors or someone successful in that space who can help you solve the challenge. It's easy to believe we all need to stand alone, but it's important to seek counsel from others, especially if they're qualified in spaces we aren't. Make sure your business plan is reviewed by a businessperson and that your contract is seen by a lawyer. Employing external resources is as important as cultivating your inner resources. Draw upon the wisdom of those around you who have been where you want to go and ask them for support to help you get to the other side.

## ASK YOURSELF

**What does "resourcefulness" mean to me?**

**Why is it important?**

**How satisfied am I with how I bring resourcefulness to my life?**

**On a scale of 1 (being low) and 10 (being extremely satisfied), rate your current level of satisfaction with being resourceful in daily life:**

1    2    3    4    5    6    7    8    9    10

- What do I know already that can help me approach the scenario at hand?

- What's a challenging situation I made it through that seemed completely impossible at first?

- Who can I call upon to help me?

- What's a totally unexpected, new, weird, or unrealistic way for me to solve this?

- What would [insert a mentor or someone you admire] do?

- Imagine your life is an epic feature film or book. What would your character do next to overcome their challenge?

## ONE-DEGREE SHIFT

1. Test out PRR (pause, research, respond) in a scenario at work. See how it goes and decide whether to implement it in other situations. Tweak it to your needs.

2. Use one or more of the visualizations in a difficult moment. Reflect on how it feels to be powerful enough to shift your state using your mind. If you find them useful, make visualization a regular practice in your day.

3. Try Ackerman Bargaining. It can be negotiating the next Airbnb you rent or purchasing your next car. Perhaps you want to try it when you pitch your next client. Go as small or grand as you like but get your feet wet employing these frameworks to make the most of your resources. You won't know unless you try! Then do a debrief. How did it go? Was it awkward? Will you try it again? What other strategy might you use instead? How might you improve it to suit your style?

4. Write out a list of individuals you can count on in tough times. How do you know they have your back? I find it reassuring that, no matter what happens, you're not alone in this journey. Does the list seem short? There are often few people we think we can count on, but when the time comes, those we never thought of can surprise us. Consider reaching out to your local community members or colleagues.

5. Talk to your family, friends, or community about a hardship you're going through that requires some resourcefulness. Have they been through something similar? How do they cultivate resourcefulness? What do they do when the going gets tough? Or, look to a mentor or author you like, and ask them about a time when they overcame adversity. No response? See if they or others you respect have written or shared about how they approach the challenge you're going through.

## TAKEAWAYS

◆ Use PRR (Pause, Reflect, Respond) the next time you're in a challenging conversation or need to make an important decision.

◆ Hone in on your unique inner resources that'll help you out in a pinch.

◆ Learn and employ Ackerman Bargaining in a negotiation situation to use your resources effectively.

◆ Make a list of trusted people in your life to remind you that you have people in your corner during the good times and bad.

◆ Call upon others to bolster your resourcefulness (because we're all better together!).

# *Twenty-Two*
# Patience

*"Do you have the patience to wait
until your mud settles
and the water is clear?"*

—LAO TZU

## CORE QUESTION

**"What's the best decision in the long run?"**

I ask myself the above question multiple times a day. Patience has challenged me most of my life. That's why I think this might be the most important chapter and why I've saved it for last. In writing this book, I've learned that the quality and skill of patience is crucial when it comes to building a meaningful life. It's easy to allow our impulses to guide our actions by making split-second decisions. As we've explored in previous chapters, there's a benefit in trusting our instincts and going with our gut. But, when it comes to building relationships—with others and with ourselves—and building a legacy, we need to employ patience.

Think about it: You've got to make a big, high-stakes decision, and you need to do it quickly or you might miss your opportunity. You feel anxious, pressured, and panicked. Are you in the optimal state to make the best decision? Are you even able to check in with your gut when you're feeling this way? At moments like these, we often lose sight of the long game. We forget that every decision we make builds into our legacy. Take a moment. Take a breath. Take a pause before you leap to a decision. Mustering up even a little bit of patience at times like these can mean we give ourselves the chance to focus, check in with our instincts, weigh the consequences, and make the decision that's best for us in the present and, crucially, for our future.

Often, it's other individuals who turn up the heat in these situations. They want a decision, a sale, or a deal and they want it now. This can be true in both business and personal situations. But ask yourself: Does someone who is determined to rush you into a decision you don't feel comfortable with really respect you? If you don't take the time to fully consider the decision, will you later regret putting your name to it? Whenever I feel someone is pressuring me and not giving me the space to consider everything I need to, I usually veer away from them, and the answer they get is invariably negative. This can work both ways. As well as using self-advocacy to ask for patience from others, we can show them respect by having patience and giving *them* the space *they* ask for by employing empathy. We're more likely to build trust in these kinds of relationships, and they're more likely to turn into long, productive work alliances.

As children, time is something we feel we have plenty of. A year in the mind of a child is an eternity. It's interesting to consider how, as we reach adulthood, we begin to rush. We always have to get to the next stage, sometimes without even truly considering whether the next stage is the right one for us. Then, we seem to grow more patient again as we reach old age—less keen to hurtle through life and more inclined to pause. We would do well to emulate the perspective of patience our elders have in our current stage of life. Rather than rushing through the day, what if we remembered to be more deliberate about enjoying the present moment?

When we took my grandmother to a long-term care facility, my heart sank. She helped to raise me and cared for many others in my family, and now it was her turn to be cared for. Visiting her new home was eye-opening, and it instantly slowed me down. The fact that our time is limited was right in front of my eyes. In a retirement home, time moves differently. There's no real rush. Everything can be slowed and savored. When it comes to decision-making, think about how quickly your older relatives would make the same decision. What might they consider from their perspective that you might be overlooking from yours? How happy will you be with the decision you make now, years down the line? Think slowly. Play the long game in the way you approach decisions. Even some of the seemingly small ones, like whether to go home for the holidays or whether to answer the phone when your parents are calling. Make choices that'll benefit you and others for years to come and not days. Easier said than done.

The rush for success can sometimes mean we don't invest the time we need to make it happen. Landing my first corporate client took patience and time. I coached a client one-on-one for a year before the idea to approach her employer even struck me. I hadn't taken the coaching job to land a bigger contract—I simply wanted to do best by the client, which meant that she trusted me and was happy to recommend me. It took a further three meetings with her boss followed by another meeting with the CEO of the company. My patience and ability to roll with their process ended up with me getting the deal and a bigger contract than I had imagined possible. Don't cut corners to get a quick win or rush forward with a proposal without giving it the due effort it deserves.

Often it takes patience to do something properly. I had a timeline in mind when I came to write this book because I thought going to the market fast was somehow better than going to the market with clarity. Writing it has taught me that creating something of value and something with meaning takes time. The very definition of legacy is bringing something to the real world with authentic actions. Truly grasping that idea over the past four years has made this book much better than if I published my first draft from 2019. Taking my time to develop and grow my ideas has allowed me to bring in stories and experiences that have added value and wouldn't have been included had I met my first self-imposed deadline. What will patience give you when it comes to crafting a career that you look back on and are proud of?

Being impatient is frequently born out of our desire to avoid missed opportunities. The drive to succeed can often transpire into an urge to seize every opportunity that comes our way. Having patience and taking time to look and see what the best course of action is might mean that some opportunities do pass us by, and that's where patience crosses over with our sense of trust. The opportunities that are right for *you* will always find you, be they work or personal.

---

IT'S A TYPE OF PATIENCE
—MAYBE SOMETHING CLOSE TO WISDOM—
THAT ALLOWS US TO LET EVENTS UNFOLD AS THEY WILL AND
TRUST THAT WE'RE ON THE ROAD WE'RE SUPPOSED TO BE ON.

---

So how do you know the difference between being patient and simply being stuck in a holding pattern? Patience is being comfortable having opportunities on the table that you're excited about and simultaneously considering them thoroughly. It feels right and you feel positive about what's going to unfold. If one or more options don't work out or aren't the right option for you, you're confident that more opportunities are around the corner and you know you can seek them out.

Patience is committing to opportunities that fit with your bigger goals and guiding values. Procrastination, on the other hand, is not putting yourself out there at all for new clients or potential employers to find you. It feels like wading through a swamp or molasses. You might say yes to opportunities, but you feel like you're settling or that the work you complete is underappreciated. When you feel like you're going around in circles and not really making progress, that isn't patience but a lack of direction. Make sure you identify which one sounds most like you in your situation. Focus on bringing an openness to find new opportunities and the patience to consider which ones are best for you.

## MENTOR'S TABLE

### Patricia Irwin

A friend and a true mentor to me, Pat Irwin was a coach, facilitator, and my teacher when I did my coaching certification. Pat fully supported the writing of this book, well before I knew I was capable of writing it, but unfortunately, she'll never get to read it. She provided me with unconditional support, but Pat passed away before I could show her the manuscript. It's entirely fitting and deserving of her legacy that she takes a seat at the Mentor's Table for the chapter on patience. Pat's choices were thoughtful and deliberate. It didn't seem as though anyone could pressure her to move faster than she deemed appropriate. Pat would not be rushed. It also never seemed as though Pat was in chaos, even when things went awry. She had a calm demeanor and an inner resolve that made it seem like she had it all figured out.

More than that, Pat believed in *everyone's* ability to make good choices for themselves and showed patience with everyone she encountered. She was never too busy to give someone an extra moment. She'd listen fully and completely to what someone had to say. She'd give people the time and space they needed to hear their inner Knowing and then trust their answer. I hope that I bring even an ounce of the calm, steady energy she exuded when she engaged with people. Pat showed how closely tied patience is with empathy. It can be easy to become impatient with others, but when we harness our empathy, it reminds us that things aren't always as they seem.

Who in your life shows up with a sense of patience? They might be a great role model to emulate as you develop your own sense of the skill. Take a deep breath and think of them the next time you feel pressured, panicked, or rushed. Consider how they would respond to the situation. It can be a reminder to give yourself some grace to recover from an illness or a challenging time. Or it might help you to remember that your time is precious and needs to be spent on things that are meaningful to you. When I encounter moments of frustration, I think of Pat and what she would do. I'm thankful for her patience with me as I learned how to be a coach. From her example, I realized that the way we manage time also gives us insight into how we manage money and other energy. She taught me that we must use our time wisely in the present moment, where we have it at our fingertips.

## Parents Everywhere

There's something magical about how parents show up with their children. I stand in complete awe of what they can do. Late nights, early mornings, sick days—there's a huge responsibility in raising children. Parents everywhere, including my own, deserve so much more acknowledgment than they get for their efforts, day in and day out. Even though I'm not a mom of any living children yet, I do my best to think of my parents in moments that demand patience.

I'm lucky that, while writing this book, I still have the option to call my mom or dad and ask for support when I'm challenged by life. If you're lucky enough to have had supportive parents, they can act as great examples of the selfless patience it requires to raise a child. If not, look to friends or admirable people around you. See how they engage with their children, how they teach them and encourage them down the right path. Consider what challenges parents face and overcome to support their children. Bring their example of patience forward when it comes to struggles at work or slower progress than you'd like.

Another way that parents have given me huge insight is that they allow me to consider the child inside us all. It's easy to think others have it all figured out, but, more often than not, everyone is as scared and uncertain as you are. We explored using this idea in *Chapter 16: Empathy*, and it's an important thing to keep in your mind when it comes to being patient with others. When I see a client doubting themselves or hesitating about taking the next step, I ask myself whether they need a little more time to consider their decision. When I feel someone is doing something to drive me nuts, I ask myself whether something might be going on under the surface, and I remind myself that they're truly doing the best they can. And when all that fails, I take a deep breath and take five. The age-old advice of parents and kindergarten teachers to count to ten when you feel yourself overwhelmed is something you might consider keeping in your everyday skill toolkit. I've learned from those I admire, and my own experience, that it's always better to take a pause than to react out of anger or frustration.

## God

"Be still and know that I am God" (Psalms 46:10). What does that exactly mean? It's saying that it's in stillness that we come to know what God truly is. You just need to be alone with your breath to feel that powerful force running through your body. It's the warm sensation of blood pumping through your veins. It's feeling the sun shining on your face. It doesn't overwhelm you with details, it's not loud or abrasive, it just tells you plainly where you're meant to go. We spend a lot of time running away from this voice and its subtle nudges. We worry about if we can handle what it might tell us if we get too quiet and too still. But you can handle hard things. Take the time to sink into the silence and you'll be glad you did.

Years ago, God probably wouldn't have made it into this book. For me, the word was directly correlated with religion. It has so many connotations. I felt disconnected from what the Bible and other religious texts teach and didn't know how to harness God's power. It's interesting because there are many ways to describe this force, yet explaining it as God brings up strong emotions for many people. Rightfully so—there's a powerful human history associated with what religious institutions have done in the name of God. But let's focus on my first definition, the force around us, that all powerful, larger than life force which holds everything in balance. Let's see it as a force of pure love.

I can't imagine a better example of patience than when I think of God seeing how we mightily try to push and pull throughout our lives, often kicking and screaming most of the way. At our worst, we focus on our problems, hold grudges, try to control others, and generally get in the habit of doubting ourselves and fearing the unknown. The patience God has for our worries and missteps is unlimited. What if we could tap into that unlimited patience? What if by leaning into our deep knowing we could overcome much more than we think we can?

All I can attest to is my experience, and I know God was in the hospital room when I delivered my third lifeless baby. He was there when I got into the car accident that could've killed me and, instead, I lived. He's been there this whole time, and all I needed to do was develop my own relationship with Him. Even at your lowest moments in life, He is working for you. I truly believe nothing I have experienced was in vain. I have learned, grown, and become the person I am because of the unique difficulties that have shown up along my path. When you remind yourself to pause and take a moment to tune in, you'll hear where He's guiding you to go next.

## ASK YOURSELF

**What does "patience" mean to me?**

**Why is it important?**

**How satisfied am I with the patience I have with both myself and others at work and in life?**

**On a scale of 1 (being low) and 10 (being extremely satisfied), rate your current level of satisfaction with how you bring patience to yourself and others:**

1    2    3    4    5    6    7    8    9    10

**Think of a situation that has been on your mind for a while that needs resolution. Before you answer these questions, pause a little longer than you would usually to consider your answer in full.**

- What's my usual knee-jerk reaction to decision-making?

- How does that impact me, others, or the situation?

- Now, put everyone else's expectations to the side for a moment. How much time do I need to think this through? Another day? Another week? Another month?

- Upon further reflection, what does my gut say is right?

- What would an outside observer think and do in this situation?

- What would the most patient person I know do?

- What decision would benefit me in the long run?

- What would I do if I had ample time to make the best decision possible?

**What are my thoughts on God?**

- How do I connect with God?

- What do I resist about God?

- What are the stories I tell myself about God?

- What do I believe about religion?

- What do I believe about worshipping with others in a church or other sacred place?

- What are the differences between God and religion?

- What gives me the strength to be patient when willpower fails?

## ONE-DEGREE SHIFT

1. The next time you need to make a decision, instead of doing the first thing that comes to mind, set up a timed brainstorming session and allow all the crazy, wild, seemingly unreasonable solutions to come out. Make it at least ten minutes before you stop writing. Then decide when you're ready.

2. Write a list of boundaries you have regarding your work, your health and wellness, and your relationships. For example, you always take Sundays off, no matter what. Or you insist on your daily yoga session. When you feel an external force pulling you away from these things, patiently consider if they're worth it. It often isn't in the long run. When you have clarity on what matters are worthy of your patience, it makes employing it much easier.

3. Consider using the "Pause" part of the PRR tool from the last chapter on resourcefulness when you feel up against the wall during your next client deal, romantic decision, or health choice. It'll give you the space to structure your thoughts and feelings so you can ensure you've done your due diligence. It's easy to skip over "pause" and "research" in the heat of the moment.

4. Take one last opportunity (in this book) to consider your relationship with God. Do you believe in a higher power or force? Why or why not? What do you call it if not God? What beliefs or experiences have driven your opinions? How do you cultivate your relationship with things unseen? How do you cultivate faith? What does this do for your ability to be patient during the difficult situations in life? What brings you a sense of peacefulness?

## TAKEAWAYS

◆ Make time to brainstorm alternative solutions to your current challenge or business situation.

◆ Write a list of boundaries that allow you to know when is best to employ patience.

◆ Employ the "Pause" from PRR (Pause, Research, Respond) to create the space needed to address a situation with patience and wisdom.

◆ Consider and reflect upon your relationship with God or a force unseen.

# Endings

HOW DO YOU "successfully" end something? Is the legacy I've created with this book what I intended it to be? I've always struggled with the ending of things. A steady stream of tears at the airport while I fly off to another city comes to mind. With every flight there are people, places, and things I'm leaving behind.

One such occasion that sticks out was when I left my husband and knew we'd be apart for two months. I felt overwhelmed with how quickly my day-to-day life would change without him around in person. And as the plane took off and I wiped my tears, I realized that I was also flying toward something. I was flying back home, to family, friends, and the places I know best. Life is filled with such competing forces, flying toward home while simultaneously away from my husband. It's in our navigation of these opposing forces that I think we find meaning and build an exhilarating life. So, I wish you the very best as you go toward your dreams and explore your fears. I hope you've found some clarity as we went on this journey of questions and ideas.

My wish for you now is to realize that you've had the answers yourself the entire time. Trust that your response is the best one you have available to you now. And keep asking questions. The key is to stay curious and be willing to explore what's around you. If you do that, then you can never fail. No subject is ever exhausted if you continue to ask questions and explore it further.

Thank you for investing your time into reading this and exploring the legacy you're building. I wish you every success in creating a life filled with meaningful moments.

# Acknowledgments

T HANKS TO ALL those who have contributed to my growth, those who have shared their stories with me, and to you for reading.

A special acknowledgment to everyone who supported my Publishizer campaign and believed in me from the beginning of this project.

And finally, another nod to my many mentors for their pivotal influence in my life and in the lives of others.

To everyone who worked on this project in big ways and small, my heart is so full knowing that my vision is now out in the world! Thank you for sharing your talent and expertise to bring this to fruition. Notable thanks to Sunbury Press and Lawrence for believing in me and this book from the beginning. Sarah, Caroline, Crystal, and Helen, your attention to detail, ideas, and support to get this across the finish line were instrumental, thank you. Ricardo, muito obrigada por participar e garantir que todas as imagens foram um grande successo. Este livro é melhor por causa da sua criatividade.

To my parents, thank you for always having my back and believing in me no matter what. Your support of my potential and dreams has allowed me to venture into the world knowing I've got something special and worthwhile to share. I'm lucky to call you both Mom and Dad.

To my husband, thanks for being by my side. For staying up with me well past midnight, multiple times, so I could meet deadlines. And for always doing the dishes so I can focus on my work. I'm glad you decided to drive south. You make this life so much better.

# About the Author

K ALYNA MILETIC is the founder of Kickstart Your Work, a world-wide network of coaches who specialize in boosting performance and engagement in the workplace. She also founded Chiefly, which is innovating to improve online meetings using real-time feedback powered by machine learning. She has been a Professional Certified Coach since 2016 and has coached over five thousand hours with clients in twenty-five countries.

Kalyna was named one of Business Insider's Most Innovative Career Coaches of 2020. She hosts a podcast called "Lead Today" and launched her own clothing brand, Lead. Apparel, to support grassroots charities. She impacts her global client base through online coaching, courses, retreats, and speaking engagements.

Kalyna loves to travel, having lived in Aruba, Bali, Switzerland, Rio de Janeiro, Fortaleza, New York, San Francisco, Dallas, and Toronto. She enjoys spending time doing yoga and is a registered yoga teacher. She explores the world with her husband, Fabio, and her dog, Max.

CPSIA information can be obtained
at www.ICGtesting.com
Printed in the USA
BVHW040509041222
653398BV00001B/1